Misunderstood

The impact of
growing up overseas
in the 21st Century

Tanya Crossman

"*Misunderstood* is a must-read for anybody trying to deepen their understanding of the TCK experience and how international mobility affects a child. Tanya Crossman's collection of unique real-life stories will not only resonate with TCKs, but will also inspire empathy and understanding for anyone who has ever transitioned."

Valérie Besanceney, author, *B at Home: Emma Moves Again* and *My Moving Booklet*. International primary school teacher.

"*Misunderstood* left me feeling refreshingly... understood! Compassionate and discerning, its blend of gathered narrative and insight left me with a sense of belonging as well as an appreciation for the many varieties of experience similar to mine. This is the guidebook I want to give people to explain my cultural upbringing."

Christopher O'Shaughnessy, International Speaker, author, *Arrivals, Departures and the Adventures In-Between.* www.chris-o.com

"If I were moving overseas with my kids today, this is the book I'd want in my hand luggage. *Misunderstood* updates the gold standard of TCK research for today's families, weaving detailed information together with compelling personal narrative, giving a voice to this generation of kids growing up overseas, and fostering understanding with those who love and care for them."

Kay Bruner, MA LCP, author, *As Soon As I Fell*, contributor, *A Life Overseas.* www.kaybruner.com

"It's hard to imagine a more thorough – or more thoughtful – treatment of the dynamics of being a TCK. Crossman's survey results alone make this an invaluable contribution to the field, but it is the compelling voices of TCKs themselves, generously cited throughout, that will leave a lasting impression. Anyone who is a TCK or who cares about them will find insights on every page."

Craig Storti, Director of Communicating Across Cultures, author, *The Art of Crossing Cultures*, *The Art of Coming Home*, and *Cross-Cultural Dialogues*. www.craigstorti.com

"Tanya Crossman's *Misunderstood* is a valuable and much-welcomed resource for Third Culture Kids who may struggle with grief and a conflicted sense of self after repeated loss of the people, places and ways of life they care about. Crossman's extensive work with, and interview of, TCKs acknowledges their pain and offers – in their own words, in their own voices – support and the reassurance that the Third Culture itself is their place of sharing, identity, home and belonging. *Misunderstood* is a treasure chest of ways in which family, friends, and TCKs themselves can provide love, understanding, assistance and the space in which to heal, grow, and ultimately thrive."

Linda A. Janssen, author, *The Emotionally Resilient Expat: Engage, Adapt and Thrive Across Cultures*

"*Misunderstood*, indeed! This book is a 'must have' for anyone who is interested in or works within Third Culture Life. The information and real-life experiences shared reflect the reality of what it is to be a 'global citizen' and the importance of having a framework to support TCKs/Expat Youth. I plan to use this book as a resource, and I highly recommend it to others. Thank you, Tanya, for supporting this population, and for providing such a valuable tool."

Dr Lisa Pittman, Licensed Psychologist (USA),
Registered Psychologist (UK), co-author, *Expat Teens Talk*

"Wow, what an insightful, well researched book. The TCK insights and stories are so personal... anyone with a cross-cultural upbringing or connection will relate to them. I wish excellent resources like this had been available when I was exploring the effects of my TCK upbringing. You will be able to understand and love TCKs in a richer, deeper and more meaningful way as a result of *Misunderstood*. Thanks Tanya for your devotion and efforts – a great addition to TCK literature!"

Heidi Sand-Hart, author, *Home Keeps Moving*

"*Misunderstood* explains ME. Tanya gives words to internal feelings I could not have previously understood as a TCK. While I read, I found myself nodding with a sense of relief and recognition, 'Yes! That's what I felt. I'm not the only one.'"

Taylor Joy Murray, author, *Hidden in My Heart:
A TCK's Journey Through Cultural Transition*

"My response to reading *Misunderstood* was to smile because it captured the essence of who I am. It reminded me of just how much potential we TCKs have to make a real impact in the world, particularly bridging the cultural divides that exist today. I'd recommend this book to anyone who has ever found themselves in between cultures – it is a compass for guiding you to your true north as a TCK."

Tayo Rockson, author, *The Ultimate Guide to TCK Living*, host of the As Told By Nomads podcast and editor of www.BrandEdU.com

"*Misunderstood* does indeed open a window on how an international upbringing may affect a child. This book will be a great resource for people working with the global population or families thinking about a global life. I loved that Crossman covers being misunderstood by friends as being hard enough, but that she also covers being misunderstood by family. Understanding TCKs and CCKs backed by her statistics makes a very interesting read. You will enjoy the two sides of goodbye, the common threads she taps into about TCKs, and information about non-traditional families. Crossman has excellent feedback from TCKs on the various lives we offer our children when we move them abroad."

Julia Simens, author, *Emotional Resilience and the Expat Child: Practical tips and storytelling techniques that will strengthen the global family*

"Tanya Crossman has done an artful job of using numerous quotes from experts in the field, along with voices of TCKs around the world, to back up her research on TCKs. Her research makes this book a valuable resource for those who study and or work with TCKs."

Lois Bushong, M.S., Licensed Marriage & Family Therapist, author, *Belonging Everywhere & Nowhere: Insights into Counseling the Globally Mobile*. Owner and Counselor at Quiet Streams Counseling. www.quietstreamscounseling.com

"Only such qualitative methodology can showcase the voices of the TCK's experience. Identifying participants by age, nationalities, number of moves, sponsor affiliation, and type of schooling, help the reader gain invaluable insights. Explaining the wider concept of Cross-Culture Kids illuminates the multilayers within each experience, as does the focus on pre/post 1985 birthdate. Another invaluable contribution to the literature for CCKs, TCKs and those who live and work with them."

Dr Ettie Zilber, Head of the International School of Arizona and author of *Third Culture Kids: The Children of International School Educators*

"Mix the ways people feel like outsiders in a casserole. Cut a hundred bite-sized pieces of theory, each spiced with a compelling story. Serve immediately. *Misunderstood* provides unlimited servings of understanding for those trying to understand TCKs and for TCKs trying to understand themselves."

Drs. Douglas W. Ota, Psychologist, author, *Safe Passage: What Mobility Does to People and What International Schools Should Do About It*

"Tanya Crossman begins *Misunderstood* with the important caveat that she is describing a 'perspective, not a person'. Through detailed narratives and interviews from hundreds of TCKs, she beautifully achieves her goal and gives us a broad picture of the world of the Third Culture Kid. *Misunderstood* is sure to be an excellent addition to the current body of TCK literature."

Marilyn Gardner, ATCK, author *Between Worlds: Essays on Culture & Belonging*. www.communicatingacrossboundariesblog.com

First Edition 2016

First Published in the United Kingdom by Summertime Publishing

ISBN 978-1-909193-85-7

Design by Owen Jones, www.owenjonesdesign.com

Disclaimer: Some of the quotes by TCKs used in this book have been edited/cut for reasons of clarity and/or brevity.

To my 'kids' all over the world.

You have enriched my life in
more ways than I can count.

This is for you.

Acknowledgements

Huge thanks go to more than 250 TCKs I interviewed while writing this book: you inspired me and challenged me to create something worthy of your stories. Thanks also to hundreds more TCKs who have shared their stories (and lives) with me over the past decade. Thank you for opening a window into your world that I might know you better – and now, to share with others what I learned.

Danny Coyle and Amanda McNeice: thank you for believing in me, and believing I could do better – without you there would be no book. Jo Parfitt, Jane Dean, and Dounia Bertuccelli: thank you for all your work to make my book the best it could be. Ruth E. Van Reken: thank you not only for all you do for Cross-Cultural Kids everywhere, but also for your gracious and kind encouragement to me.

There are also many people whose investment in me enabled this book to be written. Heartfelt thanks go to:

Danny and Jill Coyle, Iris and Tom Lowder, Melinda and Ralph Howe, Kathy and Rick Laymon, Yvonne Dutton, Rachel Heffield, Kara and Matt Banker, Joe and Joyce Jackson, John and Katie Sorrell, Christina Anderson – you have helped shape me and my writing.

Lorina and Mike Barbalas, Keith and Wendy Beeman, Beth and Scott Canterberry, Daniel and Ellen Chin, Nayree Davis, Brad and Darla Gammons, Esther Han, Deborah Kapraun, Bruce and Jo Lau, Tracy Liew, Eleanor and Steve Lyons, Denis and Lynn Possing, Amy Pu, Joanne Qian and James Shen,

Allen and Yvette Sanders, Evelyn and Gary Sun, Gordon Wang, Chris and Tammy Watkins, Kathryn and Keith Westberg, Lily Yan – your support has made this possible.

Lesley Forsyth, Keith Frampton, Amanda and Andrew McNeice, Dante and Natasha Mavec, Carla Crossman, Bev and Bruce Crossman, Bron and Harry Dorsman, Bill and Lorraine Crossman – you have influenced me (and my book) in more ways than you know.

Contents

FOREWORD

Over the past thirty years as I have lectured and written about
Third Culture Kids (TCKs)* many have said, "Well, those
issues of identity struggles, rootlessness, entry/reentry to
their passport countries, or unresolved grief might have been
true for TCKs of past generations, but I don't believe they are
relevant for today's TCKs. After all, they have the Internet.
They can stay connected with everyone and to every place no
matter how often they move."

In *Misunderstood*, Tanya Crossman shows us this is not true.
While we all affirm the countless gifts of a global childhood,
Ms Crossman has woven together quotes from past research
and the wealth of writings *about* TCKs with vignettes and
quotes *from* 21st Century TCKs. We can see those same
minefields that have sidetracked many TCKs of the past –
and kept them from living out the fullness of those gifts for
a period of time – are still present for today's TCKs.

If anything, the increased mobility across a burgeoning
number of countries for today's TCKs may be exacerbating
the development of the common characteristics David
C. Pollock outlined in the 1980s, in his now classic TCK
Profile. As the number of children growing up globally
continues to increase in our changing world, this book
comes at a timely moment, particularly as Ms. Crossman
clarifies the often foggy notion of what the third culture
is and is not. We need fresh understanding and focus for
today's TCKs as part of an ongoing reality rather than
presuming they are a historical topic.

Of equal benefit is how Ms. Crossman recognises that TCKs are one subset of the many different ways children grow up as Cross-Cultural Kids (CCKs). After discussing the traditional TCK experience in depth, she describes why this larger concept of CCKs is also significant for many 21st Century TCKs. Perhaps an evolving change from past generations of TCKs to present ones is how many deal with the cultural complexity of not only being a traditional TCK, but *also* growing up with additional layers of cross-cultural interactions within their families, as international adoptees, educational CCKs, and so forth. Perhaps this growing level of cultural complexity for many present day TCKs is one reason the Internet alone is not enough to 'fix' them in the ways people assume it should, or would.

This larger discussion also adds to the value of this book. While rightfully concentrating on the group of TCKs she has worked with and studied so intensively, the awareness that their story is part of a greater whole gives permission for readers to consider what might or might not apply from the traditional TCK experience to other types of CCKs who are not in the TCK circle at all.

At a time when it seems the world easily divides by 'difference,' considering how the lessons learned from the 21st Century TCKs quoted in this book may apply to others offers an opportunity to see first 'what' and 'why' we can share as human beings, even when our experiences are not identical. Of particular help in considering these cross-applications is the discussion of how other factors of the CCK model impact the TCKs. In those discussions there are likely more universal lessons for those who share that particular subset of the CCK experience, despite not being a traditional TCK.

Of course, what everyone wants to know is, "It's fine to understand this, but what do I do to help myself or my kids or those I work with?" Readers will find that entwined in the TCK stories are many examples of what was or wasn't helpful, so that lessons and principles learned from others can be applied to the specifics of a particular situation parents or other mentors are facing.

I have no doubt you will find this a most interesting and helpful read whether the topic of TCKs is totally new to you or you have dealt with it for years. There are many fresh thoughts and insights regarding the evolving realities of TCKs while affirming that the basic characteristics transcend generations and technology. Why? Because despite the details of how it happens, the emotional impact of growing up while navigating multiple cultural worlds filled with changing players is one that hits the human soul. And who we are as humans transcends generations, nationalities, specific cultures, and race. That is why there is so much for us to learn in reading this book, which covers interviews with people across all of these boundary lines. An important addition to our TCK literature for sure.

Children who grow up outside the parent(s)' passport country(s) for a significant portion of their first 18 years of life, usually due to a parent's career choice

Ruth E. Van Reken,
Co-author, *Third Culture Kids: The Experience of Growing Up Among Worlds*, Author, *Letters Never Sent*, Co-founder, Families in Global Transition, www.FIGT.org

INTRODUCTION

I was born in Australia. I was eight when my family moved for the first time, 13 when my father's job took us to the United States, and 15 when we returned. At 21 I moved to Beijing, where I studied in a Chinese university for a year. What began as a year abroad turned into 11 years. I stayed in China because I met a group of teenagers growing up there – not Chinese, but rather young people known as Third Culture Kids.

Third Culture Kids is a term created by Ruth Hill Useem during research she did with her husband in the 1960s. *'The term "Third Culture Kids" or TCKs was coined to refer to the children who accompany their parents into another society,'* she writes. In other words, TCKs spend part of childhood in a country of which they are not citizens. 'Third Culture' describes the experience of cross-cultural living they share.

I began volunteering with the youth group of the largest international church in Beijing. Soon I was coordinating logistics for biannual retreats, hosting hundreds of TCKs from around China. Even while working in a neighbouring province I returned to Beijing on weekends, continuing to meet with TCKs I had been investing in for years. In 2010 I quit my job and moved to Beijing to work with TCKs full time. I accepted a part-time position with an international church in the 'expat bubble' which gave me time to work with TCKs in other places as well.

I spent my time building relationships with TCKs, mentoring them, and creating safe spaces for them to express themselves and connect with others. I mentored more than 100 TCKs closely, and directly invested in the lives of hundreds more. I was a key leader in teams coordinating over 35 camps and conferences for teenage TCKs in China and Cambodia. More than 1,000 individual TCKs from 40 different passport countries on six continents attended these events. Over time my work also shifted to mentoring over the Internet, as students I invested in moved away.

Why TCKs?

I quickly realised that TCKs had struggles, like all teenagers, but many kept their worries below the surface. The smiling faces of those teenagers who exuded positivity often masked powerful emotions – emotions they sometimes had difficulty understanding, or even expressing. I saw a quiet struggle, and I wanted to help.

Thus began a decade-long journey of discovery, as I listened to, and learned from, hundreds of TCKs. I listened to their stories – both the painful and the joyful. I built trust, delved deeper, listened a lot, and looked for patterns. I learned what they felt helped them, and what held them back. I gained an insight into the hearts of TCKs – how they see the world, how they feel about life, and the forces that act powerfully upon their inner lives.

I care passionately about these young people. Over the years I have delighted with them in their successes and grieved with them through their losses. I heard their hopes, their fears, their griefs and their anxieties. I held teenagers crying over a friend leaving, perhaps the latest in a long line of lost friends. I mentored TCKs through transitions – losing friends, moving to new places, repatriation, university, graduation into an unknown future, then embarking on careers, marriage, and parenting.

I also spent years listening to adult expatriates from a variety of backgrounds. I heard fear and pain from parents doing the best they could. I heard the confusion of parents desperate to understand their kids' behaviour. I also spoke with many parents unaware of the ways an international upbringing can shape a child. I travelled to speak to groups of TCKs and parents of TCKs in China as well as in Cambodia, Singapore, Thailand, and Vietnam.

I continued to invest in individual children and families. I sat in living rooms mediating misunderstandings. I was on the other end of the phone when a parent needed encouragement. I typed tens of thousands of words in Skype chat windows as young TCKs poured out their latest frustrations. I chatted with mothers struggling to parent cross-culturally. I sat beside teens finally telling their parents about struggles they needed help with. I spent ten years entering into the lives of TCKs, and supporting parents as they learned to better understand and connect with their TCK children.

It was these conversations that prompted me to write this book. While there are many excellent books about TCKs widely available I was unable to find anything that did what I did – acted as translator between TCKs and those who cared for them. There are books that teach about TCKs, with great research and helpful insights. There are also books that share powerful and personal stories of individual TCKs. The purpose of my book, however, is to advocate for TCKs: to explain their worldview, and share their stories – in their own words.

During the writing of this book I interviewed over 270 TCKs about their experiences and conducted a survey of 744 TCKs. I was intentional about talking to a wide cross-section of TCKs from different places with different experiences abroad. Every topic discussed in the book is connected to multiple interviews and to conversations with still more TCKs I did not interview formally. Most quotes reflect thoughts expressed in multiple interviews.

Misunderstood. That is, in a single word, the heart cry of many TCKs growing up in the 21st century. As I began my interviews I noticed that every TCK brought up this feeling. After a few months, I started asking about it specifically – and the response was overwhelming. Stories poured out of TCKs, along with relief at being heard. This book speaks on their behalf, giving voice to fears and feelings many TCKs believe others cannot, or will not, understand.

This book explains how life feels from a TCK's perspective, and explores feelings TCKs may have trouble articulating. It will help you see the world through their eyes, and suggests ways to encourage and support them as they grow and mature. I hope it stirs you to listen to TCKs you know – whether a family member, neighbour, friend, or student – and learn their stories.

Tanya Crossman, Sydney, 2016
tck.tanya@gmail.com
misunderstood-book.com
Facebook.com/misunderstoodTCK
Twitter.com/TanyaTCK

WHO *MISUNDERSTOOD* IS FOR

I wrote *Misunderstood* with two main audiences in mind – TCKs, and those who care for them. I call on the experiences of hundreds of TCKs to illustrate the landscape of an international childhood – what it feels like to grow up abroad, and how this experience impacts them. This helps young TCKs see they are not alone – that others have felt the same things – and gives them an opportunity to learn from the experiences of TCKs who have gone ahead of them. For those who care for TCKs, *Misunderstood* opens a window on how an international upbringing may affect a child.

Growing up internationally

There are many ways, and many reasons, a child may grow up internationally. Perhaps their parents work or study overseas. Perhaps their family immigrates, or returns to their birth country with foreign citizenship. Perhaps their parents are from different countries. The common thread is these children grow up 'in between' – between two or more countries, cultures, languages – even if they live in the one place. Broadly, these children are known as Cross-Cultural Kids (CCKs). A CCK is *'a person who is living or has lived in – or meaningfully interacted with – two or more cultural environments for a significant period of time during childhood (up to age 18)'* (David C. Pollock and Ruth E. Van Reken, *Third Culture Kids: Growing Up Among Worlds.*)

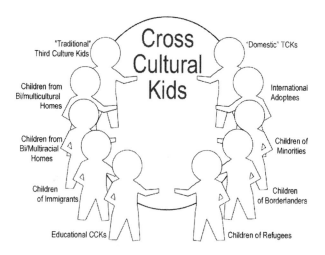

The Cross-Cultural Kid Model (©2002 Ruth E. Van Reken)

___

Misunderstood focuses on the subset of CCKs known as 'traditional Third Culture Kids' – the children of expatriates, growing up in families that live as foreigners abroad. Some CCKs fall into several categories; a few of these other categories are discussed, but only as far as the experience overlaps that of a TCK.

Other cross-cultural experiences

Third Culture Kids are not the only people who live cross-culturally, but theirs is a unique experience. TCKs live in a country they know can never be 'home', with the understanding they will leave one day. It is this sense of never being at home that makes the experience of a TCK different to the experiences of many other people who live internationally.

Many people with cross-cultural experiences who do not technically fit the definition of a TCK may find *Misunderstood* applicable and helpful. Some textbook TCKs, on the other hand, may not appreciate this label. My aim is not to classify any group of individuals, but rather to open a window into the experience of growing up internationally – to explain how it feels, according to young TCKs living these experiences.

While there is no exact formula, in my experience a child who spends three or more years abroad between ages 6-17 will identify as a TCK. Some TCKs I interviewed said they felt a shift in their third year abroad, from feeling 'I belong in my passport country' to feeling more caught in between, perhaps a sense of not belonging anywhere. That said, some children quickly feel at home abroad, and in only one or two years find they identify strongly with the Third Culture. Sometimes siblings will feel differently despite spending the same amount of time overseas – one may identify strongly with the community in which they lived, whether expatriate or local, while another never stops feeling most at home in their passport country.

In *Misunderstood* I look specifically at the experiences of TCKs who lived abroad in the 21st Century (born after 1985). The Internet has played a large role in most of these TCKs' lives, including the ways they maintain relationships across long distances. Older TCKs, and those who were less affected by the Internet, may have had a rather different experience.

What *Misunderstood* is about

This book is about stories. Most of my research consisted of collecting hundreds of stories. During more than three years spent writing and editing this book I interviewed over 220 TCKs under the age of 30, more than 50 TCKs aged 30-60, and conducted a separate survey of 744 TCKs. I sought input from TCKs with a variety of backgrounds – different schools, family backgrounds, languages, and religions (Protestant, Catholic, Mormon, Jewish, Muslim, Hindu, Buddhist, agnostic and atheist). Most telling is the different countries they identify with – a full list of more than 150 can be found in the Global Contributions appendix at the end of this book.

You will find quotes from many of the TCKs I interviewed throughout the text, sharing their feelings about their experiences. For each quote there is some biographical information. My own information, for example, would read:

> **Tanya, 34 [1st: Australia; 2nd: Australia, Cambodia, China, USA; 8 moves. Family: business. School: local.**

My passport country (Australia) and all the countries I have lived in as a foreigner are listed, along with the number of times I have moved locations. There is also a little context for the type of expat family I was part of (my father was relocated by the company he worked for) and the type of school I attended abroad (I went to local schools, along with children native to the country I lived in). Each of the sub-groups represented in these footnotes will be explored and explained. While this information is general and limited, it gives context – and demonstrates the wide variety of experiences within the TCK community.

It often amazes me that young people from vastly different backgrounds express the same sentiments, at times almost word for word. For many of the quotes included in the book there are two or three I have not included saying virtually the same thing – despite a different upbringing in a different location.

While all the TCKs I consulted speak English, for many it is a second (or third) language. Most were between 18 and 28 years old – old enough to have begun processing their experiences, but young enough to be true 21st century TCKs. There are also a few stories from older TCKs, including those now raising their own children – whether in their passport country or overseas – and from parents raising children abroad.

Describing a perspective, not a person

Just as a community is made up of many unique individuals, no two TCKs are completely alike. In this book I am necessarily dealing in generalisations and therefore not everything I have written applies to every TCK. In addition to a wide range of different experiences abroad, they have unique personalities. There is no one-size-fits-all explanation of how every TCK has felt and who they will become. Rather, this book is a window into how international life can affect the way a child thinks and feels about their world, and how this different perspective may manifest in the way they interact with others.

Reading this will not teach you everything about any individual TCK, but it will give you a head start in understanding their perspective. From there it will be up to you to take time to talk with the TCKs you meet, and allow them to teach you more about their unique life journeys.

CHAPTER ONE
THE BASICS

The Three Cultures Of A Third Culture Kid

Upon hearing the term 'Third Culture' many people assume it refers to a mix of the place a person is from and the place in which they live. If that is the case, why only three cultures? The 'Third Culture' is a concept, not a count. The three cultures of a Third Culture Kid are not three locations or people groups, but three categories of influence.

'TCKs may ask, "Well, am I a fourth or fifth culture kid? My parents came from two countries, we lived in four more when I grew up, so I'm way past only three cultures." This is a fair question, but it also shows why understanding the third culture concept is important. [...] It is a way of life shared by others with similar internationally mobile experiences,' writes Lois Bushong in her book *Belonging Everywhere & Nowhere: Insights into Counseling the Globally Mobile*

Ruth Hill Useem made a distinction between three separate types of culture – the parents' culture, the culture the TCK lives in, and the shared culture of TCKs themselves. Cross-Cultural Transition and TCK consultant Libby Stephens explains the three cultures of a TCK particularly well. She calls them the *Legal Culture*, the *Geographic Culture*, and the *Relational Culture*.

Legal Culture
The first culture is the Legal Culture – this is any country in which the child has legal standing: their passport country (or countries). This may also include having permanent

residency in a country. Some children I have worked with have more than one Legal Culture – by birth, descent, or through immigration. They may have dual citizenship or a passport from one country and permanent residency in another (and may live in neither country).

18% of TCKs I surveyed have held more than one passport; most of these currently hold two passports (some hold three different passports). An additional 17% had permanent residency in another country, either now or in the past.

Geographic Culture

The second culture is the Geographic Culture – any culture in which the child has lived. This may or may not include their legal culture(s). Most of the young people I have worked with were influenced by multiple Geographic Cultures. 40% of the TCKs surveyed had lived in four or more geographic cultures; 10% had lived in six or more.

Both Legal and Geographic cultures contribute to a TCK's understanding of the world and how it works. TCKs may absorb elements of food, dress, pop culture, body language, values and manners from each culture, blending them into a unique personal style or applying them differently according to context.

Relational Culture

The third culture is the Relational Culture. It is the culture of shared experiences – people who relate to each other because they have been through similar things. Many 21st century TCKs identify more strongly with people who have shared their childhood *experiences* than with those who have merely shared a location.

Experiences TCKs share might include:

· Familiarity with airports and travel, especially international.

· Accumulated losses of leaving friends behind, and being left by friends.

· The strangeness of their 'home' country, and the mixed emotions that go with being there.

· Funny stories of cultural mistakes – and the embarrassment of making those mistakes.

· Being part a group of friends from different cultural and linguistic backgrounds.

· Missing the very things that are supposedly 'strange' about their host culture.

· Feeling torn between a desire for change and adventure and a desire for rootedness and home.

· Confusion about what 'home' is.

The importance of the Third Culture to a TCK's identity explains why a TCK with a German passport growing up in China may feel more affinity with a Canadian passport holder growing up in Tanzania than either of them does with a child born and raised in Germany or China, Canada or Tanzania. While TCKs raised in different host countries do not experience the same specifics of culture (language, mannerisms, manners, food) they share similar experiences of being in-between and of feeling misunderstood.

"If we feel like a stranger between two worlds [...] it doesn't matter which countries we feel caught between. We share the feelings, if not the details," says Ruth Van Reken, ATCK, advocate of TCKs/CCKs, co-author of *Third Culture Kids*.

> *Even now I feel safest and most at home with other TCKs. It has caused friction in some new circles of friends where I have had an immediate bond with an established member of a community – another TCK.*
>
> **Abbie, 40 [1st: USA; 2nd: Austria, China, Germany, Hungary, USA; 7 moves. Family: embassy, mission. School: local, international, Christian international.]**

At home in the Third Culture

Today's TCKs often do not live fully in any one place, but with a foot in several worlds. That does not always mean they necessarily feel out of place everywhere they go, but it does mean the 'in between' is an important shared experience. 62% of TCKs born after 1985 said that 'feeling in between' was a significant part of their childhood experience (compared to 46% of older TCKs).

Many TCKs have told me of feeling at home in airports – where everyone they see is between places. Everyone in an airport has left a place, and people; everyone in an airport is on their way to somewhere else.

Comfort of the Third Culture

Many TCKs find comfort in belonging to a network made up of other TCKs. This might be an international school, a social group such as a scout troop, a church youth group, a group of families working for the same employer, or a combination of many groups. In these communities, TCKs are 'normal' – a precious gift.

> *I find it interesting that TCKs can bond easily with other TCKs who grew up in different places. Most of my daughter's close friends at university are other TCKs from all over the world – it is easy for them to connect.*
>
> **Yuli, parent of TCKs [1st: Indonesia; 2nd: Australia, China, Indonesia, Japan. Family: business. School: international.]**

On many occasions I have watched kids enjoy the exciting experience of meeting 'someone like me'. When you grow up believing no one can understand you, meeting someone with parallel experiences to yours can be thrilling. At one conference I organised a teen boy shared his excitement at meeting another teen with 'the same story'. The two had no overlap in their legal and geographic cultures, but the similarities in their Third Culture experiences were far more important than their differences. This illustrates why for so many TCKs it is indeed the Third Culture that feels most like home.

> *I had the opportunity to attend six great youth camps in Beijing, a nine-hour train ride from where I lived. It was great to meet other people like me, who could talk about similar experiences. This is where I learned what the term 'third culture' meant – I was not some weird combination of cultures that didn't belong anywhere, but to a group who were just like me.*
>
> **Jeremy, 22 [1st: New Zealand; 2nd: Australia, China, New Zealand, Singapore; 4 moves. Family: education . School: local, home, international.]**

A Third Culture identity

For many 21st century TCKs, the term 'Third Culture' is not a label with negative connotations, but rather a name for the living, breathing, community to which they belong.

> *I did not hear the term TCK until I was 28 years old. I suddenly realized the description was – me. I had no idea there was a term for it!*
> **Megan, 30 [1st: USA; 2nd: Germany, USA; 6 moves. Family: military. School: local, international.]**

'Third Culture Kids are hard to pin down as a group. There are just so many different types of us and we come from such a wide variety of passport countries and backgrounds. Despite the backlash against labels and the necessity for everyone to fit into a neat box, having a delineated identity can be reassuring. The reason why we are unique and why we deserve notice is that we are on the forefront of forging a new identity. [...] For a group that is characterized by a lack of community, we are surprisingly tight-knit. Distance is not an issue and we fully understand just how small this world truly is,' observes Cecilia Haynes in the anthology, *The Worlds Within.*

In the ever-smaller world shaped by the Internet and global transport, TCKs are more connected with places and people than was ever possible before. The Third Culture may not inhabit a specific piece of land, but it is home for many TCKs nonetheless.

> *The Third Culture is our home. It is where we 'belong'
> and relate to people as others do in their hometowns.*
> **Lisa, 24 [1st: UK; 2nd: China, France, Malaysia, Mexico, Peru,
> UK, USA; 7 moves. Family: education . School: international.]**

Cross-Cultural Experiences

Third Culture Kids are not the only people who live cross-culturally. Theirs, however, is a unique experience. TCKs live in a country they know can never be 'home', with the understanding they will leave one day. It is this sense of never being at home that makes the experience of a TCK different to the experiences of many other people who live internationally.

Third Culture Adults

For many people, the country their parents were born in, the country they were born in, the country they grew up in, and the country they have citizenship in, are all one and the same. This is also true for many adults living overseas, including parents of TCKs. While they live cross-culturally as adults they do so with a sense of 'home' developed in childhood. These Third Culture Adults live in the Third Culture of shared international experiences but, unlike TCKs, their cross-cultural experiences begin in adulthood.

Many TCA parents who grew up monoculturally assume that since they are living outside their passport country along with their children they share similar experiences and struggles. In many cases, however, the cross-cultural experience is quite different.

Having grown up in their passport country, these parents bring a strong cultural identity with them; their children, however, do not have the same emotional connections. TCKs must work through the mire of social and personal identity – difficult for most young people – while living between cultures.

Immigrants

Immigrants, and their children, also share the experience of living 'between' two cultures. They leave one culture for another, and often go through a difficult transition.

"Are immigrant kids TCKs?" Ruth considers. "It was that very type of confusion of terms and wondering who was and wasn't that made me start to use the broader term Cross-Cultural Kid (CCK), and TCK is one subset of that, but so is an immigrant child or bicultural or refugee or minority etc [...]. So with the CCK circles, TCKs are not immigrant kids or refugee kids, but there are things they often share, in particular in relationship to identity questions."

Immigrant kids often feel caught between two cultures – the culture they live in and the culture handed down by their parents. In some ways it is opposite to the experience of TCKs. Both are caught between the influence of their parents' culture and the culture in which they actually live. While a child in an immigrant family is expected to balance their parents' culture with assimilation in the new place, TCKs are often expected to connect most strongly to the place from which their parents came, not the place in which they live. This difference can actually be confusing for TCKs.

> *I know people who were born and raised in Australia with parents that are fully Asian. I never understood why they called themselves Aussies and had Australian accents. They have no idea about the countries of their parents, and there is a sense they are unwilling to understand or try to bring that culture into themselves. I thought they were too arrogant to get to know their own cultures. I never realised they just don't have a connection with it.*
>
> **Yanie, 23 [1st: China, Hong Kong, UK; 2nd: Australia, China, Hong Kong; 3 moves. Family: business. School: local, international.]**

Immigrants have an expectation of permanent residence in their adopted home. The child of an immigrating family begins to form an identity in one culture then moves to a place where they suddenly do not fit in; but they have reached the end of their journey – this new place, strange as it may be, is their permanent home.

TCKs have a different experience. They live in a place that is not legally their home, regardless of how attached they may feel to it. For most the expectation is they will leave, perhaps even that they have no right to stay. There is a price for getting too attached, and a cost to going 'home'.

> *Growing up in America my dad would always say,*
> *"Remember, this is not your home." It really hurt me*
> *because we never really knew how long we would*
> *be there. The question 'where are you from' really*
> *confused me.*
>
> **Longa, 18 [1ˢᵗ: Zambia. 2ⁿᵈ: China, USA, Zambia; 4 moves.**
> **Family: education . School: local, Christian international.]**

When immigrants become expatriates

Immigrants do not always stay put, however. Some move on, with their new citizenship, to a third or fourth country. Children in these families are TCKs, but with an added cross-cultural layer. They have at least three cultures to juggle – their heritage, their legal home, and the country they live in as expatriates. I call these families 'Immigrant Expats'.

Other immigrants return to live in their original home countries, now with foreign citizenship. Adults in this situation usually have a solid childhood home experience, but struggle with cross-cultural issues upon returning to that 'home' after many years settled in a new country. Rather than being truly local, they are acknowledged expats, with legal standing somewhere else – a country they can (and often do) return to. Children of these families, which I call 'Returned Immigrant Expats', are also TCKs.

Adult TCKs

What happens when TCKs grow up? Are they still Third Culture 'Kids'? TCKs are affected by their international upbringing throughout their lives. The term Adult Third Culture Kid (ATCK) refers to an adult who, regardless of their current location, grew up internationally as a child.

Pollock and Van Reken comment, *'While parents may change careers and become former international businesspeople, former missionaries, former military personnel, or former foreign service officers, no one is ever a former third culture kid. TCKs simply move on to being adult third culture kids because their lives grow out of the roots planted in and watered by the third culture experience'*.

These days, when people ask how long it has been since I returned to my passport country and I reply with "almost 10 years," the response is often dismissive. The funny thing about experiences you have in your formative years is that no matter how far in the past they may be, they will always be a part of you. Though a TCK's experiences are almost inevitably different from a national's, they are a no less real and integrated part of who they are.

Lani, 25 [1st: Australia; 2nd: Australia, Ethiopia; 2 moves. Family: mission. School: home.]

ATCKs who lived overseas in the 20th Century share many experiences with today's TCKs. That said, today's world is much 'smaller' than it once was. Most ATCKs grew up without the influence of the Internet, whereas truly global relationships are a big part of life for 21st Century TCKs.

TCKs with ATCK parents appreciate the shared experiences they bring to the table. Those who are not themselves parents can also be a great help to younger TCKs, by mentoring or otherwise coming alongside them as they journey through the experience of growing up internationally.

"When a TCK is mentored by another adult TCK who has learned how to be well adjusted and comfortable with their identity, that TCK will feel a sense of belonging with that mentor," explains Ellen Mahoney, ATCK and founder of Sea Change Mentoring. "This experience can be the source of great relief and often serves as the jumping off point for learning how to feel more connected with others."

20ᵗʰ Century TCKs vs. 21ˢᵗ Century TCKs

The lives of TCKs in the 21ˢᵗ century are different to the lives of TCKs in the 20ᵗʰ century in a few key respects. A major global event occurred in the late 1990s, which dramatically changed the experience of TCKs worldwide – widespread use of the Internet. As I talked to TCKs of all ages, I saw differences in the responses of TCKs from the pre- and post-Internet years.

Changes in travel

Early expat families travelled abroad on ships, and the sea journey between locations took considerable time. There were very few options for communicating with friends or extended family in their passport country. For these TCKs, the cultures and experiences of each place were removed from one another, creating a buffer.

'In the era when most international travelers went overseas by ship, the trip could take weeks, providing a built-in transition *period that allowed time for the grief process. In today's world of jet travel, however, there is no transition time to deal properly with the inevitable grief of losing what has been left behind...'* note Pollock and Van Reken.

While this meant these TCKs had the opportunity to really *be* where they lived, it also meant goodbyes felt quite permanent; often a family left their host culture believing they would never be back.

By 1970 air travel was the norm – international travel was becoming cheaper, easier, and faster. TCKs I interviewed who lived abroad in the last few decades of the 20th century said they often travelled internationally once a year, including visits to their passport country once every two years.

A lot of today's TCKs travel frequently. There are many benefits to this – 21st century TCKs are usually well travelled and see extended family more often than their 20th century counterparts. A drawback to this is a lack of permanence. Many young TCKs I interviewed live in one place and yet spent three months of the year in another country, or countries.

TCKs are now more able to return to the place that feels like home, if they desire. When I left Africa for college in the 1970s, I knew I would never go back, and I have not. The same was true for my husband. I think the feeling that we can never go back has contributed to feelings of rootlessness in our adult

> *lives. But my daughters went back to Hungary several times during college, and both made a trip with their husbands as newlyweds.*
> **Cynthia, 59 [1st: USA; 2nd: Belgium, Hungary, Nigeria, Switzerland, Togo; 42 moves. Family: mission. School: local, international, home, boarding.]**

Changes in education

Education is a big part of most young lives. A section on International Education in the next chapter discusses education options now available to expatriate families. There are more choices than ever before, and several significant trends in education were apparent in the survey. Half of TCKs born before 1985 attended boarding school, compared to only 10% of younger TCKs. In contrast, over half of younger TCKs had attended an international school, compared to less than a third of older TCKs.

"When TCKs, in the mid 20th century were educated outside of their passport culture, they often had the choice of being educated in a local education system or their families would educate them in such a way that they could reintegrate to their passport educational culture upon return," explains Valérie Besanceney, ATCK, international school teacher and author of *B at Home: Emma moves again*. "When international schools came into the picture, it became easier for children to transition from one country to another because they could continue their education in one language, regardless of changes in the curriculum. In the 21st century, the community of international schools has grown immensely."

The Internet also changed distance education. Quality education is available online, even for advanced classes and specialist subjects. As bandwidth continues to rise, live online classes are available. These changes mean homeschooling is now a viable option for families who in years past may have sent their children to boarding school or repatriated.

Changes in friendship

A distinctive trend in my interviews with TCKs of different ages was a difference in friendships. The core friendships of TCKs in the 20th century were generally people who lived nearby: when they moved, they developed new friendships. While they may have kept in loose contact with friends from previous locations, even made visits, their core support networks were where they lived. After moving they felt little pressure to maintain contact with friends left behind, and were motivated to engage fully in their new location. As the Internet became widespread and accessible worldwide at the start of the 21st century, the experience of TCKs changed with it.

The Internet changed the way we communicate, shrinking the distances between us. TCKs can now stay in touch with each other very easily – meeting in person once or twice a year can be enough to maintain a close friendship when they chat weekly (if not daily) online. It is not uncommon for 21st Century TCKs to have best friends in two or three different cities – even two or three different countries. They may not stay in touch with friends from early childhood (with whom they did not have an online relationship) but will often stay close with a select group of friends from middle or high school – even through multiple international moves on both sides.

> *People who haven't moved as much or as far do not understand that it is usual for TCKs to have more than one best friend. They are my best friend in this circumstance and this location. I don't expect all of those friends to say I'm their only best friend, we all have many, we all respect that and not are insulted by it.*
>
> **Callie, 17 [1st: USA; 2nd: China, Qatar, USA; 6 moves. Family: business. School: international.]**

Drawbacks

While there are obvious benefits to these tools, both for building/maintaining relationships and for education, there are drawbacks too. 20th century TCKs were more grounded in the places they lived. Many were deeply connected to local peers. 21st century TCKs, on the other hand, have less incentive (and often less opportunity) to invest in relationships with local peers. Maintaining friendships with people in multiple locations can also add to the sense of being 'between' places.

Of the TCKs surveyed, those born before 1985 were more likely to live immersed in the host culture. TCKs born after 1985 were twice as likely as older TCKs to have lived in an 'expat bubble'.

Many 21st century TCKs have a support network scattered across the globe. It is wonderful to be able to stay in touch – it opens many doors, and makes living far away easier for many. But it also increases the obligation to stay connected. Time devoted to maintaining relationships with friends and family in other places is time that cannot be devoted to building and maintaining relationships where the expat family lives.

'I have heard it said, "TCKs sort their friends by continents." That is true. What richness they have in friendships of all sizes, colors, statuses, religions, ages, and history! But then, how do they keep up with all of these great relationships? Today's world of social media has helped enormously, but a new challenge facing some is to make "in-person" friends in the new place rather than spend all of their time on Facebook with friends from a previous location,' writes Lois Bushong.

For today's TCKs, maintaining online relationships is not optional, but essential. It is truly a different *relational* world from the one in which 20th century TCKs lived.

Challenges of TCK Life

Some benefits of the TCK life are obvious – a broader world view, travel opportunities, learning language(s), exposure to a range of cultures and customs, all of which result in an open mind toward the differences of others. There are opportunities to develop empathy, to be able to put oneself in another's shoes. Many TCKs also receive an education the family could not afford were it not paid for by an employer. To list these benefits while ignoring the corresponding difficulties, however, is to see only half the story.

'*Expat Life is a life full of discovery, newness and, often, a lot of travel. However, as exciting as change can be, it can also be challenging and difficult,*' write Dr. Lisa Pittman, a practicing psychologist and Diana Smit, educational therapist, in their book, *Expat Teens Talk: Peers, Parents and Professionals offer support, advice and solutions in response to Expat Life challenges as shared by Expat Teens.*

Living abroad is not necessarily a disadvantage for a child, and growing up (and especially being a teenager) is never easy, no matter where in the world you live. There are added complexities, however, when growing up between cultures, against a backdrop of transition.

> *I have loved growing up cross-culturally. The adventures, experiences, and worldviews I have are priceless. But it comes at a huge cost. Most of the time I think it was worth it, and I have a generally positive view of my life.*
> **Emily, 21 [1st: USA; 2nd: DR Congo, Kenya, Rwanda, USA; 20 moves. Family: mission. School: local, international, boarding.]**

Being a TCK is not a 'problem' – it is an opportunity. Many TCKs have been hurt by well-meaning adults who tell them they have certain issues or problems due to their overseas upbringing. International life is the TCKs normal; their problems aren't 'TCK problems' but *life* problems.

> *My school invited along a speaker who specialised
> in TCK issues. We had no identity crisis; what was
> abnormal to others seemed perfectly normal to us.
> I applaud the well-intentioned TCK speaker, but a
> three-hour dry talk from an adult whom we didn't
> know, didn't respect, and weren't interested in was
> probably not the best way to inform us of our 'problem'.*
>
> **Justin, 23 [1st: Japan, Singapore; 2nd: Canada, Japan, Singapore, UK;
> 16 moves. Family: mission. School: local, Christian international,
> home, boarding.]**

ATCK perspectives

I heard a lot of overwhelmingly positive feedback from
ATCKs, especially those who lived abroad in the 1970s
and 1980s; many loved the experience of growing up abroad
and can be quite defensive of how great it was. While some
had negative experiences, most reported feeling a general
sense of contentment as children. As adults, they look back
fondly on their international upbringing and many still value
travel highly.

> *As a child I had only positive feelings about my
> international life. My appreciation for my childhood
> overseas has grown as an adult. I love that I learned a
> foreign language at a young age and also that I don't
> really feel like living in one place forever. It has given
> me a sense of movement and adventure, which makes
> life very interesting.*
>
> **Zach, 42 [1st: USA; 2nd: China, Hungary, Romania, USA;
> 8 moves. Family: mission. School: local, home, international.]**

ATCKs who described their childhoods negatively referenced either frequent moving or family dysfunction as a major contributing factor. Some of these ATCKs now stick to one home location, whether in their passport country or abroad. They may refuse to move away or even travel very far, finding this emotionally stressful. Creating and establishing a physical home is important to their emotional wellbeing. One explained that while he enjoys travel greatly, packed suitcases can bring up negative emotion; his solution is to unpack and put his suitcase away whenever he arrives somewhere, even if he will only be there for a single night.

Is it worth it?

I have heard a lot of questions from expatriate parents worried the decision to move overseas will have a negative impact on their children.

· "Is living overseas damaging my kids?"

· "Would it be better for my kids if we went home?"

· "Will they be scarred for life?"

· "Is it selfish for me to take this job?"

· "Is it worth it?"

If you are a parent of TCKs and worry about the potential negative impact of international life on your kids – do not be discouraged. Children gain *a lot* from life overseas. There are difficulties, but they can be addressed and processed. No two TCKs are identical, but over 80% of TCKs surveyed said they were glad to be TCKs; only 2% wished they had not lived abroad. TCKs of all ages resonated more strongly with positive words than with negative words, saying they considered their international upbringing, 'exciting' (82%), 'fun' (79%) and 'special' (76%). 90% of TCKs surveyed were thankful for their experience overseas; 65% said it was a good choice for their family.

> *The list of things that I love about being a TCK outweighs the cons by far. I love that I don't see the world as revolving around one certain country; I love that I am for the most part comfortable talking to any race, nationality or class of people; I love that I have had the incredible blessing of travelling to many countries and seeing many things; I love that I have an automatic connection with almost every TCK I have ever met; I love that I am more comfortable than most trying new and crazy things; I love that I am not okay with having a safe life; I love that I have had a small taste of the incredible amount of things that can be done in life (travelling, jobs, living situations etc.).*
>
> **Gabe, 22 [1st: USA; 2nd: China, USA; 5 moves. Family: education , adoptive. School: home.]**

Living abroad can be difficult, but it does not have to be negative overall. Parents (and other significant adults) have the power to affect how TCKs experience life overseas – to help them successfully navigate the difficulties that come with life in the Third Culture, providing tools to process and integrate their experiences.

Douglas Ota, counsellor/therapist, founder of the Safe Harbour transitions program at the American School of

The Hague and author of *Safe Passage: How Mobility Affects People and What International Schools Should Do About It* says, "Blanket statements about all TCKs are tricky. Those TCKs who 'would not trade' [life overseas] are demonstrating what is called 'integration' in their lives: they have storied their experiences and these experiences – good, bad, joyous and painful – have become part of who they are. This is a sign of psychological health."

What I gained is invaluable; the open mindedness acquired through understanding different values people can have, and understanding there is more than one way to go about things. I missed out on the normal life that a normal kid would live back home. But to tell the truth, it is not something I regret a bit.

Jeremy, 22 [1st: New Zealand; 2nd: Australia, China, New Zealand, Singapore; 4 moves. Family: education . School: local, home, international.]

Misunderstood

The unique cross-cultural experience of growing up away from 'home' means TCKs often feel misunderstood by many different groups of people at once – in their passport country, in their host country, even in their own family. They love what they gain from life overseas, but at the same time can feel separated from the people they wish to share it with.

> *As a TCK, I often feel that I cannot truly relate to those around me. I function in two worlds at once. I have gained a broad knowledge of the world while missing the more specific aspects of cultural understanding that come with spending a lifetime in one place.*
> **Heidi, 24 [1st: USA; 2nd: China, USA; 8 moves. Family: business. School: home, local.]**

Misunderstood by family

For many, the feeling of being misunderstood begins with family members who obviously love them but do not recognise the different difficulties they face. Every child goes through hard times at some point, and the difficulty is compounded should a child feel these problems are minimised or missed altogether – a common theme in my interviews. A third of TCKs surveyed felt misunderstood by parents; more than half felt misunderstood by extended family.

> *Our parents thought we were incredibly lucky to travel so much and be in international schools, but both primary and secondary school were very difficult. I never felt at ease or completely comfortable around people my age. I often felt out of place, as if I was just a spoiled child whining about all the negative aspects of her life and overlooking the positives. My parents said we were extremely lucky, but during the years spent chained to their feet, our situation often felt like an imprisonment.*
> **Aurelie, 19 [1st: France; 2nd: Belgium, China, France, UK; 5 moves. Family: business. School: international, local.]**

Some parents of TCKs have trouble understanding the culture gap between them and their children. I often see this in families who live in expat communities and send their children to international schools; these parents can assume this life is close enough to life in their passport country that it will not make a great difference to the child.

Other parents see the differences, and struggle to accept them. This is particularly common when parents identify strongly with a passport culture that has very different expectations to the host culture, or the expat culture, their children are engaged with. Examples I have witnessed include American families upset at the children's lack of patriotic sentiment, a Nigerian family upset because their children did not act 'as Nigerian children should', Australian parents concerned that their children spoke with American accents, and families from several different countries worried that their children were absorbing Western values at the expense of the parents' home culture.

Misunderstood by friends

Even if there is no tension at home, TCKs spend a lot of time explaining. No matter where they are, someone does not understand key aspects of their life and experience. TCKs do not easily fit in the boxes others use to understand identity, which often leaves them missing a sense of belonging.

41% of TCKs surveyed said they felt misunderstood by local friends in their host culture and 67% felt misunderstood by friends in their passport country. Even friends who share the Third Culture may have very different experiences – then either leave or are left behind.

> *Here in Thailand I have to explain all my Australian terms, that Christmas is in summer and still the 25th of December and stuff like that, but then back in Australia I need to explain everything! I have to explain the school system, that I'm half a year behind because we start in August. Telling stories I have to translate what was said into Thai. Even if other people have other weird habits I still have to explain mine because I picked them up in Thailand.*
>
> **Katherine, 18 [1st: Australia; 2nd: Australia, Thailand; 2 moves. Family: mission. School: Christian international.]**

Explaining can be tiring, but when a TCK chooses to let things slide, another tissue-thin layer of isolation slips between them and those around them. Sometimes TCKs (even as young adults) do not notice the strain of all the explaining until they are in a group of TCKs and feel an almost physical sense of relief. *This* community is where they feel 'at home' – neither their passport country nor any host country is as comforting or as comfortable.

This leads to a corresponding feeling they are on their own, that no one can help them. This can make it hard to reach them – many young TCKs really do not believe another person, especially an adult (with their cross-cultural differences), can really understand them.

> *TCKs often feel they will never be known completely; at best they are known slightly by people all over the*

> *world. Each person only knows tiny snapshots of parts of their lives.*
>
> **Gabe, 22 [1ˢᵗ: USA; 2ⁿᵈ: China, USA; 5 moves. Family: education, adoptive. School: home.]**

Building understanding

Some TCKs focus on the fact their TCK friends *do* understand them. Others learn to find common ground with monocultural friends, areas where they can relate to one another. Having had cross-cultural experience certainly gives a head start when connecting with TCKs, but this is not essential. One third of TCKs surveyed said they taught others how to understand them, and that this worked.

There are many overlaps in the emotions we each experiences, regardless of the different circumstances that prompt these feelings. Learning how TCKs *feel* about their lives, understanding their world, creates opportunities to connect – an opportunity anyone can take up.

When non-TCKs take the time to learn and understand how growing up internationally can affect a person, they are better able to bridge the gap – taking the pressure off TCKs to make themselves understood. But even if there is no one around who 'gets' the international part of a TCK's pain, emotions are a common human experience; the triggers differ but the core feelings are similar. I may not be able to empathise with a TCK's specific experiences, but I can often empathise with the feelings that arose from those experiences. It therefore helps TCKs greatly to learn to articulate and express the emotional side of their experiences, as this gives non-TCKs a point of commonality from which to empathise and begin to understand.

> *The truth is, I know that there are many out there who are just like me, or at least can understand how I feel. There is a sense of isolation from others who are not TCKs, but I've always felt that in time most other people can at least comprehend the feelings we have. Loneliness is a universal trait among humans, whether it's because you were always the weird kid at school or because you lived two thousand miles away from anyone who spoke English. While the reasons may be different, it's the same type of pain we share.*
>
> **Eugene, 21 [1ˢᵗ: USA; 2ⁿᵈ: China, South Korea, USA; 10 moves. Family: immigrant expat, adoptive, education. School: home (group), Christian international.]**

"When we have similar emotional experiences we can understand the other even if the circumstances for the emotion weren't identical," says Ruth Van Reken. "When relationships are broken for any reason – death, anger, moving away – we feel it. It is not a function of which culture we are from or live in. If we feel like a stranger between two worlds also for reasons rooted in our need to belong, it doesn't matter which countries we feel caught between. We share the feelings if not the details."

21ˢᵗ century TCKs *want* to be understood. They *want* to tell their stories to people who are genuinely interested to hear, and to learn about the places that matter to them. They *want* to form deep connections with others – whether they believe it is possible or not. *Misunderstood* discusses different experiences common among TCKs, to give you a head start in getting to know specific TCKs you meet.

CHAPTER TWO

DIFFERENT EXPERIENCES OF TCK LIFE

Parents' Employment

Some TCKs think their specific experience is the 'typical' TCK experience, without understanding how differently other TCKs live. This chapter explores different factors in a TCK's experience.

In most cases, a family moves abroad because of the parents' work. Different sending organisations (or 'sponsors') provide different levels of support for the children of their employees; different career tracks affect families in different ways. This is such a big factor in a TCK's international experience that some refer to themselves accordingly – such as Missionary Kids or Military Kids.

'The sponsor creates the paradigm of the expatriate family; it has its own subculture and norms to which the family members must adhere; it influences the type and quality of family life, the transition process, and, also, the education and schooling of the children. It has a strong impact on the nature of the third culture experiences of the children,' says Dr. Ettie Zilber, in her book, *Third Culture Kids – The Children of Educators in International Schools.*

While there are exceptions, most international families fall into at least one of the following five categories:

1. Mission work

2. Foreign Service – military personnel and diplomatic staff

3. International business

4. Teachers in international schools

5. Unaffiliated

6. Non Governmental Organisations

Mission work

Mission families go overseas with a religious group, usually with a strong sense of spiritual vocation. Missionaries are involved in a huge range of work, including education and development. They often have very limited financial resources; they may not be paid for their work, instead fundraising to support their families.

Children of missionaries are often known as 'MKs' – Missionary Kids. MKs usually have a strong TCK identity. 85% of MKs born after 1985 identified with 'Third Culture', compared to 78% of young TCKs overall.

Organisational support
Most missionaries are affiliated with a wider organisation which provides oversight and support; others go independently. Mission organisations often provide the most recognition of, and support for, TCKs, understanding they have different needs, and providing the most help with re-entry. In the USA there is a college organisation – Mu Kappa – that works exclusively with MKs, and a number of Christian universities provide re-entry support for MKs.

Many mission organisations have annual conferences to bring families from around a certain region together, and many of these conferences include programs for MKs who attend with their parents. For some, it is one of the only opportunities they have while growing up to spend time with other TCKs. Some organisations also provide support upon the family's return to their passport country, with individual assessments or re-entry seminars.

Not all MKs receive this level of support, however, even those under the umbrella of a wider organisation. When missionaries themselves are under great strain, this translates to their children Where a family is relationally isolated (it is possible to be physically isolated and yet have good relational support) there can be problems. The unavoidable stresses of life remain contained within the family. Most MKs I have known with dysfunctional relationships with their parents were in families with little or no organisational support. This does not mean a family lacking support is doomed, but it is important for parents to advocate for the needs of their children, and find the support they need.

Lois Bushong, ATCK, counsellor/therapist and author believes families can overcome dysfunctional relationships even without organizational support. "I believe the lack of support should challenge the parental unit to seek the necessary support they need on their own, rather than do nothing or just sit back and blame the agency," she says. "In other words, the problem is not necessarily in the lack of support from the organization, but how the parental unit responds or does not respond to the challenge is what creates the dysfunction."

Resentment

12% of TCKs surveyed identified a sense of resentment with their childhood overseas. While this is not a large percentage, half the MKs I interviewed expressed resentment about aspects of their experience, even if they had resolved this. Other TCKs may share a sense of resentment toward the sponsor, but with MKs the mixture of family, faith, and sponsor makes resentment particularly fraught.

MKs who do struggle with resentment are deeply affected, something that was clear in many interviews. Resentment can greatly upset TCKs and their families. Others suppress resentment; this unresolved emotion lingers under the surface and can negatively colour a TCK's experience of life overseas.

A number of MKs felt resentment toward their parents for choices made on their behalf. MKs are not missionaries. They did not choose the missionary life – they were brought along by parents who chose the life. They may believe in what their parents are doing, think it is great, and yet have negative feelings about their experiences. They may wish they went to a normal school, had more money, or were not painted with the 'missionary' brush. They may feel guilty about these feelings, believing it makes them 'bad people' especially when it is felt as a religious imperative. This resentment and guilt may be buried, result in passive-aggressive behaviour or only re-emerge later in life.

Resentment is a huge problem for most of us kids on the mission field. We all agree that staying positive

> *toward our parents can be extremely difficult. Instead of showing resentment toward my parents I would just do little things to drive my parents crazy. I hoped they would get tired of me and would let me go back. Unfortunately (well, more like fortunately) they never did, but I wouldn't change my time here. The mission field was probably the best thing that could have happened to me.*
>
> **Risa, 17 [1ˢᵗ: Guatemala, USA; 2ⁿᵈ: Guatemala, USA; 4 moves. Family: adoptive, mission. School: home (group).]**

MKs who feel free to express resentment they experience have an opportunity to process it – but this can be hard for a missionary parent to hear. Such feelings, when expressed, can feel like an indictment on parents for doing the 'wrong' thing for their kids. Parents may feel compelled to tell their kids why the sacrifices are worth it.

In her book, *Letters Never Sent*, Ruth Van Reken comments, *'In my life, the greatest pain I experienced came in the constant cycles of separation and loss from people and places I loved and these were primarily a result of my parent's believing they were following God's call […] I understood the price Jesus paid to be my Saviour so I 'should' be grateful. I understood that God is worthy of my life's devotion so I 'shouldn't' mind the losses along the way.'*

Most missionaries go with an idea of what they are giving up, but also with a strong sense of *why* they are making the sacrifice. MKs do not have this same sense of purpose. When well meaning adults (not just parents) try to comfort or encourage MKs by pointing out the 'good things' their parents are able to do, it is rarely a comfort to the MK. They did not go abroad to do ministry; they are children experiencing childhood. Their lives are not sacrifices for the sake of something greater; their lives are just that – their lives.

> *I am angry that my life was chosen for me, that my path has not been my own, and that my parents do not see how this is painful for me. Why did my parents choose to follow Someone they can't even see? My life is not theirs to control. It's not fair.*
>
> **Chelsea, 21 [1st: USA; 2nd: Estonia, Hungary, USA; 11 moves. Family: mission.]**

When MKs are treated as 'little missionaries' it can create a sense of distance, of being misunderstood. They did not choose missionary life, and most do not see themselves as missionaries. When MKs are able to spend time with adults who treat them simply as young people living life, not missionaries, they receive freedom to be themselves. These interactions give them space to be something other than a representative of a mission organisation.

> *I love the experiences I had as a TCK – they are a treasure trove of memories. What I don't like is that I didn't have a choice in the matter as a kid. I always felt that it was my parents who had chosen to be missionaries and not myself. The church youth leaders I knew were there for the benefit of TCKs, not as*

> *missionaries. It was really wonderful to be met by a TCK worker where I was treated as a kid rather than as a missionary.*
>
> **Karissa, 23 [1st: USA; 2nd: China, USA; 9 moves. Family: mission. School: local, home (group), Christian international.]**

While MKs are not missionaries, it can still be beneficial for MKs to get involved in their parents' work in some way. This gives them an experiential connection to what their parents do and why the family lives the life they do. While this may not be possible for all families, finding projects to do together can be helpful. However, if they feel pressured, rather than invited, this may backfire.

> *Friends who were involved with their parents' work always did better than those who did not. It creates family unity because they are all working together towards a common goal. Children always come first. Always. My parents believed this and it made a huge difference in our lives. It's true everywhere but cross-culturally it's much worse. If an MK is struggling do as much as you can to help them. Just don't ignore it, because it won't go away.*
>
> **Emily, 21 [1st: USA; 2nd: DR Congo, Kenya, Rwanda, USA; 20 moves. Family: mission. School: local, international, boarding.]**

Personal autonomy

Autonomy and control are big issues for many MKs. Their lifestyle was chosen for them; there must be space for personal autonomy within that life, even if it is the choice to remain distant from their parents' work.

Missionaries are often under heavy outside scrutiny – supporters may look into their finances, their lifestyle choices, their beliefs, and even their children's behaviour. Most MKs feel a pressure, whether implied or stated outright, to be 'good kids' so their actions do not reflect badly on their parents. They may feel boxed in, unable to express personal identity and opinions. This is especially true when children are made a public part of a family's fundraising.

> *I never resented my parents doing missionary work, I loved growing up overseas; I thought (and still do think) that we've had a much more interesting childhood. What I hated was the 'scrutiny' or 'specialness' other people expressed of us when we visited our supporting Australian 'home churches'.*
>
> **Rebecca, 28 [1st: Australia; 2nd: Australia, Papua New Guinea, Solomon Islands; 8 moves. Family: mission. School: home (group), Christian international.]**

Many react to this by striving to look perfect on the outside, making it harder and harder for them to share their inner conflict and confusion with other. Others rebel against the control they feel, trying to break far away from the life they feel forced into. MKs do best when they feel permission to be themselves, to express their honest opinions (especially at home), and have creative avenues their parents support – when they feel loved and accepted, whether or not they fit the missionary mould

Many factors impact how an MK feels about their family, their parents' work, and their life in general. While most MKs enjoy their experiences when they are young, and may be quite proud of what their parents do, quite a few distance themselves from the mission world as they get older. There are losses attached to missionary life which MKs need permission to feel and to grieve. If they have no space to do this as children, they will do it as adults.

> *Transitioning from being a pastor's kid in the United States to a missionary kid in China, I was constantly looked at through the lens of my parents' vocation. I was always recognized as the pastor's first daughter and once in China, the missionaries' first daughter. Many times, it was difficult to articulate what I was going through and I never felt I could be 100% honest in my responses because I knew I was also representing my parents.*
>
> **Pauline, 22 [1st: USA, 2nd: China, South Korea, USA; 3 moves. Family: returned immigrant expat, mission. School: Local, Christian international.]**

MKs and faith

Not all MKs are people of faith, as children or as adults. For some, the assumption they share their parents' faith can be irritating or even maddening in some contexts. Not adopting their parents' religion does not mean these TCKs are 'rebelling' or angry with their parents. Many feel compelled to adopt the outward practices of their parents' religion as children regardless of their actual beliefs; it can come as a shock to their parents when these MKs step away from religious practice after growing up and leaving the family home.

"The issue for missions that make them have a different twist than the other sectors is the God factor," says Ruth Van Reken. "Therein comes the reason many wind up losing their faith in the end, because it is the crux of the reason for their pain."

Regardless of where MKs land in terms of faith and career, most appreciate their parents' work even if they do not share their parents' faith. 77% of MKs born after 1985 would not give up their international experiences, compared to 70% of TCKs overall; 81% said they gained more than they lost, and 92% were thankful for the experience.

Foreign Service

For the purposes of this chapter, foreign service includes both employees of the diplomatic corps (diplomats and other embassy staffers) and military personnel serving abroad. There are similarities in the family situations of TCKs in Military and Diplomatic families. Both groups tend to move frequently, an experience explored further in the later section, 'Relationship with the host country'. As their parents' work is directly connected to their country of origin, these TCKs may also feel strong pressure to be patriotic, or that they are representatives of their passport country/ culture wherever they go.

Some foreign service families get stuck in an expat bubble

– where all their friends are expats and they spend most of their time in places that cater to expats. For families housed in diplomatic compounds or on military bases this can happen quite naturally, and in some places families are encouraged to stay within the compound for security reasons. This provides strong support among a community of similar families, but fewer connections to the place in which they live – something several foreign service TCKs I interviewed regretted in hindsight.

Military

Children of military families are often, sometimes self-referentially, called 'Military Brats'. These families are often the most frequent movers, which can add extra turmoil to a child constantly in transition. Many live on military bases, however, where they are surrounded by others in the same situation and have built-in support.

There is a special camaraderie that develops on a military base. With so many people shuffling in and out, people know how to make the new guy feel welcome.

Megan, 30 [1st: USA; 2nd: Germany, USA; 6 moves. Family: military. School: local, international.]

'For most of us, it's about never knowing a way of life that was not centered around military protocol, military bases, dependent schools, commissaries and base exchanges until sometime after we became adults,' notes Dr. Jim Grubbs in his book, *Growing Up In The Military.*

When military families are attached to an embassy rather than a military base these children may live in a diplomatic compound, or a compound with many other expatriates.

Diplomatic

The support for children of the diplomatic corps varies widely from country to country. Countries with large diplomatic corps (such as the US) provide greater support for TCKs. In a large embassy, there may be enough families so these kids can interact with others like them.

Until high school my family always followed wherever my father was posted. I found that in each country the friends I was closest to were from the embassy. I realized after moving to a place where I was the only diplomat kid in my generation, I only settled in with my new surroundings after I met other kids from the embassy within my generation. It's like knowing there is another person in your position attracts you to become friends and helps both get used to the new place. It's like these embassy kids are a supportive pillar to help get used to the surroundings. How the friendship develops in the future after settling in will then rest up to each person.

Vanka, 19 [1ˢᵗ: Indonesia; 2ⁿᵈ: Australia, Canada, Fiji, Germany, Indonesia; 7 moves. Family: embassy. School: local, international.]

TCKs from smaller embassies may feel quite isolated, even in a place with many other foreigners. This is especially true if there are no others from their passport country in their peer community. I interviewed several TCKs in this position; most felt disconnected from their passport culture (many had never lived there), but felt pressure to be their best selves at all times, as they were the only representative of their country most of their friends would ever meet.

Embassy children are often required to attend official events of some kind, at least occasionally. They are taught early to act appropriately, that appearances matter. These TCKs are often the best chameleons – they learn from a young age to control their outward behaviour, regardless of how they feel. Some may rebel against this sense of control, but most are well behaved in public even if rebellious in private.

National identity

A number of foreign service TCKs said their nationality was one of the first things people saw about them while living overseas – a defining characteristic. Several said this was a wearying experience. When visiting their passport countries, many of these TCKs felt extremely foreign. Some said their nationality was a label that did not really 'fit', despite feeling a deep sense of patriotism or pride in their country.

An ambassador's daughter told me her South American passport country was just a word to her – something her father did for a living. She had no emotional connection to the place her family represented, despite living in an embassy. An African diplomat's son said he dreaded visits to his passport country; he felt out of place there, which made him feel like a fraud for representing his country abroad.

Patriotism can be a challenge for many TCKs, but especially

for foreign service TCKs. These TCKs may have strong connections to their passport countries through their parents' occupations, but may not have many experiential connections in the country.

International business

With the growing global economy, more and more businesses are sending families on overseas postings, creating another group of TCKs. Of those surveyed, only 8% of TCKs born before 1980 were business kids, but that figure jumped to 30% of post-1990s. I have heard TCKs in this category self-identify in several different ways, such as 'Business Kids,' or 'Corporate Brats'.

Families from specific companies or industries may connect, having their own social circle or group identity. One example is 'Oil Brats', TCKs with parents working in the petroleum industry. If a single company is large enough to send multiple families to the same overseas locations, these families may also feel an affinity.

While there are some overlaps in the Business Kid experience, there is also a lot of variety – company culture, salary level, and whether a family is settled or moving frequently all impact BKs. Those I interviewed did not always strongly identify with other BKs. Several who lived in one country a long time, attending a local school, identified more with MKs in similar situations. Some who moved frequently identified more with peers in foreign service families who also moved a lot. BKs from families with a modest income reported feeling very distant from BK classmates with greater financial resources. It was the overlap in experience that seemed to matter most.

Support for families

Business families are often very well supported financially; salary packages may include a combination of benefits such as housing, cars, international school fees, staff (such as a driver or nanny), or home leave. It can often be hard for those outside the international business world to see past these material benefits to the actual financial situation of a family. The house, car, staff, or school that look like signs of great wealth may be provided by the company – and in reality be far beyond the family's means if they had to pay for them out of pocket. On the other hand, some children who grow up with these perks may have trouble adjusting to life in their passport country, where family members have different domestic responsibilities.

Nothing is more frustrating than people thinking, "you're rich" just because I've moved overseas. Actually no, we aren't, it's just like having a job here (sort of). My aunts and uncles thought I was the most spoiled kid in the world because we had a driver and a housekeeper. They didn't understand it was illegal for my parents to drive themselves, not only illegal but very dangerous.

Callie, 17 [1ˢᵗ: USA; 2ⁿᵈ: China, Qatar, USA; 6 moves. Family: business. School: international.]

Apart from material benefits attached to a job, there may be little if any support. An employee may receive some sort of language and/or cultural training both prior to the move and upon arrival. Very few companies provide this sort of support to employees' spouses, or children. Some companies provide limited support services, such as a translator they can call for help when needed.

The 'Trailing Spouse'

This puts a lot of stress on the 'trailing spouse' (the one who accompanies an employed partner). A trailing spouse who is over-stressed and under-supported – particularly in a country where they do not speak the language – may feel resentful toward the company or the host country, feel overwhelmed and become depressed, or develop a deep dislike of the host country, which they then speak of disparagingly. While the 'trailing spouse' situation applies to most types of employment, it was corporate spouses who expressed the most difficulty with their situations.

One 'trailing spouse' I interviewed spoke of her unwillingness to engage with the host culture for 18 months, and of discovering the impact this had on her children. They knew she was stressed, picking up on her anger and sadness. She later realised her children were enjoying their experience overseas, but felt they could not share this with her. Another mother of BKs was embarrassed to hear her child speak rudely of their host country in front of a friend – only to realise her child had picked this attitude up from the parents' own frequent complaints.

When business families, especially trailing spouses, connect with the host culture in a positive way it greatly improves their child's experience. If a company provides little support, parents can create their own network. Making friends, including fellow expatriates who can relate, makes a big difference. Most expats are happy to help if they can – everyone has been the new person before, and everyone is far from their home country support networks.

Learning about TCKs

Of all the groups I interviewed, it was the BKs who were least likely to know what a TCK was – that there was a term to describe the experience of living abroad as a child. This information was rarely provided by the companies who employed them, so these families relied on other networks to provide it.

One avenue of information is the school a BK attends. 91% of BKs born after 1985 attended an international school for at least part of their education (compared to 57% of all younger TCKs). If an international school is proactive about prompting discussions about the experiences of TCKs – great! Unfortunately, not all schools do.

When neither the sending organisation nor the child's school is a reliable source of information, parents are left to work it out on their own. Some are unaware there is information to find; others are desperate to find it. One mother of TCKs I interviewed spoke of making a three hour round trip to attend a seminar on TCKs – she was desperate for more information, but had trouble connecting with resources. Another spoke of her shock at realising that 'cross-cultural issues' applied not only to kids living immersed in the local culture, but also to her children growing up in an 'expat bubble'.

Teachers in international schools

Children of international educators are a growing sub-group of TCKs, known as EdKids. As the number of international schools has grown, so has the demand for teachers to staff them – some of whom bring children with them.

Ettie Zilber writes, *'International, English-medium and/or bilingual schools (as defined by ISCresearch.com) often employ educator couples who are accompanied by children. A recent online survey of 75 schools indicated that, on average, just over 21% of staff have their own children enrolled in the school in which they work, and just over 4% of the students in the school are children of educators who are employed therein.'*

Some international schools are part of networks of schools spanning several countries (or continents). Other schools are independent entities, but the school still acts as a sponsor for the family. An international school is an expatriate community, providing a support network for the family of a teacher. In most cases, part of the salary package for a teacher in an international school is free tuition for a child, so these TCKs are also part of the school's expatriate community – with access to information and support.

One possible issue for these TCKs is a social or financial gap between themselves and their school peers. The TCKs I interviewed were not bothered by this overall, but several spoke of feeling 'behind' their school friends at times, knowing their parents did not have the same resources as their friends' parents did. Children of international school teachers were the group of TCKs most likely to resonate with a sense of 'missing out' (37%, compared to 26% overall).

> *Some international schools are filled with kids from all around the world, so I didn't feel a financial gap there. In Peru, 80% of the students at my international school were Peruvian, and another 18% were from other Latin American countries. These kids were very elite and in the upper social class. I felt a gap there, and was not really friends with them outside of school. I feel a lot more similarities with kids who also have teachers as parents. It is fun bonding and getting to know them and their families, as you see them at teachers' functions too.*
>
> **Lisa, 24 [1ˢᵗ: UK; 2ⁿᵈ: China, France, Malaysia, Mexico, Peru, UK, USA; 7 moves. Family: education. School: international.]**

Several international school teachers spoke of knowing they could not afford to give their children everything their classmates had. While this can create friction for some, the TCKs I interviewed were generally positive. Many made connections with different types of TCKs, and cited this as helpful in feeling balanced about their lives. One said she often preferred to spend time socialising with MKs, as they spent less money than her international school classmates.

Unaffiliated

Families who move abroad without a 'sponsor' are a growing percentage of the TCK community. Of the TCKs surveyed, only 12% of those born before 1985 had unaffiliated families, whereas 31% of those born after 1985 spent time abroad independently. Their parents may be students, teachers in local schools, entrepreneurs (running a business or a charity), or missionaries not associated with any organisation. Alternatively, these parents may have moved overseas as single adults and, discovering international life suited them, settled into expat life independent of a sending organisation (usually by finding 'local hire' jobs).

TCKs I interviewed from unaffiliated families were more likely to report feeling isolated or misunderstood. Of the TCKs surveyed, unaffiliated TCKs were the most likely to report feeling misunderstood in a variety of situations, including by loved ones and by other TCKs. They were more likely to identify negative feelings about their childhoods, such as loneliness (50% compared to 43%), and were the group least likely (at 51%) to report feeling proud of their experiences.

Lacking community

Independently employed families lack the institutional support of a wider community. There is no sponsor looking out for them. The children of these families depend even more than others on their parents to provide stability and support, especially if they are not attending an international school. While 56% of unaffiliated TCKs surveyed did attend an international school at some point (more than MKs, but less than BKs), they were also the group most likely to attend a local school (37%).

> *I feel disconnected from other TCKs. I had experienced only one country other than my passport country, and didn't know many other TCKs. Those I did know were connected to organizations, and travelled a lot, or were in international schools, while I was homeschooled. Thankfully my parents recognized this, and kept me involved with other homeschooled TCKs. My parents did a great job with keeping me connected! Even though we were not affiliated with an organization, and homeschooled, I still felt extremely supported.*
>
> **Wendy, 16 [1st: USA; 2nd: China, USA; 3 moves. Family: unaffiliated, mission, adoptive. School: local, home (group).]**

Some independent families do a great job and their kids have great international experiences. Others, however, can feel on the edge of – or separate from – the community, without a place in which they naturally belong. Several unaffiliated TCKs I interviewed spoke of envying the connections they saw other TCKs make with peers from similar backgrounds. Joining TCK groups – whether school, club, team, or youth group – can make a big difference.

Unaffiliated families are not automatically setting their children up for hardship. However, it is even more important for these parents to pay close attention to their child's social connections and opportunities. It may be important to seek out (and/or set aside money for) social groups in which their child can participate – such as sports teams, art classes, or scouting troops. It is also important that unaffiliated parents educate themselves about international and TCK issues.

Parents as students

One sub-group of unaffiliated families are those who move overseas so a parent (or both parents) can pursue higher education. In many cases, the family has moved from a less developed nation to a more developed nation, where they have broader educational options than in their home country. There are often additional pressures on TCKs in these families. The family may live on a lower income meaning children may be called upon to help at home. An oldest child may feel pressure to contribute domestically. Added to the academic pressure which naturally comes with being in a family in which parents are pursuing higher education abroad, the whole situation can add a lot of stress to the life of a TCK.

I can't speak for all TCKs of student parents but there are girls I know who would tell you it's often hard trying to excel academically when you come from a developing country, you're the oldest in the family (especially girls) and the culture in which you were raised has taught you that you are duty bound to help your parents. There were times where I not only played big sister but mother and father. It wasn't only the culture shock of moving but also that I was culture bound (for want of a better expression) to help my mum and dad where I could – even if it meant cooking, cleaning, babysitting, comforting or disciplining my siblings, I did it. There were times I cut school so I could look after a sick sibling or just have time to myself. I never told my parents and I fell so behind in school work that they got more and more upset.

Yasap, 30 [1st: Papua New Guinea; 2nd: Australia, Papua New Guinea; 4 moves. Family: unaffiliated (student). School: local.]

In this situation, repatriation is often (though not always) the goal – the parents' plan is to achieve further education which will contribute to their home society. Repatriation can be difficult for their children, however, especially if returning to a less developed nation. While studying the family may have chosen not to travel (especially to their passport country) in order to save money and their TCK children have become accustomed to life in the host country. This means TCKs with students for parents may feel less emotionally connected to their passport country, which may come as a surprise to their parents. When parents are able to accept their children's upset, and create safe space for their children to express what they are feeling, the impact of the move can be mitigated somewhat.

One family I spent time with returned to Vietnam after studying in the Philippines. Their young daughter had no memories of Vietnam and found the transition, especially into a local school, very traumatic. The parents found her constant complaints about their beloved home country very distressing. They tried to help by speaking to her in Vietnamese, to improve her language, and limiting discussion of their old life, to encourage her to engage in their new life. These strategies backfired, with their daughter expressing more anger and resentment. After we talked about how the transition must feel to her – moving to a place that felt foreign, speaking a language that was taxing – the parents changed tack. They told their daughter it was okay to miss the Philippines, and she could speak in English at home any time she wanted. This gave her a safe space to express parts of herself that did not fit in at school, and the atmosphere in their home changed almost immediately.

Non Governmental Organisations

Another group of expat families are those who are relocated by a wider organisation that is neither corporate, nor mission, nor government. This group includes international charities, non-governmental organisations (NGOs), and intergovernmental organisations (IGOs). For brevity I use the term NGO to refer broadly to all three.

It is hard to generalise this group of TCKs – their experiences are extremely varied – which is part of why it is important to include them. Other TCKs often look at an NGO kid (or 'NGO brat', as several I interviewed called themselves) and make a judgment call on what their family is like – either 'like me' or 'not like me' – without recognising reality might be less black and white. NGO kids can be 'a bit like' a lot of different groups. Some NGO kids I interviewed preferred to group themselves with a different category (MKs, or BKs). Others felt no category really explained them. Many felt most comfortable simply being TCKs.

As an IGO kid who currently goes to an International Christian school, I'm always a bit hesitant in

> *answering the question "where do your parents work"*
> *right after the rest of the class says their parents are*
> *missionaries. I rarely single out myself as an IGO kid,*
> *but rather, as a TCK.*
>
> **Liza, 17 [1ˢᵗ: Cameroon; 2ⁿᵈ: Cambodia, Cameroon, Tanzania; 3
> moves. Family: IGO. School: international, Christian international.]**

Similar, but different, to other TCK groups

NGO kids can be a bit like MKs. As with missionaries, most NGO and charity workers who live abroad went with a sense of vocational calling (whether or not they are people of faith). The parents have a sense of purpose. They are there for a *reason* – something bigger than making money or representing their country. This choice to prioritise vocation means some NGO families, like many mission families, have extremely limited financial resources. When these NGO kids understand what their parent does, how their work is helping others, it can help them feel a sense of ownership and pride in their family.

NGO kids can be a bit like BKs. Many bigger NGOs pay school fees as part of an employee's package, so these kids may attend big international schools. This puts them in the same social set as business and embassy kids, and other expatriate families with high income and job benefits. Some of these NGO families are very well off, particularly if the parent is employed in a specialised role. It can be difficult, however, if the NGO kid's family is not at the same economic level as their peers'.

NGO kids can be a bit like unaffiliated kids. Some NGO workers are sent as representatives of a charity or organisation. While they are part of a larger group, as expatriates these families are without much support from people in similar situations while in their overseas post. (Whereas mission organisations often have annual conferences to which children are brought along, NGO conferences generally do not include families.)

> *Being from an NGO family can be difficult to explain to people from your home country. Which then leads to feeling you have to tread carefully in what you say about your lifestyle – such as having domestic help or a country club membership. I find the question 'what do your parents do?' a very awkward one.*
> **Ashley, 28 [1st: UK; 2nd: Cambodia, Singapore, Sri Lanka, UK; 6 moves. Family: adoptive, NGO, embassy. School: international.]**

NGO kids tend to be engaged in the local culture even if moving in expatriate circles. Their parents' work is related to understanding and helping the local people so as a family they tend to be far more aware of the lives of locals (especially if living in a developing country).

> *My parents' good example has led me to also want to do development work. They inspired me to fight racism that comes in the form of development work. Having grown up among people in the Global South I have compassion in these struggles.*
> **Thongfaa, 24 [1st: Finland, USA; 2nd: Finland, Laos, Thailand, USA; 5 moves. Family: multicultural, NGO. School: home (group), international.]**

Relocation

There are also big differences in the experiences of an NGO kid living in developing country and one living in a developed country. When living in a developing country, they may be seen as well off (especially by MKs or local peers) but feel very poor compared to peers in a developed country. It is all relative, but the change in circumstances can be jarring.

When it comes to moving on, and especially repatriation, NGO kids are also in between. Many NGOs provide financially for a move, paying for possessions to be shipped (like a corporate family) but may also provide debriefing sessions before or after a move (more like a mission family).

All this almost-but-not-quite can make NGO kids feel a bit like they do not quite belong with their TCK peers. Thankfully, and perhaps because of this, this does not stop them finding fellow TCKs to engage with. In fact, several NGO kids I interviewed saw the blend of relating to both the host culture and the expat culture as a 'best of both worlds' experience.

International Education

There are many factors to consider when choosing a school. Continuity of curriculum can be an issue for families who move frequently, especially for a child preparing to enter university. Expatriate parents may have many options to choose from; the bigger the city they live in, the more options. Most options fall into one of five main categories. Some locations have several options within each category; others have options from only one or two categories.

1. Local school

2. International school

3. Christian international school

4. Homeschool

5. Boarding school

Sometimes different children in the same family are better off in different schools. While sometimes an American parent may hope for their child to attend an American school, a British school down the road might be more suitable to the child's needs – and vice versa.

"It is important to pay attention to the language of instruction, qualification of teachers, methods of instruction and assessment. If students have learning differences, it is also important to determine whether or not the school truly has the resources to meet those needs," advises Rebecca (Becky) Grappo, founder of RNG International Education Consultants. "When there are special learning needs involved, it is more important than ever to focus on the fit for the child or teen and not just follow what everyone else in the expat community is doing."

A child struggling at a large, elite school might benefit from a smaller school with more personal attention or less academic pressure. A child in a remote location feeling socially isolated may do better in a boarding situation. A child who wishes to pursue an interest at an elite level, or a child with special learning needs, may do better in a bigger school with more resources. I have seen children make each of these moves and flourish.

For many TCKs, school is the main place (even the only place) they interact with peers, making it very important in their social and emotional development. If life at school begins to feel intolerable, life in general can feel intolerable.

"When students transition to a new school, their biggest worry is usually not whether or not the school offers the right academic challenge. Rather, their main concern is probably going to be finding someone to eat lunch with since school also fills the social-emotional needs of children and adolescents," Becky Grappo says.

There are no 'right' or 'wrong' types of schools – every child (and every school) is different – and schools vary even within the same category. The goal of this section is not to advise on *which* school to choose, but to explore *how* the type of school a TCK attends may affect their experience. The descriptions of school experiences are general, and so will not be true for every school and every student, but provide a starting point for considering this.

Local school

This term refers to a school that uses the host country's curriculum and is intended primarily for nationals of the country (whether a public or private school). 28% of TCKs born after 1985 had attended a local school, a drop from 34% of older TCKs surveyed. Diplomat kids were the least likely to attend a local school (10%).

In some locations, local school is not an option. A school may be restricted to locals only, or children of a certain religion. The curriculum may be so different to that of the family's passport country, or previous location, it would disrupt the child's education (especially for older children). In some countries, security is an issue that prevents TCKs attending a local school; some sending organisations have strict security guidelines a school must meet.

Attending a local school, when possible, has both positives and negatives for a TCK. A TCK attending a local school will be more closely connected to the host culture and more fluent in the language. However, attending a local school can also be confusing, frustrating, and overwhelming for a TCK – especially if classes are not in the child's native language. 40% of surveyed TCKs attending local schools were schooled in a second language and 15% in a language their parents did not speak (compared to 22% and 7% of all TCKs).

Primary school-aged children often adapt well to attending local school, although the initial transition period may be emotional and stressful. The older the child, the more difficult the experience can be. One mother said her children began to feel isolated as they grew older – even though they were at the same school, with the same classmates, differences in their worldviews became more obvious as the children entered adolescence.

I attended local school at a young age, and adapted well. Studies were more difficult compared to local students as my parents didn't know the language – homework took longer etc. I did essentially keep up

> *with the class for the two and a half years I was there. I felt accepted by teachers and classmates. Looking back, it was definitely worth it.*
>
> **Jeremy, 22 [1st: New Zealand; 2nd: Australia, China, New Zealand, Singapore; 4 moves. Family: unaffiliated. School: local, home, international.]**

A lot depends on the child's personality and preferences. An older child whose parents make the decision on their behalf may wilt under the weight of so many differences, and withdraw. One TCK I interviewed said she felt a pressure to attend local school, as it was what her parents wanted for her, and while she did enjoy it, when she moved to an international school she felt 'set free' – everything was easier once she was being taught in a language she spoke fluently.

Even when the child's native language is spoken in the host country, and is the language used in school, attending a local school can still be troubling for a TCK. Differences in pronunciation, spelling, writing conventions, curriculum, and classroom expectations exist between countries. Adapting to a new grading system and teaching style can be stressful, especially for a child who values academic success. For example, an American child not familiar with the metric system may experience great frustration at not understanding basic measurements in their new location.

A child who takes part in the decision and is excited by the challenge may gain a lot from the experience. When TCKs have their own reasons for choosing the local school path it helps them press on when things get tough.

As a Chinese person born and raised in the United States, I realized the best way to understand my heritage was to live and breathe China. When my dad's company relocated him to Beijing, I was eager to expose myself to the culture and connect with my roots. However, I soon began to fear that I wouldn't survive in this 'foreign' country. But I was determined to triumph over the challenges. By the end of the first semester, I was watching Chinese movies with my classmates and my grades were improving steadily. I even ran for election in the student government and was elected as Vice President, and later became President.

Lee, 24 [1st: USA; 2nd: China, Germany, USA; 6 moves. Family: returned immigrant expat, business. School: local, boarding.]

For the right child, in the right situation, attending a local school while overseas can be an excellent experience with great benefits. I have known many families who chose a local school during their child's early years, to help with language acquisition, then switched to an international school for the child's later years, when curriculum became more important. Nearly half the TCKs who attended local school also attended another type of school at some point (mostly international schools, but others were homeschooled).

International school

International schools use the curriculum of another country and are usually staffed primarily with expatriates. They are particularly common where there are legal and linguistic barriers making it difficult for TCKs to attend a local school.

Many teach in languages such as English, German, French, Spanish, or Korean (whether or not it is a language spoken in the host country) and may also be bilingual.

As Ettie Zilber notes, *'Globalization has increased the volume in human mobility and has led to an increase in the number of employees who are relocated to fulfill functions outside their home countries. Many have families who, naturally, would accompany them. The result is a proliferation of international schools [...] there are 5,232 such schools in 236 countries with a population of over two million students and almost 200,000 educators.'*

Half of TCKs surveyed had spent time at an international school, and nearly 60% of those born after 1990. BKs and diplomat kids were the most likely to go to an international school (89% and 86%, respectively) and MKs the least likely (31%). 12% of TCKs who attended international schools were children of international school teachers.

As the globally mobile community grows and the number of international schools increases, there is also a shift in the education provided in these schools. Valérie Besanceney, who teaches at the International School of Geneva, says, "Many international schools are moving away from offering solely a national (usually UK or US based) curriculum toward curricula that are specifically designed for the international community, like the International Baccalaureate."

My current school is the first in Kampala to run a hybrid program: both American and British. All the other international schools offer a specific national

> *curriculum (British, American, Indian, etc.) Our*
> *students will graduate having taken all of the necessary*
> *exams to go to university in the UK (and thus many*
> *places in Europe) as well as in the US and Canada.*
> **Kim, parent of TCKs [1ˢᵗ: Canada; 2ⁿᵈ: Canada, China, Uganda;**
> **3 moves. Family: mission. School: Christian international.]**

Many international schools have very high academic standards and charge extremely high tuition (on par with a good university education). Some international schools are restricted to foreign students, others are essentially private schools available to anyone with the means to pay. As educational fees are often included as part of the salary package for business executives and diplomatic staff these families often form the majority of the student population in foreign-only schools. In 'open' international schools, the student population is often largely comprised of children from local families of considerable means.

For some families, international school is the only good educational option available – even if the school fees are not covered by an employer, and are therefore a financial burden. This means that there can be children at international schools who do not fit the financial profile of the business/ embassy or upper class students around them; this can be stressful for both parents and children.

> *It can be an extra hardship for kids who are in an*
> *international school but whose family don't have the*
> *same resources and opportunities as the rest of their*
> *peers. Our girls survive without a car, driver or nanny,*

> *overseas holidays, large sums of money for clothes*
> *allowances and such, and have to think about the costs*
> *of after school activities or other sporting events. Most*
> *of their friends do not have these issues.*
> **Joh, parent of TCKs [1ˢᵗ: Australia, 2ⁿᵈ: Australia, Indonesia;**
> **3 moves. Family: business. School: international.]**

These are excellent schools, providing a top-level education. Attend an international school graduation and you will likely hear a litany of top universities around the world to which the graduates have been accepted. Many are full of TCKs who share Third Culture life together. Their students have opportunities to participate in fantastic extra-curricular activities.

The downside is that academic expectations at these schools are often very high. While students in all sorts of schools can feel this pressure, it seems more pronounced among international school students. TCKs who moved from their passport country to an international school during secondary school spoke of a big change in what was considered 'average'.

> *In Canada I had the best grades in my friend group.*
> *At the international school I wasn't even average.*
> *I was suddenly surrounded by really smart people.*
> *Everyone wanted good grades. That made me feel so*
> *inadequate. Eventually, with parent and peer pressure,*
> *I started to become just as concerned with grades.*
> **Cat, 21 [1ˢᵗ: Canada, (China); 2ⁿᵈ: Canada, China, USA; 5 moves.**
> **Family: returned immigrant expats, unaffiliated. School: local,**
> **international.]**

Most TCKs I interviewed considered study life to be less intense in their passport country. In some countries it is common to take lots of extra-curricular classes at school, in others it is more common to pursue other interests outside school. Students at international schools tend to have few options for outside activities but these can be a great release where available.

> *I think activities outside school are really important. We only ever saw the same 25 people, and thus formed very tight friendships with them, but being involved in a TCK youth group was really great for me, because I got to see and interact with people who did not go to my school. Seeing adults in their twenties who seemed happy was something I'd never really seen before. It was a great outlet, because it wasn't a quantified thing. You couldn't fail youth group. Being involved there had nothing to do with what my parents wanted, so that was a lot of really welcome freedom and relief.*
>
> **Arielle, 24 [1st: USA; 2nd: China, India, Kazakhstan, Kenya, Thailand, Uganda, USA; 9 moves. Family: embassy, NGO. School: local, international.]**

Christian international school

Christian international schools exist all over the world, many with a stated purpose to provide affordable education for children of missionaries. Two-thirds of MKs surveyed had spent time at a Christian international school. Of all TCKs who had attended a Christian international school, 57% were MKs, 18% were children of teachers, and only 9% were business kids.

School culture varies, but there are two main types of Christian schools:

1. The first aim to be elite international schools on par with any other top school; the school culture at these institutions is similar to that at any other international school, but with a faith-based foundation.

2. The second focus more on the holistic development of the child, with a spiritual emphasis; academic pressure may be less intense. Some are not big or well-funded enough to provide a full range of activities and services.

Christian school cultures depend on the predominant cultural influences, and the emphasis on faith. In my experience, schools with strong American influence tend to value extra-curriculars (sports, music, art) in addition to academics, and promote a strong American worldview, whereas predominantly British schools focus more on academics and have a more international, diverse worldview. Some schools accept more local students than others; this can sometimes help TCKs better integrate into the local culture, although the local students often are or become highly

Westernized. The emphasis on faith also varies from school to school. Some are Christian in name only, while others try to engage students in faith on as many levels as possible; the Christian emphasis can feel forced, or very organic.

Em, 19 [1st: Australia; 2nd: Australia, Thailand; 4 moves. Family: mission. School: Christian international.]

Many of these schools are not-for-profit businesses. Their fees are usually much lower than those of other international schools, and their teachers have lower salaries. This means the teachers are there for something other than money, because they could certainly make more of it elsewhere. Most teachers I have talked to at these schools see their work as a vocation and they are often quite sensitive to the specific needs of TCKs.

I taught at a Christian international school in China and now at one in Uganda. Salaries are definitely lower here: several teachers work in exchange for tuition for their kids and a work visa without any other financial compensation. Most of us see our work as ministry: we teach missionary kids well so that missionary families can complete their missions well. For example, many missionary mommas are gifted and called to the field but if affordable education wasn't available, they would be homeschooling their children, often not feeling competent in that work. Additionally, most teachers recognise the unique needs

of the TCKs they teach and see their classroom both as
means to bless their students with a great education,
but also as a venue to support and nurture students.
Kim, parent of TCKs [1st: Canada; 2nd: Canada, China, Uganda;
3 moves. Family: mission. School: Christian international.]

A supportive environment is compromised, however, if a school teaches faith-based elements in an overbearing manner. Forcing children to engage in religious rituals they are uncomfortable with, or adhere to religious doctrine they are not in agreement with, is counterproductive. It is possible, however, to have a faith-based foundation and approach the teaching of religion as an invitation to learn and discuss.

While a holistic approach and a supportive environment is a big plus, there are downsides as well. These schools are often less well funded, having smaller and simpler facilities with less equipment. Despite the fewer resources for extra-curriculars, students are generally encouraged to try new things. This means there can be room to fall short without major embarrassment.

These schools may not be the best fit for students wanting to pursue elite sports, and do not always support very advanced academics. Students may be able to study more advanced courses individually or through online classes but this means going above and beyond their classmates.

I was blessed to be in a Christian international school
that was small but still rigorous in academics, sports

> *and arts, providing brilliant opportunities for us*
> *to pursue our interests and be involved in various*
> *activities. We had a good relationship with other*
> *'big' international schools and American bases in the*
> *area. But students often had to fight to squeeze AP*
> *(Advanced Placement) courses into our schedule,*
> *and rarely received much needed support for*
> *our endeavours.*
>
> **Justin, 23 [1ˢᵗ: Japan, Singapore; 2ⁿᵈ: Canada, Japan, Singapore, UK;
> 16 moves. Family: mission. School: local, Christian international,
> home, boarding.]**

One TCK I interviewed was a star athlete at her small Christian international school and dreamed of playing team sports at a university level, perhaps trying for a scholarship. She attended a summer sports camp in her passport country only to discover she had been placed with students several years younger because her skills were that far behind. While this can also happen for students at bigger international schools, the difference is usually more marked for those at smaller schools.

Homeschool

For families who move a lot, homeschooling can provide stability in education – the books and programs stay the same regardless of where in the world they are located. For others, homeschooling is a way to provide quality education for children in remote locations, especially through online programs. The flexibility of a homeschool schedule can also allow students to pursue other interests. Nearly a third of TCKs surveyed were homeschooled at some point; 80% of homeschoolers were from mission families.

We have homeschooled twice – our first year in China and now, in our last year. Our kids had been in public schools before our family moved overseas. Adjusting to homeschool was as much a challenge as adjusting to China. The challenges were big, but so were the benefits. Our kids had time to focus on some personal interest skills that are still paying off today. Our daughter learned to knit in homeschool; she is now a business major with plans to develop new textiles for knitters. This year of homeschooling has been really good. We feel like it has given our youngest daughter the benefit of both her senior year and a gap year all in one. The biggest challenge has been social. It requires more effort for her to spend time with friends. They aren't automatically with her every day.

Angie, parent of TCKs [1st: USA; 2nd: China, USA; 2 moves. Family: mission. School: home, Christian international.]

TCK and author of *Hidden in my Heart: A TCK's Journey Through Cultural Transition*, Taylor Murray, says, "As a TCK, my family has moved and travelled extensively over the past eight years. Homeschooling has stayed routine and normal for us during these transitions. Also, the flexibility of homeschooling works perfectly with my family's schedule."

"Homeschooling has allowed for travel and opportunities that I would never have experienced with a school schedule tied to a specific time and place. Homeschooling is wonderful for TCKs who frequently travel, desire a flexible schedule or find it difficult to continually change schools with each move."

> *Growing up I loved being a homeschool kid because it allowed for my family to travel around. We road tripped in Europe and travelled wherever we went.*
> **Maddie, 18 [1st: USA; 2nd: Germany, Japan, USA; 9 moves. Family: military. School: home (group).]**

Homeschool families get bad press sometimes, but I have known a lot of wonderful homeschoolers. Many got great educations, including admission to excellent universities, and have never been short on social skills.

> *I was able to organize my own schedule and do a lot of other things I would not have been able to otherwise. I think this allowed me to develop my personal values early on. I had a lot of control over my classes and how I could go about them, which meant there was very little adjustment for moving into a college schedule. I personally like studying on my own and learning at my own pace. It was challenging to motivate myself sometimes, but being able to figure out my own style was comfortable and natural for me. If you have*

> *the chance to be more flexible with schooling, enjoy the full benefits of that. Don't let life work around schooling, let schooling work around life.*
> **Becca, 19 [1st: USA, (China); 2nd: China, USA; 7 moves.**
> **Family: adoptive, education. School: home.**

How homeschooling works

There is a lot of variety in homeschooling. Some families are connected with a distance education program in their passport country, with a set curriculum and schedule to follow. Some programs include real-time online classes, or students can contact a subject teacher by email. Some programs provide online exams, or exam papers for parents to oversee, a few require the student to take annual exams in their passport country.

Other families create their own homeschooling program, choosing a curriculum and pacing the lessons to fit their schedule. A family may even choose a combination of the two approaches, signing up a child for online classes while supplementing with their own curriculum.

Some families have set school hours, others set a required number of hours or tasks per day and let the children choose when to complete this. One family I interviewed set minimum hours for study each day; if the children chose to work longer, they could earn time off on another day. Another family set dates for their family to begin and end the school year, based on when they would be travelling, and plotted out what each child would need to work through each week. The children were given a choice, however – if they wanted to start the year earlier, they could, and if they finished their work before the scheduled end date, they could have the extra time as vacation.

Taylor shared that although their schedule can change depending on circumstances, they do have set times for school. They also take certain proficiency tests and exams, but most of their assessments are done through personal discussions. "I don't take exams on a regular basis," Taylor explains. "For assessment, we usually discuss what we're learning, write essays and connect it to other content areas."

School location can be flexible as well. Some children work in their bedrooms, others in a common area of the home. Some families I interviewed had set aside spaces for school work. One family had a school room at the parents' workplace and hired a tutor to teach the children while the parents worked.

Outside the TCK world, families who homeschool generally do so as a deliberate alternative to other available options. While this is also true of some expats, for others the decision to homeschool is based on price, convenience, or a lack of other options. This means some homeschool parents have not chosen to teach, instead seeing homeschooling as the only viable option for their family. Some parents find this responsibility daunting; I know families who moved in large part due to concern for their children's education.

I had parents come up to me during parent-teacher conferences and confess they barely spent any time on Science during homeschool because they didn't understand it themselves. What a loss for these kids! Obtaining the materials required for many homeschool programs, particularly upper level sciences, is daunting. Many homeschool parents are also terrified of upper level math!

Kim, parent of TCKs [1ˢᵗ: Canada; 2ⁿᵈ: Canada, China, Uganda; 3 moves. Family: mission. School: Christian international.]

What homeschooled TCKs think

Homeschooling can work very well for some families. Many TCKs I interviewed enjoyed the freedom of homeschooling, choosing what to study, when to do their schoolwork, or being able to schedule around other activities. Several homeschooled TCKs spoke of doing extracurricular activities with groups of nationals or expatriates in their local area, such as a soccer team and a theatre group.

This year will be my 11ᵗʰ year in China. For most of my life I have been homeschooled. I was taught by my mom from age seven to 13. For high school I did online school. Homeschooling has been one of the most challenging and rewarding experiences of my life. I grew so much as a person. It's learning how to motivate and inspire yourself to be better, to do better. Pushing past the so-called boundaries and working harder than you thought you could.

Ann, 17 [1ˢᵗ: USA; 2ⁿᵈ: China, USA; 1 move. Family: mission. School: home.]

"I've been homeschooled since kindergarten and absolutely love it!" Taylor says. "My three younger sisters are currently taught by my mom, just like my twin sister and I were at their age. Starting from junior high, we gradually became more and more independent. Now we study completely independently, and much of our work is geared toward our personal interests."

Even when homeschooling has worked well for a particular child or family, should the situation change it may be worth considering other options. Even if there are no viable alternatives, an honest discussion may help a child feel heard rather than powerless.

> *As I grew older and outgrew the homeschool groups we had, homeschooling began to feel more isolating. As my mother and I disagreed more, I wanted time away – but being homeschooled it wasn't an option. I had activities I went to but I avoided my parents at them because I wanted something they were not involved in.*
> **Maddie, 18 [1st: USA; 2nd: Germany, Japan, USA; 9 moves. Family: military. School: home (group).]**

The majority of homeschool families I know do an excellent job. Unfortunately, I have also mentored and interviewed TCKs who had less effective, and less pleasant, homeschool experiences. Those who shared negative experiences always referred to at least one of two key issues: working alone, and lack of social interaction.

Working alone

Sometimes parents do not have the time (or inclination) to teach. Others may feel ill-equipped to teach, preferring to provide their children with informative resources. This leaves their children working alone.

I'm homeschooled and neither of my parents teaches me and I don't have a teacher. I watch DVDs with a class on them and try to figure things out. It's really hard because I can't ask questions so I often struggle to do well. But my mum often pushes me to do well and is upset if I get below an A. It's hard and stresses me out.
Faith, 17 [1st: USA; 2nd: Cambodia, USA; 2 moves. Family: mission. School: home.]

Sitting alone with schoolbooks can be lonely, even when children are able to work through material effectively on their own. Reading in isolation is not the method by which most children learn; no matter how good a curriculum might be, most children still want an adult to talk things through with and to explain the material.

Homeschooling oneself can be disheartening, especially for a child who does not understand school material on the first reading. Over time, children in this position may become so discouraged they will try to avoid school work, as school time is simply a constant reminder of their perceived failures.

My mom didn't make our education a priority so neither did we. There was no structure. By 4th Grade there was not much she could help with, so we had to teach ourselves from the text. When we couldn't figure it out, and our parents were too busy to help, we had to look at the answers and go from there. There was no one to teach and support us to make sure we were doing what needed to be done. It was very difficult to learn without someone helping me. It made me despise learning, simply because I could not understand any of it. I had education up to 4th/5th Grade, then 7th Grade, then had to study for the GED. I could not have done it without the help of friends. I went from only a few years of education right into college. Not learning how to study, or the discipline of study, really affected my ability to incorporate into college life. I still struggle with that to this day.

Yisheng, 24 [1st: USA, (Taiwan); 2nd: China, Taiwan, USA; 10 moves. Family: unaffiliated (mission), adoptive. School: home.]

Parents do not have to be the teacher in a homeschool setting. Several families I talked to employed a tutor to work with their children while the parents worked. Several mission families had interns who spent a period of time with them to tutor the children while experiencing life abroad.

I interviewed several people who worked as homeschool teachers of TCKs. One, who worked for three different families at different times, said discipline could be a problem. Children knew if parents would be less strict, and that the parents' decision outweighed the teacher's. Another issue was curriculum. Sometimes parents expected the home teacher to create the curriculum, but this was time-consuming and difficult, especially without familiarity with what had been taught previously.

"I was homeschooled in my own country and did a teaching degree. I was pretty idealistic about moving overseas to help a family homeschool their kids," shares homeschool tutor Kerry. "Boundaries were blurry, and there were issues we did not navigate well. I was part teacher, part friend/sibling, which was sometimes confusing for the kids. I saw positives and negatives for the children. Their socialisation with locals suffered as none of their classes were in the local language. On the flip side, they did better academically with a qualified teacher than with non-teacher volunteers/parents."

Social interaction

School is a key place for most children to meet others and make friends. A homeschooled child has fewer hours of peer interaction each day than a child attending school outside. Some countries with laws regarding homeschooling take this into account. For example, the state of South Australia requires a parent to demonstrate that their child will have opportunities for social interaction as part of their home education registration. Several US states (such as Colorado and Florida) require public schools to allow homeschool students to join extra-curricular activities. Several homeschool families I interviewed were able to do something similar for their children while living abroad.

I was sequestered from the culture I was in. I am
thankful for not having to be in Chinese school
systems, but I do regret not at least being more
active in extra-curricular programs. In junior high
I participated in some classes at a local school.
This gave me a small taste of Chinese schooling
culture, and I am extremely thankful for it now,
though I wasn't always at the time.
Becca, 19 [1ˢᵗ: USA, (China); 2ⁿᵈ: China, USA; 7 moves.
Family: adoptive, education. School: home.

Lacking the opportunity to spend time with peers can have a negative impact, socially or emotionally. Even an introverted child, or one who enjoys the individualised learning of homeschooling, can be discouraged if there is a total lack of social life.

TCKs I interviewed who felt socially isolated while homeschooling spoke of a lack of motivation both for schoolwork and for investing in friendships. 61% of homeschooled TCKs born after 1985 said they felt lonely as children living abroad, compared to 45% of young TCKs overall.

At first I liked homeschool because there was flexibility
with my schedule. But after a few months I became
overwhelmingly lonely and pushed myself less and
less. I am the type of person that needs others around
me to motivate and challenge me, otherwise I just

> *do the bare minimum. Since my parents left us each to teach ourselves, I would get so frustrated from not understanding that I would just cheat. Homeschooling also keeps you from interacting with the people of the country in a more realistic way. School is normally where kids go to find friends and spend most of their time, but keeping kids at home and having them do school by themselves means they not only have trouble with the learning at times, but they are also missing out on being around other people their age.*
>
> **Risa, 17** [1st: Guatemala, USA; 2nd: Guatemala, USA; 4 moves. Family: adoptive, mission. School: home (group).]

Some expat families choose to homeschool because they live in a remote location. This may mean fewer opportunities for children to interact with peers – but it does not have to be impossible. I talked to 18 homeschool families who lived in remote areas about their creative solutions. Most centred around travelling to give their children chances to make friends at group events in areas where there were more expatriates. These events included monthly trips for youth groups or scouting troops, biannual trips for TCK conferences, and annual mission organisation conferences – most of these taking place several hours away from the family's home. Some families travelled more than 12 hours to make these trips.

These TCKs made friends who became their core social community, with relationships maintained throughout the year via various Internet platforms. Many of these families also helped their children make trips to visit friends, on some occasions by going out of their way while on a family vacation. Making this happen cost these families a significant amount of time, energy and money, but their children appreciated the effort. While these TCKs still felt lonely at times, long distance social connections were very meaningful and important to them.

Friendships maintained online helped and still help me a great deal. They served as a way to reminisce and share in the processes and challenges of life with other TCKs. My parents have been very gracious with making opportunities for me to visit friends – this includes driving long(ish) distances, being willing to host friends, and encouraging me to keep in contact. They make a point to ask about the lives of my friends who live far away who I talk to. I would encourage TCKs to be consistent and keep in contact with their friends online and through texting. But don't let those relationships be the only ones, because they can take away from building relationships in person. These may be more difficult to build, but help connect with the host culture more meaningfully.

Becca, 19 [1ˢᵗ: USA, (China); 2ⁿᵈ: China, USA; 7 moves. Family: adoptive, education. School: home.]

Homeschool groups

In areas where several homeschooling expat families live nearby, there is the opportunity for homeschool groups to develop. A third of homeschooled TCKs surveyed took part in group homeschooling.

One arrangement is for several families to homeschool together. The children from these families gather together every day, and may have a hired (or volunteer) teacher who works with them. This arrangement gives the children structure, consistency, and classmates.

> *There was a Finnish boarding school in Thailand but my parents were not willing to send us so far away as young kids so they got their organization to send volunteer teachers from Finland to teach us (after homeschooling for a year). After third grade other Finnish families moved to the same area giving us schoolmates. This was so exciting for us. We had classrooms and everything was structured like a real class. We had all the required classes in a regular Finnish curriculum (16 different subjects including languages).*
>
> **Thongfaa, 24 [1ˢᵗ: Finland, USA; 2ⁿᵈ: Finland, Laos, Thailand, USA; 5 moves. Family: multicultural, NGO. School: home (group), international.]**

Another arrangement is a network of homeschool families that share resources and have group activities. A homeschool co-op in Beijing, for example, meets one day a fortnight for a variety of group classes.

These arrangements can help both TCKs and their homeschooling parents to feel less isolated. Parents can share duties, or the cost of hiring private teachers. Students who are very extroverted or externally motivated feel more encouraged and therefore more interested in school.

> *I would not have been able to homeschool without the homeschool community we had – several families who supported each other and had fun together. That made ALL the difference!*
>
> **Linda, parent of TCKs [1st: USA; 2nd: China, USA; 3 moves. Family: mission. School: home (group).]**

Boarding school

While half of surveyed TCKs born before 1985 attended boarding school, that number drops to only 10% of those born after 1985. MKs were the most likely to have attended a boarding school, but the percentage drops steeply by age – from 59% of older MKs to 15% of those born after 1985.

To move away from family and live semi-independently at a young age can be quite challenging. This is made easier when children have their own reasons for embarking on this big change.

> *I think that if children are involved in the decision it makes it easier. My mum was willing to homeschool me if need be, but we visited a school on holidays with our friends whose kids went there, and I thought it looked fun and asked to go there and my parents were willing to let me. It was, though still painful to be apart, a mutually agreeable situation.*
>
> **Georgia, 31 [1st: Australia; 2nd: Australia, India, Nepal; 3 moves. Family: mission. School: home (group), boarding.]**

The right boarding situation can be a great thing for the right child. An extroverted child living in a remote place may benefit from the social aspect of boarding school, even though homeschool may be fine academically. Boarding school may also be good for a child needing academic support not available where they live. Attending a boarding school can be a good option for students with a need for structure and stability, especially if their family moves frequently.

> *I chose to go to boarding school. My parents never forced me to go. I wanted to go to make friends and have close relationships. I did. I made close friends that I kept close for many years. My dorm had the same people; we didn't get anyone new until 10th Grade. We had a full house; it was the largest dorm, with about 17 kids, plus the dorm parents' three kids. All the way up until 11th Grade we had the same brothers and sisters in my dorm.*
>
> **Brian, 25 [1st: USA; 2nd: Cambodia, Malaysia, USA; 8 moves. Family: mission. School: home, boarding.]**

Types of boarding school

There are various types of boarding schools available. Some are primarily for expatriate children (some for MKs specifically); others are local schools, attended by nationals of the country. Some are a combination – a local school with a significant percentage of international students. Many TCKs I interviewed attended boarding schools for expatriate children, often in neither their passport country nor the country their family was living in. Others attended a boarding school in their passport country.

A TCK's experience of boarding school is greatly affected by the type of school it is. In an expat school, TCKs live in the Third Culture, often among peers (and teachers) who understand its particular joys and stresses. TCKs who attend boarding school in their passport country leave the familiarity of the Third Culture and experience the stress of repatriation while separated from their immediate family.

Leaving school

TCKs repatriating to their passport country to attend boarding school may have a rough transition. One mother told me her teenage children were reluctant to return to school after every visit for the first 18 months, but are now thankful for their school. The upside for these TCKs, however, is that having gone through repatriation stress in secondary school, they will not have to go through it again as they start university. TCKs who attended a boarding school abroad with expat classmates, on the other hand, may find completing school, and beginning university, particularly difficult.

University peers can easily travel to where they call home for a weekend, and have the opportunity to reconnect with their friends from high school. TCKs find such a notion laughable, and are stuck pondering the relationships they've left behind in a country many time zones away. Boarding school students experience this to a greater degree because their experience at boarding school was likely very similar to their new experience at university, specifically the aspect of living in a dorm. A boarding student would find many aspects of university life eerily similar to the one they left behind, and as a result, feel nostalgic for the life they left even more strongly. It took me my entire freshman year to accept that I had to leave the life I had built behind, and came to terms with my new surroundings (which I came to love).

Jon, 24 [1ˢᵗ: USA, 2ⁿᵈ: Czech Republic, Germany, USA; 4 moves. Family: mission. School: local, Christian international, boarding]

Bonding with adults

Adults who teach and supervise at boarding schools and boarding houses have a huge impact on TCK students. TCKs I interviewed who make close pseudo-family connections with boarding school staff coped much better than those who were less connected.

Two dorm supervisors became mentors and personal friends. They were so helpful because they are also TCKs, so they understood the things I was going through – they had been through them too. They offered unconditional acceptance, and a safe place to be myself. Because immediate family is usually the only family TCKs get to experience, I think we look to make families out of the people we meet while abroad. This couple became part of my ever-growing family. I can't express how much I appreciated that

> *they became my 'step-in' family when I was away*
> *from my parents and brother.*
> **Catherine, 24 [1ˢᵗ: USA; 2ⁿᵈ: Brunei, Indonesia, Malaysia, Russia,**
> **USA. 9 moves. Family: business. School: local, international, home,**
> **Christian international, boarding.]**

A safe environment

For boarding students, school is also home. If there is a problem at school, boarding students have no safe place to retreat to. The stressful, even traumatic, environment becomes the students' 'normal' – the environment in which they spend most of their time.

One boarding school teacher I interviewed recounted several worrying incidents of bullying that occurred in the dorm setting. This particular school provided very limited interaction between boarding students and adults outside the classroom. Students were supervised but not engaged with emotionally. Most lacked opportunities to observe adults living 'normal' life, or to bond with them.

This situation was the exception, not the norm, among young TCKs I interviewed (though some older TCKs shared painful experiences). Most felt safe at school (their home) connecting this to the adults who cared for them outside the classroom.

Multicultural Families

All TCKs grow up in cross-cultural families – influenced by both passport and host cultures. A multicultural family has multiple cultural influences *within their family*. This may come from parents of different cultures, or be the result of immigration or adoption.

A child growing up in a multicultural family is influenced by at least two different cultures (and often two different languages) within their own home. These children are a subset of CCKs, but are not necessarily TCKs. This section concerns children from multicultural families who are *also* TCKs. These include:

1. Parents from different cultures

2. Immigrant Expats

3. Returning Immigrant Expats

4. Cross-Cultural adoption

Parents from different cultures

Children with parents from two different cultures are often called 'bicultural' kids. I have spent time with many bicultural families, and interviewed bicultural TCKs, from a variety of backgrounds, such as Argentine-German, Australian-Finnish, and Chinese-Nigerian. Most raised cultural identity as an important issue in their lives.

In *Third Culture Kids*, Pollock and Van Reken write, '*In 1960, one-quarter of American children living overseas had parents from two cultures, according to Ruth Hill Useem. In 1995, Helen Fail found that 42 percent of her ATCK survey respondents had grown up in bicultural families.*'

Identity is a complex issue for many TCKs. For bicultural TCKs there is an added layer of complexity. Some bicultural TCKs have dual nationality – they are citizens of both parents' home countries. Those with citizenship in only one of their parents' countries still have a strong cultural influence from the other parent.

A bicultural kid living permanently in a single passport country is provided with a place to belong, and a stable foundation for identity. Although the second parent's culture impacts them as well, the influence is different.

Bicultural TCKs are often more evenly influenced by both parents' cultures. They may live in one country as a foreigner while holding a passport for the other country, or live in a third country. This is a wonderful heritage, but can be tricky for a child to navigate, especially when asked the dreaded question, 'where are you from?'

Finding identity in one culture

Some bicultural TCKs handle the complexity of identity by drawing more heavily from one side of their parental heritage. 71% of the bicultural TCKs I interviewed identified more with one parent's home country as children. Several others spoke of switching between the two – changing not only language but even personality according to context.

Identifying with one culture more than the other gave these bicultural TCKs an anchor point – a primary 'home' country/culture they could point to. They knew it did not tell the whole story, but it was easier than explaining the whole story, especially when they felt the listener would not understand anyway.

I interviewed several sets of bicultural siblings, and they often had different primary identities. For all the bicultural kids who identified with one culture, different factors affected the process, such as:

· The language(s) most often spoken at home

· The language they were schooled in

· The language(s) classmates spoke natively

· The country their curriculum came from

· The predominant language/culture of any expat community they spent time in

· Which country they most look like a native of

· Which parent's home country they visited most often

· Which extended family members they had the most contact with, or felt the most connected to

· Negative experiences in, or associations with, one parent's home country

A negative experience while visiting a parent's home country can deeply affect a child's attitude toward this culture. One young woman told me about overhearing strangers in her mother's home country say nasty things about her mother – that she betrayed her people by marrying a foreigner, for example. This produced in her a deep hatred of her mother's country and its people. It took years for her to begin to let go of this prejudice, and she still has very little interest in spending time there.

I grew up in the Philippines, where my mom is from, but I grew up speaking English and attending an International School with an American curriculum. So even though I grew up in my mother's country, I was still in my father's culture, in a way. Looking back I realize I have come to identify more with Asian culture. I have always been closer to the Filipino side of my family because I've lived near them but never near my American relatives. Now that I'm at a primarily Dutch American populated school, I've found it very difficult to connect with other American students and have retreated to the familiarity of an international group: Koreans who have lived outside Korea and attended international schools much like the ones I attended.

Beulah, 19 [1st: USA; 2nd: China, Philippines, USA; 6 moves. Family: multicultural, mission. School: local, Christian international.]

Embracing both cultures

Regardless of childhood and adolescent attitudes toward their parents' cultures, most bicultural TCKs appreciate knowing about their cultural roots. 92% of the bicultural TCKs I interviewed expressed a deep sense of connection with both cultures, even those who identified with one more than the other.

Most bicultural TCKs want to feel they can belong in each of their parents' home countries, and be accepted by the people there. There may be sadness or even bitterness in a child who feels excluded by locals in a parent's home country.

> *Having parents from two different countries has been the most confusing aspect of the question 'where are you from'. Sometimes in the US to avoid attention I say I am from Finland. When they ask about my life in Finland I realise I didn't really live there. I have feelings of wanting to belong fully to both cultures and be seen by people from those countries as fully a part of them.*
>
> **Thongfaa, 24 [1st: Finland, USA; 2nd: Finland, Laos, Thailand, USA; 5 moves. Family: multicultural, NGO. School: home (group), international.]**

Many bicultural TCKs I know spent time in their early twenties deliberately investing in their sense of cultural identity – learning more about a piece of their heritage they felt less connected to, and finding a balance they were happy with.

While finding a balance helps a bicultural TCK understand and identify with both cultures, identifying with two distinct cultures is not always easy. Biracial TCKs in particular spoke of feeling their outward appearance did not match how they felt inside. While this is a feeling many TCKs express, biracial TCKs carry their difference on the outside. One biracial TCK (with an African father and Asian mother) told me she felt she had to 'prove' herself to both sides of the family, that she stands out in every family gathering, no matter which side of the family she is with.

There is an upside, however. Another biracial TCK told me he has come to like his 'different' appearance because it reflects the cross-cultural life he has lived as a TCK. If nothing else, it seems that being part of a bicultural family gives these TCKs a good reason to not fit in the monocultural box.

Helping bicultural TCKs connect

Many bicultural TCKs I interviewed spoke of ways their parents had helped them connect with their cultural heritage, and were grateful for these efforts.

Several families were deliberate about celebrating holidays from both countries, no matter where they were living. One foreign service family changed their home language according to the country they were in. If they were in a country where the native language was Spanish, they only spoke English at home; if they were in an English-speaking country, or a country where they spoke English at work/school, they only spoke Spanish at home (even while on holiday).

Several bicultural TCKs spoke about Third Culture communities being a place of great comfort – the one place their background was easily accepted. Most knew other TCKs with similarly mixed backgrounds, which helped normalise their multicultural experience. Several parents of bicultural kids also said they felt more comfortable living in Third Culture situations – where neither of their home cultures had the 'advantage'.

Being a TCK from a multicultural family comes with several challenges. It is sometimes hard to be sure about your identity, and to find a balance between what different people want from you. Some family members say you act too Asian or too Western and

> *you struggle to find your identity or where you belong. Being multicultural also comes with benefits, like being trilingual and having great international experiences. I think it also contributes to multicultural kids being really open-minded about many things that others have trouble relating to.*
>
> **Sarah, 18 [1st: USA; 2nd: China, USA; 7 moves. Family: multicultural, returned immigrant expat, unaffiliated. School: international, Christian international.]**

Immigrant expats

Immigrant kids are another type of CCK. Some become TCKs as well, as their parents move the family abroad after taking citizenship in their new country. These families are both immigrants and expatriates, so I call them 'Immigrant Expats'.

Immigrant Expat families usually have three major cultural influences: the parents' original culture, the family's new passport country, and the culture(s) they spend time in as expatriates. These families often incorporate traditions and languages of all three countries/cultures into their daily life. The influence of the three cultures on these TCKs' individual identity is more even than it might be otherwise, especially if there is a significant community of expats who speak the parents' native language.

Korean–American expats

A good example of Immigrant Expat families I have met (in several countries) are Korean–American expats. While there are many other cultural combinations, these families serve as a good example.

In most cases the parents were born in Korea, the children in the USA, and the family lives in a third country. Many of these TCKs speak all three languages fluently (including the local language of their host country), and use a mix of all three at home. I have seen Korean-American kids in China attend a Korean kindergarten, a Chinese primary school, and an American high school. They have an American passport, live in China, and are culturally very connected to Korea. They often have friends from all three cultures – American and Korean TCKs as well as local Chinese. Korean-American TCKs have told me they feel far more culturally Korean than cousins who have lived their whole lives in the USA, even though none of them had lived in Korea.

My parents were born and raised in Korea and moved to the States after high school. They took what they thought were the best parenting methods from both their backgrounds (Korean and American), and employed them hand-in-hand. My siblings and I were raised to respect our elders, but to not be afraid to question their decisions when we saw fit. We celebrated both American Thanksgiving and traditional Korean New Year. We visited relatives both in Korea and in the States. And all this happened as we grew up in China.

Eugene, 21 [1st: USA; 2nd: China, South Korea, USA; 10 moves. Family: immigrant expat, adoptive, education. School: home (group), Christian international.]

Struggles for Immigrant Expat TCKs

These TCKs share the struggles of Immigrant Kids. For example, if they are not as emotionally connected to their ethnic background as their parents, the difference can cause friction, or emotional distance.

Additionally, the aspects of their parents' birth culture they absorb are usually learned from older relatives rather than from peers, so they may feel out of touch with peers from their parents' country of origin. This can also be true for Immigrant Kids, but TCKs in expatriate communities may spend time with peers from their parents' original home country who notice this.

> *My parents are a lot more culturally connected to Korea than I am, but they teach me a slightly outdated Korean culture that existed 25 years ago. Consequently, older Korean adults like me, but I find it harder to get along with Koreans my age.*
>
> **Allie, 18 [1st: Canada; 2nd: Canada, China, USA; 9 moves. Family: immigrant expat, mission. School: Christian international, home.]**

TCKs from immigrant expat families are often excellent chameleons – switching their language, mode of speech, attitude, and even body language dependent on the cultural context. The drawback to this adaptability is that in a mixed group, with people from different cultural backgrounds, these TCKs may feel a sense of confusion – no matter how they act or speak, it will seem strange or disrespectful to someone.

*I brought my white Canadian friend to meet my
parents' Korean friends and found myself wanting to
run away. What language was I supposed to speak?
What body posture was I supposed to assume? Polite
smiles or hearty laughter? Direct eye contact? If I was
only with my friend, I would be joking around loudly.
If I was just with my parents' friends, I would be doing
a lot of listening and polite nodding.*

**Allie, 18 [1st: Canada; 2nd: Canada, China, USA; 9 moves. Family:
immigrant expat, mission. School: Christian international, home.]**

Returning immigrant expats

While some Immigrant Expats move to a third country/
culture, others return to their country of origin. This is not
a true homecoming, despite any expectations of extended
family members. The parents return to their homeland as
expatriates, no longer possessing any advantages offered to
native citizens, but with different pros and cons that come
with foreign citizenship. The country will have changed since
they left, and their status as expats also changes things.

*As my husband and I made plans to move to my
parents' birth country for the first time, my parents
wanted me to be aware of the expectations placed
on me by locals. I am ethnically Korean; my husband
is ethnically European. In many ways, locals will
impose expectations more loosely on my (obviously)*

> *foreign husband than on me. Although I have never lived in South Korea, many locals will expect me to acknowledge, internalize, and apply Korean cultural, traditional and social expectations, as if I had spent my entire life in South Korea.*
>
> **Pauline, 22 [1st: USA; 2nd: China, South Korea, USA; 3 moves. Family: returned immigrant expat, mission. School: local, Christian international.]**

TCKs in these families move to their parents' birth country often for the first time. Despite the family connection, it can be a huge shock to the system – especially if they have never visited extended family there before. For some of these TCKs it is a harder transition than going to a new country, where the family has no connections. By virtue of their ethnicity, they may be expected to speak the language fluently, or feel 'at home' very quickly – which often is not the case.

> *I moved to my parents' mother country after living in the US for most of my young life. It was definitely a weird kind of culture shock – growing up in a Filipino family made the Philippines seem almost familiar. But I definitely needed to work on speaking the language, understanding what kind of behaviour was considered socially acceptable, etc. Growing up in the US, I think my parents (as well as most immigrant/ expat families) tried to teach their kids the values of their home country while making sure they fit in or*

assimilate into their country of residence as much as possible. It's a struggle to keep that balance.
Justine, 29 [1ˢᵗ: USA, (Philippines); 2ⁿᵈ: Guam (USA), Philippines, USA; 3 moves. Family: returned expat immigrant, business. School: local.]

Balancing two cultural backgrounds is difficult. Sometimes it's easier to be accepted as a foreigner by other foreigners than to be accepted as a local by other locals. Some of these TCKs therefore deliberately hang on to their identity as foreigners, refusing to identify in any deep way with their ethnic origins.

Returned Chinese

I have worked with a lot of these families in China, where they are known as 'returned Chinese'. These are families in which the parents were born and raised in China, but moved overseas for work or study and gained citizenship there. In most cases their children were born and raised in their parents' adopted home, before the family moved to China for work.

These families have an interesting dynamic. The parents may feel China is home, but they no longer completely belong, as both they and the nation of China have changed. Their children, on the other hand, usually feel completely foreign. The difference in their experiences can create conflict.

Without a question, my parents consider China to be 'home' but I've never thought so. I was born there, but I gave up my Chinese passport long ago. My family all

> *live there, but I am not close with them. Even when*
> *I lived in Beijing for three years in high school, I felt*
> *like a foreigner. I prided myself on being a foreigner*
> *and belonging in the international community. I hung*
> *out with other foreigners, ate at foreign restaurants,*
> *went to places only foreigners go to. I think it made*
> *my parents a bit uncomfortable knowing how little I*
> *associate with their culture.*
>
> **Cat, 21 [1st: Canada, (China); 2nd: Canada, China, USA; 5 moves.**
> **Family: returned immigrant expat, unaffiliated. School: local,**
> **international.]**

Most of the Returned Chinese children I knew attended international schools and did very well there, but I also know several who struggled in local schools. Although they could speak some Chinese, they did not know all the vocabulary necessary for their academic subjects – a language gap most parents were surprised by. The resulting drop in grades was discouraging for both children and parents. In one case a teenage girl blossomed almost overnight when moved from a local school to an international school.

I particularly admire the way one Returned Chinese family I know is raising their children with a taste of both worlds. Their day-to-day life is in large part spent in an English-speaking expat bubble – an international school and international church. This gives their TCK children a safe place to belong and feel at home. At the same time, they do a number of things to connect deeply with China. They take regular trips to the parents' hometown, visiting with grandparents and other extended family members. This keeps the kids'

Chinese at a high level of fluency, and connects them to what China is like for Chinese, rather than for expats. Their family has also joined with other expats they know to raise money for charity projects the families then work on personally – building a library for a small village school, for example.

A special thing these particular parents do for their children is recognise the culture difference between them. With this is mind, they keep their kids connected to their Chinese heritage without expecting them to be 'Chinese'. Their children have the freedom to incorporate elements of both cultures into their lives in whichever way they choose.

Balancing cultures

Some returned immigrant expat parents do a great job straddling the two worlds that are important to their children; others completely miss their children's feelings. The fact the parents are often experiencing an unexpected sense of culture shock themselves – feeling more foreign or finding their birth country more unfamiliar than they expected – definitely helps these parents understand their children's feelings. Their situations are still different, however, and parents who do not notice the differences risk alienating their children.

When a returning immigrant expat family is able to balance their two cultures well, these TCKs are often very well-adjusted and at peace. They feel a deep sense of connection to both countries, experiencing and appreciating the best of both their worlds.

Cross-Cultural adoption

In some ways, adoption may feel more 'normal' in an expat community. An expat family may choose to adopt from the country in which they are living, families who had not originally intended to adopt may feel prompted to do so as a result of their overseas experience, and other families may experience the reverse – an interest in living overseas followed an international adoption. This means adopted TCKs may have several peers in similar situations with whom they can relate.

TCKs who were adopted have specific struggles with cultural identity, especially those adopted outside their own ethnicity. These identity issues come up in most cross-cultural adoptive situations, but when an adopted TCK lives in their birth country as an expat, there is additional identity confusion.

Living in their birth country

It is not uncommon for adopted TCKs to live in the country from which they were adopted, for several reasons. Some of these TCKs were born in the country their adoptive family was already living in. In other families the parents pursued an international adoption because of an interest in the country/culture, or later developed an interest in the country/culture as a result of the adoption; this interest then prompted an international move (or influenced the decision to accept a transfer).

There are certain thoughts I frequently hear from adopted TCKs living in their birth countries (and sometimes regarding visits to their birth countries):

- "I am the same genetically – why do I look so different?"

- "I sometimes wonder if I am related to the people I see on the street."

- "I saw a woman who looked like me and wondered if she could be my birth mother."

- "When I point out my (adoptive) mother to locals they don't believe me."

- "Locals tell me I am too fat, or that I don't speak the language well enough."

- "I look at locals my age and wonder how we are different. Why they were wanted by their parents, but I was not?"

- "It's hard for me to see locals begging or in bad situations. For all I know we could be related."

The situation is more complicated when an older child is adopted by a foreign family already living in the child's birth country, and they remain there. A child who remembers their life as a citizen of the country before being adopted by a foreign family may struggle to work out which country they belong to – the country in which they were born and still live, or the country their adoptive family is from.

My family adopted my brothers while we were in Guatemala so instead of having the struggle of moving them back we ran into the struggle of becoming a family even when they are still around everyone they know. Although they have been living with us for a while it is becoming evident that making them feel

completely secure in our family will not be an easy thing at all.
Risa, 17 [1ˢᵗ: Guatemala, USA; 2ⁿᵈ: Guatemala, USA; 4 moves. Family: adoptive, mission. School: home (group).]

Learning their 'story'

Many TCKs also respond positively to the opportunity to visit the place they were born – whether to see the spot where they were abandoned, the orphanage they used to live in, or any other physical connection to their pre-adoptive life and background.

Rebecca (Becky) Matchullis, ATCK, mother of TCKs (biological and adopted) and certified coach recommends adopted TCKs learn about their past. Her advice to them is, "Find out as much as you can about your past. Frequently look at photo books of your life, to ground you in the history that you do have recorded. If you don't do this, things can become tainted as a teenager or young adult."

Adopted TCKs may be excited about visiting their birthplace, hoping for answers or some sort of emotional resolution/ closure. Seeking answers, however, does not necessarily result in finding answers. This sort of visit may be interesting, even emotional, but is unlikely to answer any of the doubts or questions deep in the heart of an adopted TCK. This can be a heavy disappointment to a TCK who hoped for some sort of breakthrough.

"There is a great chance of identity crisis [for adopted TCKs] that continues longer than what other TCKs experience," Becky says. "Adoptive kids don't have roots in their ethnic or family-of-birth history. When the teen years come and they are going through the developmental stage of figuring out who they are, there are many missing pieces to the puzzle. This makes it difficult."

> *For an adoptive TCK it's hard to adapt into a 'normal' environment. For me I've had hard times trying to fit in especially in America. And when everybody talks about their biological parents (and they aren't adopted) it's hard for me, because I don't know about mine. I don't know what happened to them or what they are up to. I never lived in my birth place but I've visited there and I just wonder, out of these millions of people here, who or how many could be related to me. Do I have any brothers, any sisters? Aunts, uncles? Those are questions that never leave me.*
>
> **Magz, 17 [1st: USA; 2nd: Cambodia, China, USA; 5 moves. Family: adoptive, immigrant expat, mission. School: home (group), Christian international.]**

This is a lot for a child or adolescent to process. What seems to help many of them is having a safe space for open discussion about the circumstances of their adoption, what they feel about it, and any issues that arise as a result. This may include a desire to know the 'story' behind their adoption – why their birth parents chose to give them up, or how they came to be orphaned.

> *I lived with my birth mother and family until the age of one when I was put up for adoption. I spent a year*

in the orphanage in the capital. It was the best way to keep me fed and to have a place to sleep. By the time I was two I had trouble walking and was malnourished. A foreign couple came into our class to help out and I grew particularly fond of them. They visited me and helped me walk. I even got to spend some weekends at their house. My birth mother told them they should adopt me. I think it was that my birth mother took me out of the orphanage and brought me over to their apartment and asked them to take care of me.

Ganbold, 24 [1st: USA, (Mongolia); 2nd: Afghanistan, Mongolia, Pakistan, USA; 17 moves. Family: adoptive, NGO, unaffiliated. School: home, international.]

Different reactions

In some cases, the adopted child has a strong emotional reaction to their situation. Adopted children within the same adoptive family will often react differently, so it seems to be less connected to the adoptive family and more connected to the child's personality and/or pre-adoptive situation. There are three common reactions I have observed, but they are not mutually exclusive; many TCKs will go through different reactions to their situation at different times.

Not all adopted TCKs have these reactions; some are not at all conflicted about their adoption. They are bonded to their adopted family and feel free to talk openly about their feelings, even when they are difficult to understand. For those who do struggle, however, it can be an additional burden when others miss the perspective from which they view their situation.

The first common reaction of adopted TCKs is to want nothing to do with their birth culture. They may lie to locals about their ethnicity or history. They may be so quick to assert their adoptive identity they come across in a very confronting manner. They may refuse to learn the language of their birth country or, knowing it, refuse to speak it. They may refuse to speak to or associate with locals, preferring to have expatriate friends with whom they speak the language of their adoptive family. They may be highly patriotic, talking about how wonderful their passport country is, and comparing it favourably to other countries; their patriotism may be extreme enough to annoy or even offend others. This group of TCKs cling to their adoptive culture, using it as a shield against questions of identity. It is as if they have made an inner vow, "This is the country my [adoptive] family is from, this is the country I am a citizen of; if my nationality is clearly acknowledged by others I will know I belong; I will know who I am."

The second reaction is the opposite – ardently embracing their birth culture. These TCKs try to pass as locals, developing a fluent command of the language and surrounding themselves with local friends. They may dislike being seen in public with their adoptive family (especially any members of the family from a different ethnicity). This group of TCKs is also creating a shield against their internal struggle with identity, but in this case the inner vow is, "I was born here, I live here, so this is where I'm from; if I can belong here I will know who I am."

The third reaction is to get stuck in questions of identity and belonging. The lack of answers, and absence of clarity, leads to a deep insecurity. Some of these young people can be quite paranoid. They may think locals see them as foreign and foreigners see them as locals. They may fear they will never fit in (or be accepted) anywhere. These TCKs may outwardly express ambivalence about which country they belong to, but inwardly feel deep anxiety. They may fear being labelled or forced to make a choice. They may ride the fence – acting as an expat around expats and as a local around locals.

These reactions are ways in which adopted TCKs process their situation and the conflicting emotions they may experience. As they work through these issues, they can come to integrate the different aspects of their cultural identity – allowing for celebration in place of conflict.

At first I didn't like being seen as Khmer and really didn't want anything to do with it. I refused to learn the language but my parents forced me, which made me dislike it even more. I saw myself as American and didn't want many Cambodian friends. However as time went by I became confused with who I was because the reality struck me and people kept reminding me that I am Cambodian and nothing I can do will change that. I started embracing my culture more but Americans back home started seeing me as more Khmer. It took me about six years to realize how proud I am to be Cambodian yet I am still American. I feel like I know who I am and that I can have two homes because I truly believe that 'home is where the heart is'.

Maly, 18 [1ˢᵗ: USA; 2ⁿᵈ: Cambodia, USA; 5 moves. Family: immigrant expat, adoptive, mission. School: home (group), Christian international.]

Non-traditional Families

The traditional 'nuclear family' arrangement – married parents living with their children – is very common among expatriate families. TCKs in non-traditional families may feel isolated and unable to process their family experiences as their TCK friends often have little or no exposure to their situation.

It can come as a shock to TCKs there are so many divorced and single-parent families out there. Several TCKs I interviewed were surprised by this upon repatriation. For those from non-traditional families, this can result in feeling less self-conscious about their home life than before.

> *Growing up overseas in expatriate communities I never had any friends with divorced parents. When I left the expat world after high school I was really shocked at how prevalent divorce is, and how many of the people I met were affected. I'd really never thought about it before that.*
>
> **Jaey, 23 [1ˢᵗ: Singapore; 2ⁿᵈ: Australia, China, New Zealand, Singapore; 11 moves. Family: business. School: Christian international.]**

Non-traditional families include:

- Single parents (unmarried, divorced, widowed)
- Blended families (remarriage, step-siblings, half-siblings)
- Separation or divorce while living abroad

TCKs growing up in non-traditional families, regardless of the family's specific situation, rarely advertise their different situation. Some of these TCKs go years with no one (except, perhaps, their closest friends) even knowing they have a single parent, or that one of their parents is not biologically related. Several TCKs from non-traditional families I interviewed said only their closest friends knew about their family's situation.

Single parents

When living abroad, the practical support of extended family and long-time family friends is unavailable, or at least highly restricted. This makes life overseas harder for single parents, who are therefore less likely to pursue it. Those who do go abroad alone tend to be strong and independent, qualities their children admire. These TCKs are often fiercely proud of the parent they live with, especially as they get older; they see first hand how difficult life is for a single parent overseas.

I never hid that my parents are divorced because I felt that would mean I was embarrassed by my mother. Which I never am or was. She is strong. Independent. Everything I want to be as a woman. People think down on my mother when they find out – like it's her fault for some reason. This was made more difficult due to the small circle of people I interacted with. Most were missionary kids with healthy families. One time a group for single mothers was created at my church.

> *Two families showed up, one of them being mine. It was awkward and I felt lonely for my mother. It's rare for a single mother to venture into the world with her children. My mother was strong and fought against all the stereotypes. But I feared them and so didn't talk much about it.*
>
> **MeiHe, 22 [1st: USA; 2nd: China, South Korea, USA; 14 moves. Family: military, non-traditional, unaffiliated. School: home, boarding, international.]**

Families in which the parents are not legally married are also less likely to seek or accept overseas positions, as many countries will not issue dependent visas for an unmarried partner.

Divorced/blended families

Divorced parents may be barred from international moves due to custody arrangements. Some companies/organisations that send employees abroad require the non-custodial parent to give permission in writing before approving an overseas assignment.

Some countries also have strict rules for providing passports to children of divorced parents. These legal hoops prevent some families from pursuing or accepting overseas assignments. Children of divorce who do end up abroad may have limited contact with their non-custodial parent. Most TCKs of divorced parents I interviewed saw their non-custodial parent very rarely.

Most divorces are difficult for children – when you add cross-cultural families and international moves, additional issues can be involved. One teen boy I met grew up in Australia with his Australian father and Chinese mother. After his parents divorced, his mother returned to China and subsequently married a Chinese man. This boy, a native English speaker not very comfortable in Mandarin, later ended up attending an international school in China while living with his mother, step-father and half-brother – all three of whom were both legally and linguistically Chinese. He was left feeling an outsider everywhere – including in his own 'home'.

Feeling isolated

As non-traditional families are less common in expatriate circles, being known as the kid with a divorced, widowed or remarried parent can make a child stand out from his peers as 'different'. Camouflaging this fact, without outright lying (something most of these TCKs tried to avoid) is a simple way to appear more like everyone else. Even those who do not feel deep hurt about their situation, and don't mind questions, may find it an awkward topic to broach.

Many people don't know that I lost my mom when I was younger. It's hard to say but not knowing that much about my mom, it makes me have a different attitude towards what people ask about her. Questions about her are not hurtful to me. I did not know her that well so the impact is less for me than for one who has known their parent for a long time then lost them.

**Edward, 17 [1st: USA; 2nd: China, Macau, USA; 3 moves.
Family: mission, multicultural, adoptive, non-traditional.
School: international, Christian international.]**

In addition, most TCKs in a non-traditional family know very few other TCKs in similar situations. Their friends may be sympathetic, but have no idea how to help, or what to say. The things they do say may be unintentionally hurtful. This can be difficult for any child, but TCKs are often less aware of, and therefore less sensitive to, the situations of non-traditional families. If there is a strained relationship with a non-custodial or step-parent, innocent but unthinking questions may trigger deeply emotional responses.

> *It is always easier to let people assume my parents are still married until they ask. I would simply let people assume until their assumption needed to be challenged. When people find out that my parents are divorced they always ask if we are on speaking terms or things like that – which is personal, and none of their business. When people ask me what happened to my dad it sends me into the black hole of the past. This is also difficult for my husband because he was adopted by his step-mother. The assumption people make about her not being his 'real' mom is probably why they kept it secret for so long.*
>
> **MeiHe, 22 [1st: USA; 2nd: China, South Korea, USA; 14 moves. Family: military, non-traditional, unaffiliated. School: home, boarding, international.]**

After this happens a few times, these TCKs internalise the idea 'sharing just makes things worse' or, at least, it does not help and possibly makes others uncomfortable. The result is that when they struggle with the specific pain and emotion that goes with their family situation, these TCKs tend to turn inward.

The situation of a TCK struggling after parents' divorce comes up in *Expat Teens Talk*, by Dr Lisa Pittman and Diana Smit, who advise that teens share their feelings with a safe person. In this situation a counsellor is often best as they can stand outside the situation, while understanding the impact in a way that friends may not.

Relationship with the Host Country

TCKs do not all feel the same way about their host country. Some love their host country, some hate it, and for others it is a love-hate relationship. The way TCKs feel about their host countries has a profound impact on their overseas experience but, in turn, the way they feel is often influenced by many factors.

In this section I discuss five common experiences of life abroad, and how they affect the way a TCK relates to the host culture:

1. Full immersion in the host country

2. One host country

3. Multiple moves

4. Latecomers

5. Hating the host country

Full immersion in the host country

Fully immersed TCKs speak the host country's language fluently, attend local school, most of their friends are locals, and most of their meals consist of local fare. Immersion is the stereotype most monocultural individuals hold about TCKs, but fewer TCKs live fully immersed in a host culture now than in the past.

The percentage of TCKs surveyed who lived in a local community dropped by age – 58% of those born before 1985, 42% of those born after 1985, and 39% of those born after 1990. MKs were more likely to report living in the local community (54%), and business kids less likely (29%). Fewer than half of the surveyed TCKs who attended a local school felt they had been fully immersed in the host culture.

> *I had some local friends but as I got older and had Finnish classmates I did not make more local friends. Now as I think about going back to work in Laos I wish I had a better insight to the pop culture of my generation.*
> **Thongfaa, 24 [1st: Finland, USA; 2nd: Finland, Laos, Thailand, USA; 5 moves. Family: multicultural, NGO. School: home (group), international.]**

Friends and family in the TCK's passport country may assume they lived immersed in the host culture. It can be very awkward for TCKs who have not had an immersion experience to answer the questions which assume this.

> *The embarrassment I feel when people realize I can't adequately read Chinese, especially after learning that I've lived in China since I was two, is a horrible thing.*
> **Eugene, 21 [1st: USA; 2nd: China, South Korea, USA; 10 moves. Family: immigrant expat, adoptive, education. School: home (group), Christian international.]**

TCKs who spent their time abroad in an 'expat bubble' – living in foreign-style housing, attending an international school with TCK peers, eating 'normal' food, and so on – find these inquiries particularly distressing. Some feel very embarrassed, others are taken by surprise – suddenly realising how little they know about 'real life' in the country in which they lived.

> *Questions about how I like my host country can be tough to answer. I lived in the expat bubble so I know I wasn't as immersed in the culture as others may have been. Some people can be pretty judgmental about whether my experiences are valid. I end up feeling a fake because I don't know the local culture as well as an interested person who travels there often.*
> **Jaey, 23 [1st: Singapore; 2nd: Australia, China, New Zealand, Singapore; 11 moves. Family: business. School: Christian international, international.]**

Blending in

Full immersion is easier when a TCK is able to 'blend in' – when they look like they could be a local, something that is easier to do in a diverse country, or one with a high immigrant population. In most countries with low ethnic diversity, especially those with a long cultural history, a person of a different ethnicity stands out regardless of their language ability. An inability to assimilate, to be accepted by locals, can be painful for TCKs who identify strongly with their host country.

> *Though most of my friends are TCKs, I consider myself close to fully immersed in Japanese culture. Firstly, I am Asian and so can pass as Japanese (or an interracial person); secondly, I speak Japanese without a foreign accent. Although my TCK friends are the ones I'm closest to, I don't have trouble assimilating and blending in compared to Caucasian friends, who although they speak perfect Japanese, will never be fully immersed due to their appearance.*
>
> **Justin, 23 [1st: Japan, Singapore; 2nd: Canada, Japan, Singapore, UK; 16 moves. Family: mission. School: local, Christian international, home, boarding.]**

In ethnically diverse countries it is much easier for a TCK to be accepted as one of the crowd, so it is easier for these TCKs to become immersed in their host culture. While they may still stand out (having a foreign accent or different clothing) there is a sense that, should they want to, they could become a citizen of the host country.

Some TCKs who could blend in choose not to, hanging onto a foreign identity. I did this as a teenager living in the US – clinging (quite stubbornly) to my Australian accent and vocabulary for a sense of identity. I know several expatriate families in which one sibling deftly blended into the host culture, while another chose to remain obviously foreign.

TCKs who feel like immigrants

In some cases, immersed TCKs may see themselves more like immigrants than TCKs. They know their parents come from their passport country, but do not really connect to it as their country too. These TCKs feel so much a part of life in their host country they more than identify with it – they do not consider themselves foreign at all.

> *I don't remember life before moving to Estonia at age two. I grew up speaking two languages fluently. The majority of my friends were Estonian. I attended Estonian schools, an Estonian church, took piano lessons at an Estonian music academy, and was a member of an Estonian rhythmic gymnastics league. I even looked the part. I did not discuss my family or home life, because this made Estonians realize I was not Estonian, a concept that confused me because I belonged. At 14 I found out I was a TCK when, for the first time, it was pointed out to me that I am not Estonian. It was as if I had been lied to about everything over the course of my whole life. No one even recognized the heartbreak.*
>
> **Chelsea, 21 [1st: USA; 2nd: Estonia, Hungary, USA; 11 moves. Family: mission. School: local, Christian international, home (group).]**

One TCK I interviewed grew up in Australia, and fell so behind in his command of the family's native language that his parents sent him to his passport country for a summer of intensive language tuition. Upon returning to Australia he realised he felt more at home there than in his passport country, and began looking into taking Australian citizenship.

As Pollock and Van Reken point out, *'There are many positive things about TCKs who identify closely with the local culture, but sometimes the cultural immersion is so complete that the TCK chooses to never repatriate. While there's nothing inherently wrong in this choice, it can be a painful one for a TCK's parents because they may feel their child is rejecting them along with their culture.'*

I interviewed several TCKs who gained citizenship in their host countries, and others who gained permanent residency. While there is something great about having a legal connection to a country they feel attached to, many still feel they don't entirely belong even if their peers accept them.

One young woman told me the first time she felt truly herself was years after taking up citizenship in her host country, when she was living in her birth country for the first time. She carried the comfort of being a citizen of the country she called home, even while away. She also had the comfort of living in the culture of her parents. Most of all, as a legal foreigner she had a legitimate reason to be different. The experience made her feel less mixed-up, more comfortable and more confident in her own skin – even after returning to her acquired passport country.

One host country

TCKs who spend most of childhood in a single host country usually identify strongly with their host country and culture. TCKs who do not spend much time in expatriate circles (especially those in less developed areas) are even more likely to feel a strong connection to their host country.

Deep attachment

While TCKs who live in a single host country may feel more settled in some ways, they are still caught between at least two different places. Living between only two places can make the relationship with their passport country more complicated. They are deeply connected to and rooted in the host country; in some cases these TCKs feel a far deeper connection to their host country than to their passport country. A deep attachment to the host country complicates connections with extended family members and others from, or in, the passport country.

> *It bums me out that my husband has never seen all the cool places I have seen and may have a difficult time understanding my bond to Asia as half of my home, when he sees my tiny-white-girl outer appearance. I feel Chinese in ways, but it's actually kind of a hopeless feeling trying to explain a dual identity.*
> **Karissa, 23 [1st: USA; 2nd: China, USA; 9 moves. Family: mission. School: local, home (group), Christian international.]**

Many of these TCKs feel no one understands that the inside and the outside just do not match – the country they are supposed to call home does not *feel* like home. Some dream of gaining citizenship in their host countries – even where it is not a practical possibility.

This is not to say these TCKs do not appreciate their passport countries, but their appreciation may be second-hand (based on their parents' feelings) or less felt emotion and more intellectual fact.

Other TCKs can develop an antagonistic attitude toward their passport country – something that can be painful to parents and downright offensive to others from the passport country.

One girl I met was adamant her host country had the best climate, the best food, the most beautiful landscape, the most beautiful language, and the nicest people. On the other hand, she complained bitterly about the horrible weather, tasteless food, boring landscape, ugly language, and rude people of her passport country. In her case, this hatred was largely fuelled by a difficult experience – living in her passport country for the first time as a young teenager. Everything was unfamiliar, and she spent the whole year in shock; upon returning to her host country she never wanted to leave it again.

Many TCKs I interviewed talked about negative aspects of their passport cultures, or expressed preference for aspects of their host cultures.

> *I have felt like my host country is better than my passport country, especially the people and the culture. I really do see a stark and unpleasant contrast between the cultures. I used to hate everything about Australia except for my friends and family there, but now I've learned to love it in a strange sort of way. It's hard to admit that I do. I have people and even places there that I love and every time I leave it gets harder to do so.*
> Jo, 14 [1st: Australia; 2nd: Australia, Cambodia; 3 moves. Family: mission. School: Christian international.]

Visiting as adults

While these TCKs may struggle when returning to a passport country, an even more emotional experience can be going back to a beloved host country after time away. This is especially true if they have already finished high school, or their family no longer lives there. Expatriate communities are quite transient, so they may discover they know almost no one there anymore. Friends they went to school with have all left. Family friends have left. Things have changed – such as landmarks, or the level of development.

> *Even though I was in the same place for 12 years, home for me was wrapped up in a community that no longer exists. Many of the places I knew are totally gone. The last time I visited I felt like I was in a new place. Very few of my old friends were there, and so many of the places I cherished were gone. It was a very sad feeling. I wanted to feel as if I was returning*

to my roots, but they had moved on, or evaporated, so to speak.

Logan, 24 [1ˢᵗ: USA; 2ⁿᵈ: China, Hong Kong, USA; 6 moves. Family: mission. School: home (group).]

Author Taiye Selasi, in a TED talk called, *Don't ask where I'm from, ask where I'm a local,* touches on this when she says, "Perhaps my biggest problem with coming from countries is the myth of going back to them. I'm often asked if I plan to 'go back' to Ghana. I go to Accra every year, but I can't go back. [...] We can never go back to a place and find it exactly where we left it. Something, somewhere will always have changed, most of all ourselves."

There is an additional shock for TCKs who grew up in 'expat bubble' communities. They may not be able to afford the lifestyle they lived as a child. They may discover they have very little connection to the local culture – a lack of language, a lack of local friends.

For TCKs who lived a more immersed life in their host country, the experience may be different but the emotion no less strong. TCKs who lived as immersed children may discover they are less accepted by locals as a foreign adult returning to visit. Locals the TCK was deeply connected with as a child saw the TCK as not really foreign, but strangers do not have that relationship and may treat the TCK like any other foreigner.

Experiences like this can be crushing to a TCK who has, through years elsewhere, held onto the idea this place was home, the place they felt they belonged. For some it can be a shocking and devastating experience.

While a visit like this may be a difficult or bittersweet experience, not the 'homecoming' expected, it can also be very healthy. For some it is an almost essential step in moving on. It may help 'close the book' on a previous life, giving the emotional freedom needed to move on to new opportunities or locations. Some TCKs I interviewed described a visit to their childhood home as the push they needed to finally start putting down roots in the place they now lived.

Some TCKs do have very positive return visits, feeling welcomed and at home. Several TCKs I interviewed said it gave them space to say a real goodbye – one they were emotionally unable to process when they first moved away.

Whatever an individual's situation, whatever their attitude toward the host country, a return visit can help a TCK process childhood experiences and therefore connect better in their current life – wherever in the world they happen to be.

I went back to Bangladesh on my own about three years after we moved away. The hardest part was not having my family there. However, I did feel very welcome and 'at home'. All my old friends and Bengali family members treated me the same and that made it hard to leave again.

Hannah, 20 [1ˢᵗ: Germany, USA; 2ⁿᵈ: Bangladesh, China, Germany, USA; 10 moves. Family: NGO. School: local, boarding.]

Frequent moving

Some TCKs move frequently, from country to country, or back and forth between their passport country and one or more other countries. Many TCKs who moved frequently (7 or more times before age 18) shared some sadness about all the transition in their childhoods. Those surveyed were a little more likely to say they had 'missed out', and less likely to call the experience 'awesome' or 'fun'. Despite this, 93% were thankful for their overall experience.

Making friends

Frequent moves mean these TCKs are constantly starting again. TCKs I know who moved every year or two were very practiced at first meetings. Most gave quite favourable first impressions and were able to build rapport quickly. One of these TCKs called meeting people a 'survival skill' – a skill she had honed by repetition, which allowed her to survive the frequent moves by building a new social circle quickly.

While these TCKs often had a solid social circle, they did not always have close friendships. While some of these TCKs do want to go deep in their friendships very quickly, most told me they generally hold back large parts of their hearts. Investment in another person is simply storing up pain for when the inevitable goodbye comes.

One said he considered friends a social necessity, but deeper sharing was risky.

> *Because we'd move so much, I quickly stopped making the effort of building friendships. After all, one of us would end up moving away so why bother making myself vulnerable and opening up if, after a short time, we'd be pushed apart and never see each other again?*
>
> **Aurelie, 19 [1ˢᵗ: France; 2ⁿᵈ: Belgium, China, France, UK; 5 moves. Family: business. School: international, local.]**

This makes TCKs who move frequently during childhood both easier and harder to get to know. The skills of meeting people and making friends make them easier to connect with initially (and, several told me, serve them well in work settings). Getting past surface conversation can be more difficult.

> *I remember feeling 'popular' but looking back, the majority of my friendships were quite shallow and superficial. I did not open myself up to the different possible friendships I could have had. I did not properly invest time or emotions in my 'friends'. I was prepared to say goodbye to those people from day one.*
>
> **Siyin, 21 [1ˢᵗ: Singapore (Hong Kong); 2ⁿᵈ: China, Hong Kong, Singapore; 4 moves. Family: business. School: international.]**

The cycle of making friends, leaving friends, and starting again is tiring. TCKs who move frequently may go through periods in which they are not interested in building relationships. Several TCKs I interviewed spoke of the pain of leaving friends behind, and wondered what life might have been like if they had not moved so often.

If I have only one regret about my childhood, it is the fact that we moved so often. Every four years we'd move; trips to the States were always the hardest. Even now, there are some days where I daydream about a life if my family had stayed there. I would have attended high school with all my friends. I could have been unafraid to bond with them, as I wouldn't have to leave them. I might have been able to ask out the girl I had a crush on, the one I was afraid to ask because I knew that I was going to leave anyway. I know it's a silly, childish thing to think about, but sometimes it still hurts.

Carl, 21 [1st: USA; 2nd: Japan, Singapore, USA; 10 moves. Family: multicultural, mission. School: home, Christian international.]

Family and 'home'

One TCK I know has a passport from Finland. She lived in five countries before the age of 15 – but never in Finland. She was born elsewhere in Europe, and through several moves (living on three continents) only ever went to Finland to visit extended family during holidays. Finland is 'home', but her only real connection there is her grandparents. She spent no more than a few years in each country, so it was hard to feel she was 'from' any of them. She does not really know what it feels like to be 'from' a place at all.

I'm not sure what is considered to be a move anymore. People may say going from your home to another place, but I don't know where home is, especially in

> college with my parents living in a country I have
> never lived in before. There is no place that seems
> more home than another.
> **Emily, 21 [1ˢᵗ: USA; 2ⁿᵈ: DR Congo, Kenya, Rwanda, USA; 20 moves.
> Family: mission. School: local, international, boarding.]**

Family is often very important to TCKs who move frequently; if the family is moving together, then the family unit is the one constant through the transitions. Several TCKs I interviewed spoke of feeling 'lost' without their family, especially after leaving to enter university.

'Often TCKs whose parents move every two years rarely consider geography as the determining factor in what they consider home. Instead, home is defined by relationships,' write Pollock and Van Reken.

The mother of a military family I knew worked hard to create traditions that made every new house in every new country feel like home. The first things unpacked in their new home were their curtains. One of her children told me those curtains created a sense of ownership: "This is *our* living room; this is *my* bedroom." For this family, a simple thing such as curtains created a sense of belonging, continuity, and security.

> Our kitchen was always yellow and strawberries, and
> the living room always had maroon coloured furniture
> and curtains when possible. I'm not sure if it was on
> purpose, or just what my mom liked, but it definitely
> helped places feel more like home.

Emily, 21 [1st: USA; 2nd: DR Congo, Kenya, Rwanda, USA; 20 moves.
Family: mission. School: local, international, boarding.]

Connecting with the host culture

When a family moves frequently, there can be a sense of
culture-weariness – not wanting to start from scratch with
yet another language, not wanting to be seen as a tourist yet
again, not wanting to work out how to get things done in
another foreign system.

While this is totally understandable, kids who grow up like
this can later feel they missed out on something. Many
have expressed a sadness that they spent years in a country
without developing any friendships with local peers – all
their friends were fellow expats. Upon repatriation these kids
are asked questions about the country, culture and language
– causing many to realise for the first time how little they
really know about a place they may think of as 'home'.

*I wish I had just one Korean friend after living in
Korea for four years.*
Johanna, 25 [1st: USA; 2nd: Mexico, South Korea, UK, USA;
6 moves. Family: embassy. School: international.]

Alternatively, they may grow nostalgic for a particular
country, but the place they miss no longer exists – their
expatriate friends have all moved on, and their understanding
of the local culture and language is often limited.

Deliberate engagement in local culture – whether through

travel, language or culture classes, or activities where they meet local peers (such as sports) – helps these TCKs feel a connection to the culture in which they live. While they may find this tedious at the time, in retrospect these often become highly treasured memories.

Connecting with the passport country

TCKs who move back and forth between their passport country and different host countries are likely to have a strong bond with their passport country – it is the place to which they always return. Frequent reconnection to the passport country makes it 'home'. These TCKs (especially if from a foreign service family) may have a strong sense of patriotism and national pride. Despite this, their inward attachment to their passport country is still not the same as that of their monocultural peers; a wider experience of the world gives them a broader perspective.

TCKs who move from country to country have a very different experience. They are less likely to bond deeply with any one place, but feel like global citizens, belonging no more to one place than to another. They will answer the question 'where are you from?' differently depending on where they are and who is asking.

"Often it depends what their mood is that day, if they want to give the long or short answers about their lives, or what they think the person is actually asking," Ruth Van Reken explains. "But that is the time many feel the slight pang of not knowing or feeling like they belong to a particular place and that many around them don't give them permission to feel connected to lots of places to be 'from'."

This is not to say these TCKs hate their lives – most enjoy the excitement of visiting new places and meeting new people. But beneath this can be a quiet loneliness these TCKs cannot quite explain. How do you miss something you have never had? They hear the word 'home' but can only imagine how it feels to be so emotionally connected to a single place. They are usually proud of the wide range of experiences they have had, but at the same time they also know there are gaps – in gaining variety they lose continuity.

> *I don't love moving so much. I can't tell you how jealous I've been of girls who have lived in one place their entire life. I've always wished for the marks on the door frame in the house that shows how much I've grown in the past 10 years, and knowing the neighbour since I was in diapers. I feel the loss of the life I could have had if we had stayed in one place to begin with. Moving so much has made me who I am today, and I would not change that, but that doesn't mean I'm not sad about it.*
>
> **Callie, 17 [1st: USA; 2nd: China, Qatar, USA; 6 moves. Family: business. School: international.]**

Restlessness

As young adults, the thought of staying in one place for an extended period of time may trigger 'itchy feet'. Quite a few of those I interviewed chose to study abroad for a semester during their university education. Others chose jobs that required travel or relocation, or found a new job in a different location when the urge to move hit.

> *I was required to stay in one place for four years to finish my university degree. By the end of the second year, I was so restless and fidgety because I craved moving as 'it was time'. The average time I stayed at a city before I moved was two years, so it seemed about right to move after the second year.*
>
> **Shannon, 22 [1ˢᵗ: Canada, Hong Kong; 2ⁿᵈ: Canada, China, Hong Kong; 9 moves. Family: business. School: local, boarding, international, Christian international.]**

Brooke, a 22-year-old TCK, discusses this in *The Worlds Within, An anthology of TCK art and writing: young, global and between cultures*, writing *'Yes, it's hard not having roots; mainly because I have no idea where I would like to start a career. When you are so used to leaving you grow restless being in a place too long. I feel like I will be able to put that feeling at bay by continuing to travel once or twice a year to a new place. Because that's all it really is; a strong feeling to see more, because you know more is out there that is beautiful and different than any other place you've seen.'*

Latecomers

Those who made their first international move in high school may not identify as TCKs. They have a stronger connection to their passport countries, having spent most of childhood there. I worked with 'latecomers' who were uninterested in engaging in the culture of their host country, seeing it as a temporary place before they would go home. I also worked with latecomers who wanted to soak up as much as they could.

One year I was connected with two families making their first move overseas. Both families had children starting their final year of high school. These two latecomers had very different reactions to the experience. The first threw himself into activities, making friends and getting to know more about his new location. The second withdrew into herself, investing in studies rather than in people, thinking she would not be there long enough for it to be worth the effort. The first student developed several close friendships he maintained after returning to his passport country for university. The second student said that she looked around at the end of the year and realised that while she did not have a bad experience, there had been the potential for more.

Struggles

Some latecomers cling to their passport country identity, uninterested in being affected by the host culture. Some prefer to maintain relationships 'at home' via Internet communication platforms, leaving less time and energy to build friendships in the new location.

Latecomers may feel they do not fit in with TCK classmates. They are entering a cross-cultural environment and do not have the shared experiences that make up the Third Culture, certainly at the beginning. Some latecomers struggle to make new friends, especially if they feel unwelcome. Their Third Culture classmates may be slow to include new students; some can be dismissive of a latecomer's lack of Third Culture experiences.

At first, I didn't want to try that hard with friendships because I was 'only' going to be there for two years.

> *My efforts to make friends and to belong were rebuffed at first by a few classmates. However, I quickly became involved, even if not everyone liked me. There were others who welcomed me and tried to include me. The growing pains in my first year paved the way for a successful final year of high school.*
>
> **Victoria, 20 [1st: USA; 2nd: China, South Korea, USA; 3 moves. Family: immigrant expat, mission, unaffiliated. School: Christian international.]**

Latecomers may look forward to returning to their passport country – to a place they know, and are normal. The problem is that things change – they have changed, and passport country peers (and pop culture) may have changed as well. Instead of comfortably sliding back in, they may have to work at being 'normal' again – should they wish to do so.

> *I kept up with a few friends from home during my first year, but barely during my second year, because I belonged more in China. When I went back it came as a shock that people stayed almost the same while I had changed so much. I had to work to belong again. To this day I still do not belong in the 'old crowd' because I changed so much. Facing people at home who remained the same, it was awkward for me to relate to them, and I felt pressure to act the way I used to around them before my move, because I didn't know how else to handle it.*
>
> **Victoria, 20 [1st: USA; 2nd: China, South Korea, USA; 3 moves. Family: immigrant expat, mission, unaffiliated. School: Christian international.]**

Although latecomers may struggle at the start they often develop a deep fondness for their host country and enjoy the people they meet. They benefit from the broadening of perspective that comes with life overseas, often while maintaining a grounded sense of 'home' in their passport country.

Hating the host country

Everyone dislikes elements of their host country from time to time – it is part of the process of adapting to a new place. Some TCKs, however, exhibit irrationally deep hatred toward their host country.

'Hate' is a strong word, but it is appropriate for this phenomena. These TCKs are experiencing strong emotions beneath the surface and choose to lash out at their host country, perhaps seeing it as an easy target, and safer than lashing out at the people in their lives. For some TCKs, host-country hatred is almost an addiction: they realise the irrationality of their outbursts, and may be embarrassed by it, but cannot stop the strong feelings rising up within them.

Lois Bushong agrees and says, "It is safer for a child to be angry at a country or a school than at a parent. They are typically very loyal to their parents. Instead of saying they are angry with their parents for moving them, some find it safer to talk about how much they hate a particular country."

TCKs' hatred often takes the form of rants about everything that is 'wrong' or upsetting about a host country. They may look down on the food, clothing, or customs of the host country. They may complain about the habits or manners of the host culture. Sometimes this may be expressed by being overly patriotic, overly proud of everything about their passport country. They may constantly compare elements of the host country to their passport country, and every comparison favours their passport country. In their opinion, everything is better 'at home'.

These are not objective opinions based on truths about the two countries (although these TCKs can give you long lists of their reasons). In reality, the TCK is exhibiting a stress reaction caused by the overwhelming experience of moving abroad. A child in this situation cannot be reasoned out of their hatred. Instead, they need extra care and compassion to help them process their feelings about the move, and difficulties they may have experienced in the process.

Pretty much all TCKs I know have experienced a form of host-country hatred. I've talked about it a lot with friends and all say they have hated it at one point. I became more comfortable being mad and negative toward the country. I hadn't realized that was what I was doing until a woman sat down and talked to me. She told me I needed to figure myself out before I acted so strongly against a place I had only lived in for a few years. After that I re-evaluated myself and my emotions and realized I was acting out because I didn't know what to do with myself. I felt like I needed to be mad at something and the country was the easiest and most harmless thing to act against.

> **Risa, 17** [1ˢᵗ: Guatemala, USA; 2ⁿᵈ: Guatemala, USA; 4 moves.
> Family: adoptive, mission. School: home (group).]

While anger is one of the stages of grief (discussed in *Chapter Three: Transition and Grief*) a problem can occur if anger and hatred becomes part of a TCK's identity. One TCK I know created an email address expressing hatred of the country he lived in; while it embarrassed him later, at the time the hatred was part of his identity.

I experienced a degree of host-country hatred while living in the US (from age 13–15), which continued after I moved back to Australia. It took years for me to recognise this as an expression of the confusing emotions I experienced. In time I became very thankful for the years I spent in the US, despite the difficulties I experienced. Almost every TCK I interviewed had this revelation at some point.

> *I witnessed that moving to Beijing was a big culture shock for a lot of my peers, myself included, especially for those who hadn't travelled much before. It often took a while, but China – and Beijing in particular – had a way of growing on people; I know I fell in love with the richness of the culture and history once I got to know it better.*
>
> **Saz, 24** [1ˢᵗ: Malaysia, New Zealand; 2ⁿᵈ: Australia, China, New Zealand; 5 moves. Family: immigrant expat, business. School: international.]

Whether a child loves or hates their host country (or their passport country), it is important they have space to express and explore these emotions. TCKs may have very conflicting feelings about their host and/or passport country – feelings can be threatening and overwhelming to the TCK. Having a safe place to express these feelings gives great relief.

Emotions are not 'good' or 'bad', 'right' or 'wrong'. It may be difficult for an adult to listen to a child's complaints about a place to which the adult has a strong attachment, but the child needs to feel accepted and safe to express those feelings. While TCKs need not be encouraged to publicly say things that may offend others, they definitely need a safe place where it is okay to feel whatever they are feeling, and know they will not be rejected for it.

CHAPTER THREE

TRANSITION AND GRIEF

Transition

Change is a constant in the lives of TCKs. Change is physical – a new location, a person who is physically absent. Transition is the process of handling the emotional fallout of physical changes.

Many people – including TCKs – do not understand the subtle but crucial difference between 'change' and 'transition'. Change happens instantly. Transition is a process that takes a long time. Transition begins the moment one becomes aware of an upcoming change. Transition continues until after one becomes emotionally at ease with all the consequences of the change.

Transition starts with recognising something is about to change, or has already changed. It means grieving the loss of what was, and becoming comfortable with the newness of what now is.

Most TCKs enter a new period of transition long before a previous process of transition has been completed. They are not completely comfortable with one change when another is piled on top. And another. And another. Their best friend moves away, they change schools, their sibling goes away to college, their family moves to a new country.

In the past two years, my two best friends moved, my dog passed away, my grandmother passed away. My sister went to college. Then my family moved back to

Texas (for the first time since I was five years old), and my dad got a new job where he goes to Angola for 28 days, is home for 28 days, then goes back to Angola and so on. Now I am applying to college and finishing up high school. I know exactly what it is like not being okay with a transition when another one occurs.
**Callie, 17 [1ˢᵗ: USA; 2ⁿᵈ: China, Qatar, USA; 6 moves.
Family: business. School: international.]**

The transitions in expatriate life can be tiring for adults, too. In her memoir, *As Soon As I Fell*, ATCK and professional counsellor Kay Bruner writes, *'We celebrated every transition with a gathering of whoever happened to be in town at the time. As time went on, the farewells mounted and became more painful, as each departure added to the load of losses I carried.'*

Despite this weariness among adult expatriates, a parent who grew up in a fairly constant environment, in a single country, has a very different experience of life abroad than that of a TCK. The emotional background upon which their experiences happen is very, very different.

Transition has always been a part of my life. I knew how to fly before I could walk. I had more stamps in my passport by the age of one than I did words coming out of my mouth. Growing up, I learned the skills of packing a 50-pound bag to perfection and quickly found the strategies of sleeping comfortably

> *on 13-hour-long plane rides. I even know how to*
> *repeat the airline safety instructions in multiple*
> *languages. My life has always felt like a constant*
> *of people walking in and out, and of course never*
> *throwing out the packing boxes.*
> **Corrie, 20 [1ˢᵗ: USA; 2ⁿᵈ: China, USA; 11 moves. Family: mission.**
> **School: home, international.]**

Transition is a constant part of life for many TCKs, to the point that they really do not know what it is to live without the emotions of ongoing transition. They do not have the emotional security of constancy. The TCK life is one of unending transition, and its constant presence becomes wearying.

Take a moment to consider how living in a constant state of transition might affect the way a child feels about their life, their world.

> *I had to say goodbye to a close friend knowing I*
> *would not see her for at least five years. I missed her*
> *so much. Immediately after she left, I could not make*
> *new friends. I think I was still sore from the goodbye.*
> *I still talk to her online but it really isn't the same.*
> *I do believe I will see her again, although I know the*
> *relationship will never be the same. A lot can happen*
> *in five years, and people change.*
> **Joy, 16 [1ˢᵗ: Singapore; 2ⁿᵈ: Singapore, Thailand; 4 moves.**
> **Family: multicultural, immigrant expat, mission, unaffiliated.**
> **School: home.]**

Some TCKs respond to the overwhelming pressure of constant transition by shutting down emotionally. Others live in a state of denial – that change does not matter. Others experience near constant dread – fearing the next person or place they will have to say farewell to.

Linda A. Janssen in her book, *The Emotionally Resilient Expat: Engage, Adapt and Thrive Across Cultures*, comments, *'Life is full of transitions, with expatriate/cross-cultural existence having more than its share. We would be well-served to learn how to deal with them, and in doing so, we dip into [...] the reserves of emotional resilience within us.'*

Anticipating separation

Many TCKs absorb a belief that 'everyone leaves' – it was a phrase TCKs used repeatedly during interviews. This is a logical belief for anyone living an expat life – if you do not leave regularly yourself, it is pretty likely close friends leave you. If a friend moves away with little or no warning it strengthens the belief that no relationship can be relied upon to last.

While many TCKs are concerned with knowing how long a person will be around, there are different responses to the stress of this uncertainty, and not every TCK reacts the same way.

Some TCKs run headlong into relationships, determined to soak up everything they can before the inevitable goodbye. They can come across as needy or draining – especially to non-TCKs. Several TCKs related problems making friends in their passport country because they were seen as 'too intense'.

Others strive to never be taken by surprise, desiring to be the one who leaves, rather than the one who is left. They may refuse to engage with a person who will be in their host country short term, hoping to dull the emotional impact of another goodbye. They may also break off relationships with people or groups as soon as they learn someone will be leaving (even if the move is months away). As adults they may hop from school to school, or country to country, in an attempt to control the goodbyes – if I am the one who leaves, no one can leave me.

> *I lived with a mentality that 'everyone leaves'. I just recently moved off to college and I had a really close friend get mad at me for pushing her away and trying to do anything I could to minimize the hurt I knew was coming. Honestly I still expect us to eventually lose touch anyway because people move on. That's all I've ever known.*
>
> **Maddie, 18 [1st: USA; 2nd: Germany, Japan, USA; 9 moves. Family: military. School: home (group).]**

Building walls

Self-protective behaviours related to emotional closeness are common, but some TCKs are quite deliberate about it, building big emotional walls to hide behind. It is an attempt to create control in the midst of a life full of change – upheaval over which the TCK has little or no control at all.

For some TCKs the 'wall' is more like a tough exterior –
a shell to shield them from painful experiences of any
kind. They may come across as 'strong' (creating positive
reinforcement) or 'cold' (which may prompt further retreat
from the pain of rejection).

> *Today I still feel the negative repercussions of moving
> as a child. I find I have problems with denial and
> hardening my heart to bad things, which I think has
> come out of moving and having to put on a brave face
> right away so I could make friends.*
> **Elisabeth, 19 [1st: USA; 2nd: China, USA; 2 moves.
> Family: unaffiliated. School: Christian international.]**

TCKs who rely upon the strategy of wall-building have
absorbed the idea that the best solution to inevitable
goodbyes (and grief) is to keep their heart so deeply buried
that nothing can touch it.

Patterns of behaviour
There is a often a mixture of different responses in each
individual TCK. Many put people in different categories –
some they will jump in with very deep, very quick (especially
other TCKs), while others are kept at arms' length.

A lot of these behaviour patterns (such as diving deep,
leaving first, or wall building) are totally subconscious. Many
TCKs only begin to recognise them as young adults. It can be
both difficult and painful to challenge and change patterns
of behaviour that feel normal.

My life feels like a series of learning how to stack stones on the wall around my heart. I've mastered the skill of plastering masks on my emotions, and only now I am beginning to understand the true destruction of this path. Rooted deep inside me is this lie that says, "Everyone will always leave." Being at college has made me notice how deeply rooted some of the grief from all my transitions is. With people walking in and out constantly, it takes me a long time to allow anyone to have a glimpse of what really goes on inside.

Corrie, 20 [1ˢᵗ: USA; 2ⁿᵈ: China, USA; 11 moves. Family: mission. School: home, international.]

Loss

While there are many different types of international experiences, and every TCK is unique, the biggest shared experience in the Third Culture is that of *loss*, and the grief that goes with it. The rest of this chapter discusses how grief affects TCKs, and how to grieve losses well. First, it is important to consider what those losses might be.

There are so many different elements of loss associated with a change in location, or a friend moving away. These losses can include:

· Leaving a house/neighbourhood that felt like home.

· Losing pets unable to travel to the new location.

- Losing the 'safe place' represented by a particular school or social group.

- Losing the homey feel of a social group when a key member moves away.

- Loss of social status in a new place.

- No longer being 'in' but starting again as the 'new kid'.

- Loss of academic status – no longer being top of the class upon starting at a new school.

- Emotional cost of 'starting again' (whether leaving or left).

- Gradually losing the closeness of a friendship with time and distance (a drawn out loss).

- Visiting friends in a previous location and realising one no longer belongs/fits in (a delayed loss).

- Distance from extended family – physical and emotional.

- Being too far away to attend important events in a previous location, such as a school formal, wedding, or funeral.

- Losing one's passport country accent (sounding like a foreigner when at 'home').

- Losing familiarity with a place that was once 'home'.

- Having no way to visit a place that was 'home', as friends/family no longer live there.

- Losing the safety/comfort of family when repatriating alone for university.

Each of these losses is significant, and a single move may include several of these at the one time. TCKs usually have little or no say in the decision to move (sometimes parents have little choice themselves), which can increase the sense of loss.

Losing valued skills

Another set of losses involves skills the TCK loses, or fails to learn. Skills that were highly valued in the one culture may become obsolete in another. This can be very frustrating for TCKs; they may feel incompetent when in the place supposed to be 'home'. It may result in a loss of confidence – a fear they are unable to manage.

> *In New Zealand some of my skills are not very useful. I can navigate Beijing's many subway stations, bargain successfully and order lunch in Chinese, but I missed out on learning skills that are second nature for my Kiwi friends. I've had to learn how to shop with no bargaining, be polite in my home country, talk to strangers in English, and much more. The first time I took a bus alone in New Zealand I wasn't sure of where I was going. I instinctively thought to myself, "I speak Chinese, so everything will be okay." My next thought was, "Oh no! That's not going to work here!"*
>
> **Bethany, 20 [1st: Canada, New Zealand; 2nd: Canada, China, New Zealand; 10 moves. Family: multicultural, unaffiliated. School: local, home (group).]**

Skills that are unused in a new place – including the ability to speak a particular language – may be lost over time. This can be extremely distressing for TCKs. Losing a skill that was once familiar can feel as though a big piece of their identity is slipping away. This is especially common in younger TCKs who picked up a foreign language quite naturally as a child, only to lose it after moving away. TCKs in this position may refuse to speak the language they are forgetting, either out of fear they will make mistakes, or out of sadness for such an emotional loss.

> *My wife and I were conversing in Khmer at the dinner table. Our oldest child, then 11, was listening in and, I thought, understanding. I asked her a question in Khmer, and she didn't reply. I persisted, asking another question. She asked me – in English – to stop. I asked her why she didn't want me talking to her in Khmer, and she said it was because she couldn't understand me anymore. She put her head down on the table and started sobbing, momentarily overcome by the sadness of having left so many people she loved and the deep regret of forgetting the language that connects her to her past life.*
>
> **Thomas, 43 [1st: USA; 2nd: Cambodia, Uganda, USA, Venezuela. Family: mission. School: boarding, Christian international.]**

Anything that a TCK misses, or feels sad about leaving behind, any change that makes them upset in any way – whether sad, angry, or fearful – is a loss that is worth addressing.

Even when nothing can be done to change the situation – especially when nothing can be done – recognising and grieving these losses helps TCKs.

Valérie Besanceney says, "It is so important to acknowledge the losses and challenges of moving in order to truly celebrate the positives."

Grief

Grief is not a bad thing – it is a natural healing process. It is also a sign that a person has loved something enough to feel hurt by its loss.

'We only grieve when we lose people or things we love or that matter greatly to us, and most TCKs have a great deal they love about their experience of growing up among worlds,' write Pollock and Van Reken.

Grief is a signal a loss has occurred and needs healing, just as physical pain is a sign an injury or illness has occurred and needs healing. Left untreated, a physical wound can fester until blood poisoning occurs – at which point the ignored injury poisons one from the inside. In the same way, hidden grief can gnaw away at a person from the inside and taint relationships with others. The many losses TCKs experience result in layers of grief and each needs to be grieved and healed.

Jonathan Trotter, pastoral counsellor and writer for mission blog *A Life Overseas*, experienced grief first hand both as an inner-city trauma nurse and in losing close relatives in his youth: a sister when he was six, and both parents to cancer (at age 17 and 25). "Grief is the soul's way of dealing with hard stuff," Jonathan says. "When we're physically ill, our body has ways of stopping us, forcing us to rest and heal and focus on what hurts. Grief does that for the soul, forcing a pause. A detox, if you will. So without grief, without the appropriate venting of feelings and emotions and tears, we miss a prime modality of healing. And frankly, we're not designed to deny grief. Perhaps for a time, as a coping mechanism, but in general, denying grief and its effects is not natural."

The grief of moving is made up of a hundred little losses. Each changed relationship, each group of people lost, each place left, must be mourned. There are lifestyle changes, changes in the food available, and even changes to the way one is treated by strangers. The same goes for a person left behind – life may be different in the light of their loss, with reminders of the person (or people) who are no longer there.

I have lived a very privileged life, but I have experienced a lot of grief. While I have never had a close relative or friend die, I have said goodbye to more people than I can remember. Investing so much time and energy in friends only to lose them, over and over, starts to wear us down. In many ways I have lost perspective on those things that do last. Adults need to help TCKs gain perspective about their experiences, help them go through the grieving process for every

> *friend that leaves, and prepare them for the time*
> *when they too will have to move on.*
>
> **Johanna, 25 [1st: USA; 2nd: Mexico, South Korea, UK, USA;**
> **6 moves. Family: embassy. School: international.]**

"Grief is cumulative," Doug Ota explains. "Don't try to escape your losses. Face them. Find assistance if you need it. Your feelings are your friends. They're trying to teach you something so you can become whole."

Pre-grieving and post grieving

Some people grieve in advance of a loss – they see it coming and feel sad. (This is also known as Anticipatory Grief). An internal countdown turns normal activities into sources of grief. Soon they will not be able to visit this friend's house, or that restaurant, or play in the local park. They may linger over every 'last time' and cry a lot as a separation looms. They look around and realise, "I will never do this again."

Others grieve after the change occurs. It may be due to a sense of denial prior to the change, but some people are just wired this way. Their grief comes after the change, when they see the space where a person or place or activity used to be. It is at this point the post-griever realises, "I will never do this again."

> *I know a lot of people who in the days before they*
> *leave, or before someone they know leaves, feel really*
> *sad all the time, but it's not like that for me. I never*

*feel sad until a half hour before the person I know
leaves. It hurts too much, so I numb myself to the
pain, block it out, and refuse to think about it until
it's actually happening.*
**Faith, 17 [1st: USA; 2nd: Cambodia, USA; 2 moves. Family: mission.
School: home.]**

Neither way is better or worse than the other. The pre-
griever may feel overwhelmed, but they are able to grieve
while still with the people they care about. The post-griever
can concentrate on the 'work' of preparing for a change, but
when the emotion hits they may be around new people who
do not understand the source (and depth) of their grief.

Secondary grief

When I first moved to China, my cousin (who had lived
overseas for several years) gave me some really helpful
advice. She told me homesickness would come in waves.
After a few months, when I settled into my new life, I should
expect a wave of homesickness seemingly out of nowhere.

A secondary bout of grief is quite common. It often comes
around the point where the new life becomes routine, no
longer novel. This new place (even if the 'new' place is their
passport country) is not a holiday spot – it is their final
destination, and they are not going to go back to their old
'normal'. They are really not going to see that person, eat
that delicacy, or do that activity. That person is really not
coming back. Sometimes, it is when the busy-ness of moving

and settling into a new routine slows to 'normal' that a TCK has space to finally feel grief that had been held at bay.

> *In my first month I dove right in to volleyball and catching up with old friends and family. I didn't have a lot of time to think about how much I missed China. After volleyball ended the dam kind of broke. I was sitting in my room looking at photos and just cried. I missed being able to talk to someone in Chinese just outside my door. I missed the community I lived in. I missed my life. I would find myself crying randomly and not really knowing what specifically had triggered it.*
> **Anna, 18 [1ˢᵗ: USA; 2ⁿᵈ: China, USA; 2 moves. Family: military. School: international.]**

An unexpected second wave of grief can be really upsetting. When parents and other adults in a TCK's life are not prepared for these later periods of grieving, they can easily discount how deeply the TCK is hurting, or feel a need to rush the child through the grief – for example, reminding them how happy they were last week.

> *I did not feel homesick at all during the first semester of university. I purposely did not often contact people back in China because I knew if I did, I would feel homesick. However, after winter break, I was bombarded with homesickness. After spending three weeks with my family in Korea, it was really hard for*

> *me to go back into college life. Thinking about Korean*
> *food, watching Korean TV, and looking at pictures*
> *would trigger those sad feelings.*
> **Dan, 20 [1ˢᵗ: South Korea, USA; 2ⁿᵈ: China, USA; 9 moves. Family:**
> **mission. School: international, Christian international, home.]**

Grief over time

TCKs who experience a lot of grief as young children may remain very sensitive toward goodbyes as they grow older. They may realise they are reacting more strongly than others, or more strongly than they think the situation warrants, but that does not stop the feelings.

I explain loss like a pebble thrown into a lake (or a boulder – depending on the magnitude of the situation). The impact of each loss causes ripples – a series of troughs and peaks that gradually diminish until they disappear. Grief can be like this: there are highs and lows, and they will take some time to abate. When a loss is grieved well these should be like fading ripples – smaller over time until they fade into calm.

> *Three years ago I started to truly engage with how much*
> *grief is a part of my life. About a year ago, some close*
> *friends decided to leave. This time, instead of shoving*
> *the emotion down, I decided to embrace it. I wanted to*
> *really say 'goodbye'. Every time I felt sad, I let myself*
> *feel it. Some of those days, I laid down in bed for a while,*
> *and let myself be tired out by the grieving process.*

Danny, 37 [1st: Ireland, USA; 2nd: China, Hong Kong, USA;
6 moves. Family: mission. School: international.]

"Exhibiting emotional resilience doesn't mean we won't get upset or overwhelmed at times. Instead we acknowledge those feelings and work our way through them," Linda Janssen says.

The grieving process looks different in each person. There is no right or wrong way to grieve, and no specific timeframe in which to do it. Some TCKs are very expressive about their grief in the months leading up to a move, others are not. Some TCKs are quickly ready to jump into a new life in their new locations; others take months, even years, to finish grieving the loss of community and relationships in the old location before they can begin making deep connections in the new one.

Unresolved Grief

It can be overwhelming to grieve many losses at once. The easiest solution is to suppress that grief – to ignore it. This 'unresolved grief' becomes an emotional burden the person carries until they face it and grieve the loss, however belatedly.

With the amount of loss most TCKs experience, repeated again and again over time, the grieving process can feel unending or become exhausting. It is not surprising that most will, at some point, suppress the grief of a loss.

'What they [TCKs] loved and lost in each transition remains invisible to others and often unnamed by themselves. Such losses create a special challenge. Hidden or unnamed losses most often are unrecognized, and therefore the TCK's grief for them is also unrecognized [...]. These hidden losses also are recurring ones. The exact loss may not repeat itself, but the same types of loss happen again and again,' write Pollock and Van Reken.

Outlawed grief

Jonathan Trotter coined the term 'outlawed grief' to describe a situation in which a person is persuaded (whether deliberately or accidentally) that it is not okay to express their grief. He explains, "Outlawed grief is sadness that's somehow labelled as 'wrong.' Sometimes grief gets outlawed for 'spiritual' reasons, and sometimes it's more patently selfish. That is, someone says 'I can't deal with my grief or yours right now, so you need to stop.'"

Many TCKs I interviewed shared stories of ways in which they 'learned' to suppress their grief. TCKs from a variety of backgrounds told me stories about occasions when, even as a small children, they were told not to cry about a move or other loss.

There are lots of ways adults unintentionally give TCKs the message their grief should not be expressed, saying things such as:

- "Look on the bright side."
- "But you will have so many great experiences there."
- "It will be so good for you."
- "You can still stay in touch by email and Skype."
- "You/they will be back before you know it."
- "You're so lucky."
- "This is a great opportunity for you/your family."
- "You'll be glad later."

> *I always knew we would only stay in China for three years, but by the time we were getting ready to leave, I didn't want to leave. My parents did their best to comfort me. They said moving back was best because I was getting ready for college and everything would be easier back home. I understood what they were saying and agreed with it, but that didn't really change not wanting to move.*
>
> **Anna, 18 [1st: USA; 2nd: China, USA; 2 moves. Family: military. School: international.]**

It is very tempting for adults to try to soothe an upset child with a list of good things about the change in situation, or encourage a depressed child with hopeful thoughts about what will happen in the future. The problem is that a child who is still expressing their grief, in whatever manner, is usually unable to really hear and accept these positives yet.

Instead of comfort or hope, the message they receive is that their grief is not acceptable.

Whatever the reason, when a TCK grieving a loss is told these things, the message conveyed is 'you should not feel sad about this'. Young TCKs in particular may come to believe they should not express grief – and it becomes 'outlawed'. Some think of a lack of expressed grief as being strong (and inwardly fear they are weaker than others). Emotions are bottled up, and the weight of unexpressed grief grows.

> *Whenever we would get ready to move it was surreal, just a thing that happened. I was terrified of the hurt, but didn't want to appear weak. I would cry alone and then force myself to snap out of it after a while because I couldn't move back. I was told to "be strong because the move is hard on your little brother" as if it wasn't hard on me too. Whenever we moved eventually I learned to suck it up because new friends didn't care a ton.*
> **Maddie, 18 [1st: USA; 2nd: Germany, Japan, USA; 9 moves. Family: military. School: home (group).]**

Pollock and Van Reken discuss lack of permission as one of the reasons for unresolved grief, writing that, '*Sometimes TCKs receive a very direct message that lets them know it's not okay to express their fears or grief [...]. In such situations, TCKs may easily learn that negative feelings of almost any kind, including grief, aren't allowed. They begin to wear a mask to cover those feelings and conform to the expectations and socially approved behaviour of the community*'.

Compartmentalising

Another tool many TCKs talked about was compartmentalising. These TCKs feel their losses, but keep their feelings private, or kept different areas of their life as separate as possible – so the emotion from one area could not spill over into another area.

Compartmentalising sometimes offends people in these TCKs' lives, as they feel the TCK is not 'upset enough' about a shared grief experience. Perhaps the TCK seems not to be showing sadness over an upcoming separation, or the passing of a family member. It does not mean the TCK in question is not feeling sad, but perhaps the sadness is only expressed when the TCK is alone, or in a different context. The weight of 'shared grief' may be too much, so it is compartmentalised away when with people who are also mourning.

One TCK spoke of an extended family member scolding her outside a funeral, offended by her composure during a time of mourning. This TCK was in fact greatly upset and barely holding herself together while around others; the accusation hurt her deeply.

Relieving the stress of unresolved grief

As unresolved grief builds up, the unexpressed emotion must somehow find a release. As Pollock and Van Reken write, *'Unresolved grief will always express itself somehow. Often it will be in ways that appear completely unrelated to feelings of grief and apparently focused on very different events.'*

The methods by which TCKs self-regulate unexpressed emotion vary. For some it is completely internal – extremely intense thought patterns, or crying alone when the pressure becomes too much to bear. Some share explosive bursts of deep emotion with close friends (almost exclusively fellow TCKs). For others these emotional explosions are expressed by lashing out verbally at parents or siblings. Or, they may lash out physically (punching or throwing inanimate objects) so they will not lash out at the people around them. 'Hatred of the host country' (discussed in *Chapter Two: Different Types of TCKs*) can also be an expression of unresolved grief.

A particularly dangerous kind of suppressed grief is when a TCK attempts to repress all feelings, to live in a state of numbness, where none of the negative emotion can touch them. This cannot really work; the suppressed emotion escapes in some way, often resulting in self-destructive behaviours. Self-destructive behaviours can also be used as a way to self-regulate emotional stress levels.

Pollock and Van Reken write that this sort of behaviour, *'becomes a way in itself to numb the pain of longing for some type of security and home base. The sad thing is that until the loneliness and longing are addressed, the TCK will stay walled off, often in very destructive behaviour.'*

As much as I pushed stuff away for years of moving, I couldn't always avoid it and it would often come out in arguments with my parents about anything. Anger about who knows what would surface with

a vengeance. However, the high school pressures
build up and the need to succeed made survival more
important. I didn't have time for anger surges and so
at one point I did resort to cutting as a release and a
way to feel and then be rid of emotions quickly.
Maddie, 18 [1ˢᵗ: USA; 2ⁿᵈ: Germany, Japan, USA; 9 moves.
Family: military. School: home (group).]

'Some of the self-destructive behaviours that I have seen in
TCKs suffering from unresolved grief are: eating disorders,
addictions, rebellion against the work of their parents and their
God, violence in their marriages or families, and deep depression,'
Lois Bushong noted.

These outlets provide short-term relief from the pain
and confusion of holding everything inside. Most of the
TCKs I've discussed this with do not see their outbursts or
self-destructive behaviours as a sign of 'real' trouble, but
just what they need to do to get through. They may even
recognise these behaviours are unhealthy, but know no
better way to lower their stress levels. Two different teenage
girls (from different backgrounds, attending different
schools) who had been caught cutting each told me they
were frustrated by all the people trying to help, that they
were too busy with school to deal with counsellors and
freaked out parents.

Often I feel pressured to please everyone, get As in
school, not because people place this on me, but because
of bottling my feelings I need a release. When I cry I

have to do it alone, and then feel guilty for it. Without
faith I would have resorted to cutting or alcohol.
Wendy, 16 [1st: USA; 2nd: China, USA; 3 moves. Family: unaffiliated,
mission, adoptive. School: local, home (group).]

Some may feel guilty, ashamed, or confused about their behaviour. Their own actions can be a mystery to these TCKs, as these behaviours may not be chosen deliberately but are instead almost instinctive reactions to an overwhelming rush of emotion they feel they have no control over.

One of the biggest dangers for TCKs who develop a pattern like this (suppressing emotion until they can hold it in no longer) is that, once learned, it is difficult to shake. While bottling emotions seems like an effective way to get through childhood losses over which the TCK has little or no control, it is a system that relies upon explosive release mechanisms. Long term, this system can prevent, rather than encourage, emotional growth and maturity.

My last move was unrelated to my TCK life, but
damage from all the previous moves had built up to
a point-of-no-return. I had thought that I would
finally be able to make friends who I could share and
connect with as deep as I'd like. However, my parents
pressured me to transfer schools to be closer to family,
which I finally decided to do. I haven't really been the
same since. I have employed the generous help offered
by vodka, Marlboro, and marijuana to blow some

steam off, and though I know it's probably not a good
path to travel down for the most part, I like where
they take me. My point is that moving and losing can
and will affect TCKs throughout the rest of their lives.
Whether or not they do turn to negative outlets for
relief is a toss up, but suffice to say it's not a feeling
most of us enjoy. Bottling up emotions, no matter
how good of an idea/defence mechanism it probably
seemed at first, will always come back to bite you
where you least want to get bitten.

Carl, 21 [1st: USA; 2nd: Japan, Singapore, USA; 10 moves. Family: multicultural, mission. School: home, Christian international.]

Grieving Well

While grieving is a natural and necessary process, it can be very difficult for parents and other family members to give TCKs room to grieve. Seeing their grief pains adults who genuinely want the best for them. Moreover, parents may feel guilty for initiating a move, or powerless to help a child losing friend after friend as they move away. I have seen parents break down crying, distraught by watching their children in pain, feeling powerless to help them, and worrying the choice to live overseas has harmed them.

Sometimes children are not the only ones who need to be reminded they will not always feel this way. Parents, too, need to know their child's grief, while valid, will only last for a season. No matter how deep their sadness, if grieved well it will be resolved and integrated. And while the losses they experience are painful, the benefits are just as tangible. Giving a child space to grieve helps them through the hard part of being a TCK, so they can gain more from the positives of a life overseas.

Ruth Van Reken says she often reminds parents, "Grief is not a negation of their [the TCK's] past, but an affirmation. You don't grieve for losing things you don't care about, so if the child is sad to leave or that separations are coming, it's because they have loved this place, these people, and what they gained from that place and people is part of their life fibre now forever, but it is appropriately sad that it is changing.'

Modelling grief

One way adults can help TCKs learn to grieve well is by 'modelling grief'. This means that the adult expresses their own grief in front of the child, allowing the child to see what it can look like to express grief.

Modelling grief is extremely helpful, especially for TCKs who spend most of the early years abroad. It is important for them to learn what grief looks like. This means it is important for parents to engage in the grieving process, and to let their children see some of this. Actions often speak louder than words; showing one's own sadness over losing a friend is more powerful than simply telling a child it is okay to be sad.

Modelling grief can be both easier and harder for adult TCKs.

Many understand the magnitude of their children's grief, and the importance of grieving. However, loss and goodbyes may be strong emotional triggers even in adult life.

> *A few days ago, some friends left for good, and I was trying to explain to my six-year-old daughter how to say goodbye to them. I was trying to tell her to do something I'm not totally convinced about myself. We sat there for a minute as we both realized that this was not going to be easy. It's really odd trying to teach my kids how to do something I am only learning now after 27 years of doing it wrong. It's really hard to tell my girls it's a good thing, because my heart isn't really convinced yet. My mind says yes, but my heart says hell no! I'm pretty sure my kids pick that up, and I'm pretty sure they are not sure if they should go through the grieving process – because it hurts! Right now, my main thought is to just be with my daughters in the grief of saying goodbye, rather than coach them – to just be present, and let them know that this is really painful. I wish someone would have done that for me 27 years ago.*
>
> **Danny, 37 [1st: Ireland, USA; 2nd: China, Hong Kong, USA; 6 moves. Family: mission. School: international.]**

Providing space and comfort

To let children know their feelings are valid, to model good grieving, to make the expression of feelings acceptable and even expected, is to give them a great gift. To do this, parents often have to put aside a natural aversion to seeing children upset. Ignoring, downplaying, or putting a happy face on a child's loss can 'outlaw' grief.

One of the most important things families can do is create space for children to grieve – to talk about the people and places they miss. Parents can make their home a place where expressing the pain of grief is permissible. When a child is grieving, they need a safe space to express their feelings. Pointing out the positives can wait until the child has had a chance to mourn the loss.

'Offering comfort is a key factor in any grieving process – even when that process is delayed by decades,' advise Pollock and Van Reken. *'Remember, comfort is not encouragement. It is being there with understanding and love, not trying to change or fix things.'*

Jonathan Trotter has simple practical advice for parents: "Talk less, hug more. I think parents need to say much less than they think they need to say. In general, a wise parent is one who holds their grieving child and simply says, 'I'm so sorry. I know this hurts so much.' And then maybe, in a moment of silence, asks 'What do you miss about _____?'"

Self-awareness for parents

It is important that parents are aware of their own grief, especially when experiencing their own losses related to international life.

"Often, parents feel threatened by their child's grief. Or they feel guilty. Parents must deal with their own grief," says Trotter. "If the parent has unresolved grief deep down in their soul, whenever their child brings up grief or displays grief, it will unnerve the parent, causing discomfort, reminding them of pain."

> *It's so easy for parents to project/impose their own pain when grieving. Once my husband left and my son said "I don't like dada going away, I miss him". My response was "I know, I miss him too." I very quickly made his comment about me, not his pain. It's such a skill to listen well and provide comfort and not just 'fix'.*
>
> **Anne, 37 [1st: Australia; 2nd: Australia, Burundi, Canada, Liberia, Malawi, South Africa, South Sudan, Sweden, UK, USA; 30 moves. Family: mission. School: local.]**

"When your child starts crying or grieving in some way, take note of your own emotions," suggests Trotter. "What does your child's grief stir up in you? If it creates an uneasiness or a desire to soothe ASAP, take note. Your child's pain is probably triggering your own. Resist the temptation to defend yourself. Comfort your child in the moment, and make a note to deal with your own stuff."

Five Stages Of Grief

The Five Stages of Grief is a theory first introduced by Elisabeth Kübler-Ross in her book *On Death and Dying: What the Dying Have to Teach Doctor's Nurses, Clergy & Their*

Own Families. While no model is perfect, and every individual experiences grief differently, the Kübler-Ross model is a good tool to help understand some of the different ways TCKs respond to the grief they experience. Understanding this model can help TCKs permit themselves to grieve, rather than continuing to suppress how they feel.

The five stages are:

1. Denial

2. Anger

3. Bargaining

4. Depression

5. Acceptance

Grief is not truly linear; a TCK may experience these stages in a different order, spend more time on one than another, move back and forth between stages, or experience more than one at a time.

There is often a period of shock before the grief of a loss is felt, especially if news of an impending move is sudden or unexpected. This shock is usually short lived (sometimes only a matter of minutes) but I have seen it last weeks or even months. One TCK, speaking to me of an upcoming move, said, "I know I *should* feel grief, but I honestly don't feel anything."

These TCKs may not experience the grief of their loss until after the change occurs. Unfortunately, this means the grief they experience may take them by surprise, and at a time when they have less support to help them process it.

Stage One – Denial

Denial is, in essence, trying to pretend a loss does not matter. If I can believe this person or place is not important to me, it won't hurt to lose them. I know many TCKs who became stuck at the denial stage. Unresolved grief can sometimes be the result of an extended period of denial.

Things TCKs in denial commonly say include:

- "I don't care"
- "It doesn't matter"
- "I was never that close with them"
- "It's no big deal, this happens to everyone"
- "Whatever, I'm used to it"
- "What's done is done"
- "I'll be fine"

Sometimes a TCK says these things knowing it is not how they feel inside. They simply wish to be able to power through, and these phrases become mantras to make the pain go away.

'Some TCKs and ATCKs refuse to admit to themselves the amount of sadness they have felt [...] Others admit these separations were painful but claim to have gotten over them,' write Pollock and Van Reken.

It's not that I didn't know my emotions or how to express them. I've always been incredibly expressive. It was more that I didn't give myself adequate time to deal with them. To grieve you have to dwell in those feelings for a while. At the time, I was not willing to do that. I felt I needed to power on and keep moving. I guess I was in denial about how I was dealing with them. I guess I thought I had dealt with them when in reality I had just preoccupied myself with something else. I was really good at taking care of everyone else's problems, and ignoring my own.

Christyn, 30 [1st: USA; 2nd: Egypt, Israel, Jordan, UK, USA; 12 moves. Family: mission. School: international, home.]

Adults sometimes misread this as a TCK being very mature and understanding – having a positive perspective. TCKs themselves can be fooled into believing that suppressing their grief is the mature or responsible thing to do – and the pain of accumulated loss grows. Remaining in a state of denial means the TCK is building a wall of losses that have never been grieved.

After teaching this material at a conference I was approached by a 17-year-old boy. He had lived abroad his entire life and was preparing to move to his passport country to attend university. He had heard a lot about transition over the years, but in learning about the stages of grief became aware of a long list of losses he had never grieved. The weight of carrying this unresolved grief around while putting on a smiling face to the world was wearing him down – and now he realised why. At the end of our conversation he sighed and said, "I have a lot of work to do."

Stage Two – Anger

Anger is one of the most misunderstood stages a TCK goes through. While it is not always a conscious shift, Anger happens when a TCK realises the loss really does matter to them. This is the opposite of Denial (trying to believe it does not matter). The Anger stage is where a person recognises a loss as well as the lack of control in the situation. There is a lot of frustration wrapped up in this. A TCK at this stage may complain, "It's not fair!"

If a TCK is left behind, the logical object for their anger is the person who leaves; if they are the one leaving, the logical object for their anger is their parents. The close relationships they have with these people can make it hard for a TCK to express any anger, even as a form of grief. (Again, this can be a reason for hatred of the host country).

It is important that parents and other adults recognise anger as a form of grief, and part of the natural grieving process, rather than rebellion. TCKs need space to be angry about things they cannot change. Pressuring them to accept the situation does not help; they will naturally progress to acceptance once they have experienced and expressed the emotions the loss has stirred in them – including anger.

Pollock and Van Reken note that, *'The anger may be directed at parents, the system they've grown up in, their home country, God, or other targets. Unfortunately, once again people don't always stop to find out what's behind the explosion. The judgment and rejection of the TCK's experience increases the pain and fuels further anger and rebellion.'*

For some, anger becomes second nature – complaining about the move, the place they live in, and so on. These TCKs may come to a place of acting out an anger they no longer feel. A gentle challenge issued in a loving manner may be helpful.

A 13-year-old girl once told me she had decided to stop being angry. She had felt the grief of leaving her home in Africa very deeply and spent months lashing out at her parents and at the Asian country they had brought her to. More than six months after the move her father sat her down and explained that while he wanted to hear how she felt, it upset him when she was rude to him, her mother, and the people in whose country they were guests. He asked her to consider whether her words were fair. Disarmed by his gentleness, she stopped and thought about it, and realised she did not really feel angry anymore. She was still sad, but decided it was now time to start engaging in the new place.

When I came back to Australia I was angry at a lot of things. I was angry at poverty, war and brokenness. I didn't know how to reconcile the two worlds I had encountered and felt trapped between them. Whenever I felt myself slipping into the apathy of the western world I was now a part of, I felt it my duty to re-acquaint myself with the suffering of the world. I thought it better to be angry with purpose than ignorant. It wasn't until I did some research that I realised my hurt and anger may have been in response to feeling misunderstood, and that grieving the losses others endured was a way of grieving my own loss.

> *Perhaps the emotion – however undesirable it may seem, was a way of keeping that world alive.*
> **Lani, 25 [1ˢᵗ: Australia; 2ⁿᵈ: Australia, Ethiopia; 2 moves. Family: mission. School: home.]**

Stage Three – Bargaining

A TCK at the Anger stage recognises a loss they have experienced, and that they are powerless to prevent it. A TCK in the Bargaining stage may look for things they could or should be doing, or not doing, to make things better. This stage is all about trying to 'fix' what feels broken. For TCKs, the Bargaining stage of grief is often characterised by hanging on to what was, and looking for ways to minimise a change.

For many 21ˢᵗ Century TCKs, this is expressed with a *lot* of time online – regular Skype dates, long emails and hours on social media. Many parents are concerned when they see their children in this stage, as they recognise the need for new connections. It can help to understand this is a natural stage, and in most cases will not last more than a few weeks or months. If a child seems stuck here, they may need space to talk about the changed friendship(s); some TCKs are so fixed on the idea of not losing relationships that meant so much they may be hiding from the truth that they have already changed.

> *For months after arriving back in the States I spent long, long hours instant messaging and writing emails*

with my friends back in Ecuador, wanting nothing more than to be 'home.' It took several months for me to open up to the possibilities of happiness and new friends, but once I did, they came simultaneously.

Kendra, 24 [1st: USA; 2nd: Costa Rica, Ecuador, USA; 12 moves. Family: mission. School: Christian international.

A teenage TCK once told me about trying to maintain a close relationship with a best friend who had moved overseas. He poured so much of his energy into trying to stop this one friendship from changing he was not open to new friendships, even neglecting friends who still lived nearby. At the same time, the friend who had left was in a new place, meeting new people, making new friends. Their lives had diverged, and their relationship was changing. This TCK felt the shift happening, but desperately wanted to believe that if they tried hard enough, talked on Skype enough, their friendship could stay the same.

The underlying belief a TCK in the Bargaining stage holds onto is that there is something they can do to hang onto what their life used to be. If they talk a lot online, they think, friendships will not be lost and can instead be maintained indefinitely. The problem, of course, is even a friendship successfully maintained in this way has already changed. The old friendship is lost, and a new one has to be renegotiated.

'One day' was my favourite thought all throughout high school. One day I will be out of here, one day I will go back to Africa, to anywhere. Making promises

> *to myself was the only way I could cope with the*
> *permanency of my new reality, to give myself some*
> *feeling of control. Eventually I had to come to terms*
> *with the fact that if I pursued my future with the*
> *objective of repeating the past, I would inevitability*
> *be disappointed. The past had moved on without me,*
> *and if I put up with the present to live for the future I*
> *would miss out on what was in front of me.*
>
> **Lani, 25 [1st: Australia; 2nd: Australia, Ethiopia; 2 moves.**
> **Family: mission. School: home.]**

'The Bargaining stage is a beginning step for how to deal with the losses productively,' Pollock and Van Reken note. *'We can't outsmart or outrun it.'* Bargaining is a way to process grief, a process of recognising a loss matters.

Stage Four – Depression

Eventually, all attempts to prevent or fix the pain of loss are shown to be ineffective. When TCKs recognise things have changed despite all their best efforts, they reach what Kübler-Ross calls the Depression stage. Once TCKs reach this point they can actually *grieve*.

The 'Depression' stage of grief is about sadness – not clinical depression. It is the stage at which a person recognises and feels sad about a loss. This sadness may involve crying, reminiscing, hurt feelings, lack of energy, unwillingness to connect, and being sensitive to reminders of the loss.

Sadness will pass, but a deeper despair, hopelessness, or apathy may signal depression that should be treated by a mental health professional.

'This stage is when the reality of the loss hits. We can no longer deny what is occurring, the anger wasn't enough to stop it, the bargaining made us realize we can't outsmart or outrun it, and it seems we are left powerless. No wonder we are sad [...] The problem, however, is when TCKs, ATCKs, or anyone gets stuck here because they have never been able to name the grief and mourn the loss in healthy ways,' observe Pollock and Van Reken.

The tendency TCKs have to get stuck in the Denial or Bargaining stages means sometimes the Depression stage is quite delayed; a TCK may be confused as to why they are suddenly feeling sad about a loss that occurred months, or even years, earlier. Even when sadness was felt and expressed earlier, a deep sadness may arise when a TCK sees a final end to something they have been hanging onto – a friend who is less close now, a place they finally realise they will not be returning to. To make things harder, many TCKs have trouble finding a safe place to express their sadness. Adults can help greatly by validating the child's sadness and recognising it as a necessary and healthy part of their growth.

Some TCKs give up trying to build friendships at this stage, perhaps thinking they will never have a close friend ever again. Trying to 'fix' a child in this stage will not help them – they need time and space to be sad about what they have lost. A helpful thing to say is, "This feeling won't last forever, but right now it's okay to be sad." This reminds the TCK there is hope, without pushing them to just 'get over it'.

*My parents have always blamed the depression bit
on themselves, and then after a while, blamed me.
As if it is all in my head, whether or not I feel sad about
moving. What they don't understand is that I am 17
years old and I can be very bitter about this.*

**Callie, 17 [1st: USA; 2nd: China, Qatar, USA; 6 moves.
Family: business. School: international.]**

Sadness is the goal the other stages have been building toward. The harder we fight against the sadness, the longer it takes to get here. One of the reasons outlawed grief is so destructive is it teaches TCKs to suppress sadness – which means they also avoid healing. Suppressing grief keeps the loss alive and hurting – like a wound that scabs over but remains infected beneath the surface. Feeling permission to express sadness any time it arises helps TCKs process loss and grief well. Deliberately wallowing in sadness, trying to make oneself feel bad, is of course unhealthy. Naturally expressing grief as it wells up, however, is the healthiest thing one can do.

Stage Five – Acceptance

Just as suppressed grief negatively affects a person, grieving well has a positive impact.

*I left dynamic friendships and security in the States
when I was 15, then came back a year later to find that*

> *my friends had moved on without me. I felt so lost for years. I couldn't figure out my identity, couldn't cope with all the 'hello-goodbye' relationships, and became very bitter. Once I finally allowed myself to mourn and acknowledge that my feeling of loss was not only acceptable, but understandable and common, I reached a new place. It took me a long time to get there. I had to learn how grieve first.*
>
> **Katrina, 23 [1st: Taiwan, USA; 2nd: China, USA; 6 moves. Family: immigrant expat, business. School: home (group).]**

'Acceptance' can be misunderstood as an end to loss, pain, or grief. Acceptance does not, however, mean forgetting or ignoring a loss. There may always be a sense of loss – a space unfilled, a loved one absent, an experience missed. The stage of Acceptance is about acknowledging that gap.

"Acceptance does not mean it stops hurting," says Trotter. "Acceptance does not mean I finally carry on as if nothing ever happened. No, acceptance is an active integration of the loss into the full context of my life."

For some TCKs grieving the losses of relocation, the Acceptance stage comes gradually, until one day they turn around and realise they are fully invested in their new location and no longer hurting over the changes to old friendships. Others wake up one day after months of sadness and suddenly feel ready to move on – not to forget what was, but to start investing in what is. Sadness has been expressed fully and the TCK is ready to create new attachments.

One mother recounted the pain she felt hearing her daughter cry herself to sleep every night when the family first relocated; having expressed her sadness readily, however, her daughter went on to connect more deeply to the local culture than her siblings did.

> *Leaving Peru and moving to China was hard. I reached the Depression stage upon arrival in China and hated it; I cried every night. Then after about two months, I went up to my mum and said, "I'm going to be okay here." My three years in Beijing were some of my favourites, mostly due to the wonderful people I met there.*
>
> **Lisa, 24 [1st: UK; 2nd: China, France, Malaysia, Mexico, Peru, UK, USA; 7 moves. Family: unaffiliated. School: international.]**

However acceptance comes, there is often a sense of freedom. Memories become a source of joy rather than a source of great pain. Stories are told out of gratitude for what once was, not in an attempt to hold onto something lost.

Learning to grieve losses allows TCKs to acknowledge how they have been affected by experiences, people and places. Grieving well allows a TCK to integrate their experiences, each taking its place in the TCK's life story, shaping who they become.

Using the five stages

Grief takes time. It is a process, and one that must be walked through over time. Some losses are small, and the grieving period may be shorter. Bigger losses may take years to process fully. Some losses remain, but grieving well helps TCKs integrate their experiences and relieves the burden of unresolved grief.

The Five Stages of Grief is a tool – it helps show what grief can look like, and why it takes time. The process might look smooth and logical on paper, but in real life it is often messy and confusing. The stages may be experienced out of order, or simultaneously. That is okay, even normal.

"It's worth noting that Acceptance is not a final stage," says Trotter. "I don't think once you get to Acceptance the stages of grief are somehow completed. I live most of my life in the Acceptance stage, however, there are times and seasons when I cycle back to Anger or even Depression. I don't stay in those stages very long, but I definitely revisit them."

Finally, it is important to know that one can still be grieving what used to be while beginning to engage with what is new. It is okay to make new friends while still missing old friends. Enjoying life in a new place is not a betrayal of a previous life.

CHAPTER FOUR

GOODBYE AND HELLO
(LEAVING WELL AND STARTING AGAIN)

Leaving and Being Left

Goodbyes are hard. Really hard. They are emotional and painful. TCKs say goodbye a lot – either they leave, or they are left. Many of these goodbyes are forever goodbyes – the TCK knows they will likely never see this person, or place, ever again. Even if they do see each other again, the relationship will never be the same. Time, distance and a change in shared experiences will alter it.

It was sad to leave. Goodbyes are the worst thing for any TCK as far as I can tell from conversations I've had with other returned TCKs. It doesn't matter how much we try not to bawl our eyes out. We may be smiling when we wave the final goodbye but it's still so darn hard. I'm not sure much can prepare anyone for the emotional onslaught of sadness that saying goodbye brings.
Olivia, 22 [1st: Australia; 2nd: Australia, China, India; 4 moves. Family: unaffiliated. School: home, Christian international.]

The two sides of a goodbye

There are two sides to every goodbye – and both are painful. The one who moves away leaves everything familiar, a lot of losses, both big and small.

On the other side of the goodbye is the one left behind. While they have not moved, there is a space where the person who left used to be – a place that used to be filled and which is now empty. Often it is more than just the person – it is the activities they used to do together, time spent at that person's house, and many other things that can be hard to define.

> *It was almost always harder for the ones I left behind. They were offended. Shocked. Upset. Felt abandoned. That hurt me, too. And I missed them terribly and was afraid of all the changes ahead of me.*
> **Melody, 31 [1ˢᵗ: Argentina, Germany; 2ⁿᵈ: Argentina, China, Colombia, Germany, Mexico, Uruguay, USA. Family: multicultural, mission. School: local]**

'*The loss the leaver feels when hugging her best friend goodbye is the mirror image of the gaping hole the best friend experiences on the other side of the embrace [...]. The distinction between mover and 'movee' is not nearly as important as you might think. Though there are two people involved, mover and movee, there is but one connection linking the two. Because of mobility, they are grieving the loss of the same thing,*' writes Doug Ota in his book, *Safe Passage*.

While the one who moved away is dealing with a great quantity of loss, building a new life can be easier in some ways. Their new routine has no space where old friends belong. While they may miss this school friend, or that after-school activity, it is in some ways more abstract – as the friend has never lived in this place, and they are not in the same venue where the old activity took place.

> *Sometimes it is harder for those left behind. Those*
> *who leave have gone ahead into something new that*
> *will keep them distracted to some extent, whereas the*
> *person left behind only sees a great big hole where the*
> *friend used to be.*
>
> **Abbie, 40 [1ˢᵗ: USA; 2ⁿᵈ: Austria, China, Germany, Hungary, USA;**
> **7 moves. Family: embassy, mission. School: local, international,**
> **Christian international.]**

Transition fatigue

After years overseas a TCK has said goodbye many, many
times. It gets tiring, emotionally exhausting. For many there
comes a point at which it just does not seem worth it to make
more new friends. It might come after losing a best friend
three years in a row. It might come when only one person
of a group does *not* move. It might come after being the new
kid so many times there is no energy left to break into yet
another social circle.

> *Just before my final two years of high school, my*
> *family moved to a different country for the fourth*
> *time. I didn't know it then but I was emotionally tired*
> *and worn out. I did not bother going through the*
> *process of making new friends, only to have to say*
> *goodbye again in two short years.*
>
> **Siyin, 21 [1ˢᵗ: Singapore (Hong Kong); 2ⁿᵈ: China, Hong Kong,**
> **Singapore; 4 moves. Family: business. School: international.]**

Many TCKs hit a point at which they are no longer interested in meeting new people, no longer able to say goodbye to those who leave. The accumulated pain of goodbyes gets to be too much and feelings are bottled up. A new friendship is seen as just the start of yet another goodbye.

There is a weariness about finding oneself in the same situation again and again. Some TCKs feel a sense of hopelessness. They have 'been there, done that' enough times there no longer seems to be any point in trying – no matter what they do they end up in the same place yet again.

> *After a big move I feel shell shocked from the loss and have no desire to put myself in a place where it could happen again. But it's lonely not having those great friendships so I start to open up and get to know people and then we move again. I do believe life is better when lived out with people, but it's hard to remember that right after a move.*
> **Emily, 21 [1st: USA; 2nd: DR Congo, Kenya, Rwanda, USA; 20 moves. Family: mission. School: local, international, boarding.]**

Welcoming new arrivals

Sometimes, the left behind TCK becomes good at befriending new arrivals. All too often, though, they run out of energy to keep welcoming in new people.

> *I've lived here so long I've seen many people come and go and it never gets easier. Sometimes I struggle to make new friends because I know they are going to leave.*
> **Faith, 17 [1ˢᵗ: USA; 2ⁿᵈ: Cambodia, USA; 2 moves. Family: mission. School: home.]**

Some TCKs who live a long time in one country become very insular. They may have a small group of long-term friends that is very exclusive and difficult to break into. It is an understandable self-protective measure, reacting against the pain of constant goodbyes. While they cannot be completely protected, sticking to a small group of long-term families reduces the number of times they will be left behind. But a new kid left on the outside can feel very isolated and alone. They may be outwardly welcomed with warmth, but never invited into the inner circle; this can be discouraging and painful. I've also known TCK groups who were very strong on farewelling a member who left, but not very good at welcoming someone newly arrived.

Welcoming new arrivals well may seem daunting, but Doug Ota's book, *Safe Passage*, explains in detail why it is important to help TCKs both leave and arrive well, as well as a framework for how to do so. Ota describes the 'Safe Harbour' program at the American School of The Hague, which includes training and empowering Student Ambassadors to help ensure smooth transitions for students (and equivalent programs for arriving parents and staff). A week-long orientation connects new students with an equal number of Student Ambassadors, providing new students with opportunities to:

- Find out about life at school

- Find out about life outside school

- Find out about their course of study

- Sign up for classes

- Get to know other students (including time to socialise through games and meal times)

Student Ambassadors are also involved when students leave:

- Planning and hosting 'Goodbye Homerooms' for each grade.

- Arranging tributes from peers in both words and gifts.

- Coordinating each leaving student signing 'signature boards' – literally leaving their mark – which are displayed permanently in the school cafeteria.

Saying Good Goodbyes

Several TCKs looked at the title of this section and laughed. One called the phrase 'good goodbye' an oxymoron; another said they should be called 'badbyes' instead. While this reaction is understandable, even amusing, it underlines the importance of helping TCKs learn to say goodbye well.

After a lot of losses, a lot of goodbyes, a lot of moves, some TCKs get really good at it. They are proactive about making time for 'one last' everything. They write letters to people they are leaving behind. Many TCKs, however, go the other way. They start to ignore goodbyes. They avoid them. They refuse to say the word, perhaps using 'see you later' instead. The finality of a true goodbye is too painful.

> It is much easier to have a real goodbye with people you are not particularity close with. It is when you do not know what life is like without a person that you cannot face the goodbye.
> **Callie, 17 [1ˢᵗ: USA; 2ⁿᵈ: China, Qatar, USA; 6 moves.**
> **Family: business. School: international.]**

A proper goodbye has a huge impact long term. Good goodbyes promote closure, making it easier for TCKs to engage well with new people on the other side of the goodbye. Encouraging TCKs to say goodbye well is a way adults can be supportive through times of loss.

> I think one of the most important things adults can do is encourage good goodbyes. Even writing that makes me flinch; my first instinct is to avoid a real goodbye. It's too painful when you have to say a lot of them, but it helps re-entry to know you left the host country well. I think a good goodbye starts with being able to acknowledge that the goodbye really is important. After realizing that, then it actually has to be said. Do what you can to make sure the relationship is being left well – which may include dealing with an unresolved hurt or telling a friend how much they

meant to you. That's not always possible, but it does help resolve the relationship and make the person leaving ready for new relationships.

Grace, 25 [1ˢᵗ: Singapore, USA; 2ⁿᵈ: China, Hong Kong, USA; 4 moves. Family: multicultural, mission. School: home.]

There are a few elements to a good goodbye:

· Acknowledging the relationship will be different after the move (whether leaving or being left).

· Recognising what each person/group/place has meant to the TCK.

· Expressing this recognition – saying thank you for what each person has been/done for the TCK.

· Allowing oneself to feel sad about the loss.

"As an international school teacher, I put a lot of emphasis on saying goodbyes and leaving well," Valérie Bescanceney says. "As a writer, I have tried to provide children with a story they can identify with and a workbook to allow them to write their own 'moving' story."

Journaling and sharing stories can be helpful, as well as practicing thankfulness. Parents can help by asking their children specific questions addressing the points above – uncovering the list of people and places that matter to the child, and why they matter. The next step is to help the child walk through a process of farewelling each of these people and places – encouraging them to talk to or write to the people, and to visit/take photos of the places.

Many TCKs find it therapeutic to write a letter or card to each of the people who are important to them before they move. Others like to give a gift – something to represent the relationship. Meeting with each one in person can be wonderful as well, but there is often simply not enough time to do this – leaving can be hectic.

While these tools may be helpful, TCKs must have a sense of control over this process. Saying goodbye can feel difficult, even daunting, especially when a TCK has said goodbye many times before. Making suggestions or encouraging/facilitating the process is great, but forcing a child who is not ready to do something 'because it will be good for you' will likely backfire.

> *To help my young son deal with his sadness, we ask how he would like to say goodbye to someone/ something so that he feels that he has a little control over the separation. For example, he chose to give the Christmas tree a hug last month.*
> **Anne, 37 [1st: Australia; 2nd: Australia, Burundi, Canada, Liberia, Malawi, South Africa, South Sudan, Sweden, UK, USA; 30 moves. Family: mission. School: local.]**

Some TCKs feel too exhausted with goodbyes to do justice to this kind of exercise. Where possible, however, it is a very helpful and even healing thing to do. It means they separate on a good note – knowing the person realises how important they have been in the TCK's life. There is nothing left hanging – they can part ways at peace with the relationship. If they never meet again, they are free from regretting what was not said, or not resolved.

In my own goodbyes, I often start by assuming I will see the person again one day (so it feels less overwhelming), but then consider if this did turn out to be our last time together, is there anything I would want them to know? This distinction has helped TCKs I have mentored to say a real goodbye while still holding on to the hope they will again see people and places they care about.

Leaving School

Completing high school (called 'graduation' in some communities) is a *big* time in a teenager's life – no matter where they live. For TCKs the experience is often a mix of bitter and sweet, celebration and separation, and can be quite a rollercoaster. The situation is different for a TCK who lives immersed in the local culture, with local friends, and plans to remain in the host country after graduation (whether studying or working). For many TCKs, however, this time is also intimately connected with goodbyes.

'Graduation' was a word that most people in my grade did not want to say, because 'graduation' meant 'goodbye'. I used to say this a lot to my parents but they just kept telling me that "back in my day we only had snail mail and you guys get email and Facebook and so many other opportunities to stay in touch." I gave up trying to make my point – it's not the same. If home is where the heart is then after we all graduate

> *my home will be in Korea and America and other places I've never been to, because that's where my friends will be.*
> **Katherine, 18 [1ˢᵗ: Australia; 2ⁿᵈ: Australia, Thailand; 2 moves. Family: mission. School: Christian international.]**

While high school classmates in a monocultural setting may head in different directions, the effect is more pronounced in expatriate communities. It is common for TCKs in expatriate communities to leave their host country after completing high school in order to pursue higher education abroad. It is the time at which they leave the place they love and feel connected to – often knowing they will not return. Even those who stay in the host country watch nearly all their TCK friends and classmates leave, scattered to different countries.

Some TCKs feel they are graduating not just from high school, but from life as they know it.

> *The biggest and longest period of grief I have experienced, which I might still be in 10 years later, is when I graduated high school. I knew that I was not only leaving a place but a lifestyle. It's a really depressing feeling at 18 to feel like the best years of your life are behind you. Those last three years of high school in Cairo were my favourite overseas experience.*
> **Christyn, 30 [1ˢᵗ: USA; 2ⁿᵈ: Egypt, Israel, Jordan, UK, USA; 12 moves. Family: mission. School: international, home.]**

While this happens to many graduates even in a monocultural setting, the distances involved for TCKs are much greater – literally around the world. They may go to a different continent for school, leaving their family behind. There is also often a sense of finality –they may never see their school friends again. While this is less true with the ease of international travel in the 21st century, there are a lot of unknowns, which can cause extra grief and anxiety for a graduating TCK.

> One of the difficulties of graduation was not being able to go back. Most college students around me went to a high school in the town they grew up and their parents still live there. Their friends may have gone off to other colleges and they had to say goodbye for a short time, but come vacations they go home and see their friends again. Not so for me. My high school wasn't the place my parents lived nor the place most of the other students' parents lived either. So when we graduated we exploded to all parts of the world – in many cases away from our parents, too. We might see our parents once a year if we are lucky, but friends from high school generally don't live where our parents do so even if we go 'home' they won't be there. While it is a small world and crazy things happen I will probably not see at least half of my high school classmates again.
>
> **Emily, 21 [1st: USA; 2nd: DR Congo, Kenya, Rwanda, USA; 20 moves. Family: mission. School: local, international, boarding.]**

Supporting school leavers

Leaving an international school or expatriate community can mean losing the safe Third Culture space a TCK has lived in. It is the moment in which their world disintegrates – and each piece flies away to a different place. There is a lot of loss involved. This means completing high school can be a much more emotional experience for TCKs than it is for monocultural teenagers. So while it is exciting, and the achievement should be celebrated, it can also be a very sad time for TCKs.

Parents can help graduating TCKs by recognising how painful it can be, and giving them space to grieve. Rather than helping TCKs stay in denial (saying things like "don't worry, you'll stay in touch") it helps to make time to listen to fears, worries, or sadness that may be welling up. It can be hard to hear their pain, but witnessing TCKs' grief by simply listening is one of the best things to do for them. The loss is inevitable, and neither you nor they can prevent or change it.

Graduation was, to date, the hardest thing I've been through. Everyone around me kept saying that college would be the best years of my life, but I couldn't see how that could be true. They kept on saying, "Congratulations for finishing high school!" In my head I thought "thanks, this is the worst day of my life" but of course I couldn't say that out loud.

Emily, 21 [1st: USA; 2nd: DR Congo, Kenya, Rwanda, USA; 20 moves. Family: mission. School: local, international, boarding.]

Local experiences

Another way parents can help school leavers is to fund or facilitate some sort of local experience for the TCK to share with a group of friends. Making memories together in the place where they lived together recognises the importance of both the place and the people they will be leaving.

The goal is to bring together students who will be leaving both each other and their host city/country. By doing something together they create lasting memories of each other and their host culture, which will stay with them and help with closure as they transition into a new season of life.

Celebrations I have seen include:

- Taking a biking/hiking trip in the host country
- Doing a cooking class or sharing a special meal
- Doing a photo shoot in local dress
- Doing community service or volunteering at a charity
- Travelling to a special part of their city/country
- Working on an artistic project (such as a painting or video)

The Unexpected – Tragedy and Crisis

While TCKs experience grief connected to their international life, much of it can be expected and anticipated – the general presence of grief and loss, at least, if not the specific instances of it. When change and loss happen unexpectedly, shock is added to grief. Strategies a child developed to help cope with constant change and loss may not work, interrupting or preventing the grieving process.

Grieving from a distance

Sometimes tragedy happens far away – in a previous location, or passport country – and they aren't there:

- A grandparent passes away

- A cousin gets cancer

- A friend's parents divorce

- A former classmate takes his own life.

I have supported many different TCKs processing these, and other, tragedies from far away. These same tragedies can happen to any family anywhere in the world, but distance (both physical and emotional) changes the experience for TCKs.

Grieving long distance can be difficult. The TCK may feel emotionally disconnected from the person, or from the event. They may feel powerless to help, or comfort, their loved ones. They may feel isolated from people who 'get it' and could grieve with them.

During my freshman year of college there were a lot of deaths: my grandpa, my dad's best friend, my youth pastor's son, a girl at my school in Egypt, and

> *a teacher and two kids from my school in Egypt in a*
> *tragic accident. The deaths from the school were hard.*
> *It was extremely painful to not be able to collectively*
> *grieve with one another. I longed to be with my*
> *friends who were grieving and in the same position*
> *as I was: in college and not there. I also longed to be*
> *able to go back home to Egypt and be with everyone*
> *who was there. In a strange way, I felt like it was my*
> *responsibility to be there to grieve alongside everyone.*
> *It devastated me because something horrific had*
> *happened and it had happened to a special community*
> *that I was/am a part of. I also had friends who were*
> *close with those people. I felt their pain and was*
> *desperate to be near them to grieve alongside them.*
> **Christyn, 30 [1ˢᵗ: USA; 2ⁿᵈ: Egypt, Israel, Jordan, UK, USA;**
> **12 moves. Family: mission. School: international, home.]**

TCKs grieving long distance need to know their grief is valid, and it is good to take time and space to grieve well. Many TCKs also experience anxiety and guilt about being so far away when something bad happens on top of the grief of the actual situation. Connecting with friends grieving the same loss – whether online or in person – can be a great comfort.

Tragedy in an international setting

In addition to the tragedy that happens far away, sometimes it hits nearby. Death, divorce, illness, burglary, assault.

Some TCKs develop phobias or odd mannerisms as a response

to the trauma or tragedy experienced abroad, especially those who are young at the time. One TCK I know was subject to a frightening home invasion while living in Tanzania as a young child. The electricity was cut, so the resulting trauma occurred in near pitch black conditions. He became afraid of the dark, to the point of carrying matches with him everywhere he went, so he could always have light no matter what happened. In his case the fear, and accompanying habit, disappeared as soon as the family moved on to a new foreign location.

While these situations are difficult in any context, there are added complexities when they happen abroad. A family may be caught between the laws (and languages) of multiple countries. They may be far away from support networks that would have helped them otherwise. They may not have easy access to the resources they need – or be unsure *how* to access them in their host country.

"It [tragedy/trauma] can have a tremendous, negative impact on the TCK as an adult. It can impact not only them, but also their loved ones for several generations," Lois Bushong says. "It is important to not brush these types of events under the carpet, but the sooner they are resolved, whether in counselling or special teams trained in trauma counselling, the chances of trauma being an issue later in life drop significantly."

Differences in laws can leave individuals vulnerable and unprotected, falling through the cracks with no system that covers their specific situation. When it comes to custody issues in particular, local laws may be at odds with the laws of a family's passport country, or not be applied to foreigners.

Even where local laws do apply, a family may be unaware of procedure, and local officials may be hesitant to get involved. It adds a layer of confusion and stress to an already confused and stressful situation.

> *My sister and I were taken away from our mother and put in our father's custody. It was a nightmare. I was about nine and very confused. I didn't know where my mother was, I didn't know what was happening. After 10 days we were reunited with our mother and had to leave the country. I learned something that stuck with me – nothing is certain, everything can change in an instant. I could not count on always being safe.*
>
> **MeiHe, 22 [1ˢᵗ: USA; 2ⁿᵈ: China, South Korea, USA; 14 moves. Family: military, non-traditional, unaffiliated. School: home, boarding, international.]**

Support from expatriate communities

One benefit of being connected to an expatriate community is these communities tend to be extremely helpful and supportive during times of tragedy. Expats tend to be very aware extended family and other support networks are far away, and quick to step in and assist.

When a family is dealing with tragedy, open ended questions such as 'what can I do?' may not be helpful – the family may not even know what they need, or not know how to think about it. A yes or no question such as 'would it be helpful if I...?' or 'can I take care of ... for you?' may be easier for a family in crisis to process and answer.

The following services are ways that I, and expatriate communities I have belonged to, have supported individuals and families when tragedy struck – whether a job loss, serious illness, relationship breakdown, break in, or death of a child. While these may be helpful, especially when a family does not know where to start, help should be *offered*, rather than organised without permission.

- **Contacting their embassy** – regardless of the specifics of a tragedy, embassies usually have information and contact lists that can help. Some families have little or no contact with their embassy until a major problem arises, so offering to make the call and find the information on their behalf can be a big help. It means they will not have to tell their (traumatic or stressful) story to yet another stranger, while trying to absorb information offered.

- **Contacting their insurer** – similarly, there may be a *lot* of questions and forms that need to be dealt with, and helping with the process can take a lot of strain off a family in crisis.

- **Offering translation** – even when a family speaks the host country language, unless they are extremely fluent it may be difficult to concentrate when stressed, especially if specialised vocabulary is involved. Offering to go with them to deal with authorities, to make/take phone calls on their behalf, and so on, may help.

- **Running errands** – errands are often more time-consuming or mentally/emotionally taxing in a host country (especially in a second language). Offering to take care of everyday things like grocery shopping or paying bills can be a big help.

- **Providing meals** – for many expats, meals take more organisation or preparation in the host country. Letting someone else think about getting food on the table (especially when there are children who need to be cared for) can take a load off, and may mean a grieving person eats when they otherwise would not have the energy to prepare food. There are also a range of websites that allow a roster to be created and curated online, for example, www.takethemameal.com and www.signupgenius.com.

- **Providing childcare** – similarly, if parents need to deal with authorities, spend time in hospital, or need space to grieve privately, babysitting can be great.

- **Creating safe space for children** – often during a period of tragedy the children in a family are in a different emotional place to their parents. They may need space to relax and do something recreational away from 'heaviness' at home. It may help to have a family friend arrange some sort of outing, or a sleepover with a school friend – something that feels 'normal'.

Unexpected relocation

Sometimes a family may be forced to leave their host country due to political instability or natural disaster. This may be rare, but when it happens it happens all at once, with little or no warning. A family may have no time to pack, bringing only a few essentials. Material possessions of great sentimental value may be left behind. They may have no chance to say goodbye to friends, both local and expatriate. They may leave with no idea when, or if, they will be able to return. They may not be able to leave together, and may be separated for some time.

> *We were in Mongolia to pick up my adopted sister but my mother had to stay there for an extra couple weeks to finalize papers. My father and I travelled to Pakistan, where he and I started to get our house ready. My father had a chance to visit Afghanistan, and I stayed with friends in Pakistan while he was gone. During this time there was a military coup in Pakistan that created difficulty for our family as we all were in different countries. We all finally got reunited after two weeks.*
>
> **Ganbold, 24 [1st: USA, (Mongolia); 2nd: Afghanistan, Mongolia, Pakistan, USA; 17 moves. Family: adoptive, NGO, unaffiliated. School: home, international.]**

On top of the trauma of the situation, the suddenness affects the grieving process. There is no time to prepare emotionally for the change. There is no time to get used to the idea that they will be living somewhere else. There is no time to process the change with their peer community before they leave.

Following a traumatic incident, a family may choose to repatriate, or move somewhere new – where they can start fresh without constant reminders of what they have been through. Or they may choose to move closer to support networks such as extended family who can help care for them as they grieve and process. Death or serious illness among extended family in their passport country may also result in moving closer to 'home'. In some cases of divorce, there may be a forced relocation (as with the loss of a dependent visa, or the need to process legal matters in the passport country).

While the reasons and benefits of such a move may be clear, most of the time such a move is, to a TCK, not 'going back' but 'going away'. It means leaving their support network, their safe place, and everything familiar.

> My little sister was stillborn weeks before we moved from Germany back to the States. The community there was one I will never forget regardless of how young I was. Food and support were everywhere. Some friends took a song, gave it new lyrics and sang it at a memorial mass they put together for us. The community overseas had pulled us into a blanket of love and helped us carry on but as amazing as that all was all too soon we were flying to Texas and moving away. We returned to the States empty-handed, broken-hearted, and away from the support we needed so desperately. The friends who were there during her death were left behind, we had a funeral in a place that I didn't recognize as home, and then we moved to a different state. Few people there even knew anything had happened, and I didn't know how to tell new friends about something so heartbreaking to eight-year-old me. In the span of a few months I had lost friends, a sister, and a home.
>
> **Maddie, 18 [1st: USA; 2nd: Germany, Japan, USA; 9 moves. Family: military. School: home (group).]**

Sometimes, an unexpected relocation happens when a company gives a parent a new assignment and the family has no choice but to leave. Even as a corporate transfer rather than an evacuation, sudden moves can be very stressful for children. The lack of warning means the grieving process may be delayed. A flurry of activity leaves the family emotionally numb, or in shock, unable to really feel or process their feelings until after the move has happened.

These moves are especially traumatic for a TCK who was looking ahead to a longer time in their host country. They may have planned to finish school, go on a specific trip, or take a specific extra-curricular activity. That there may be an equivalent (or better) option in the new location does not erase the grief of what the TCK loses by moving away.

Others may leave the host country on a routine trip and be unable to return. While this lacks the urgency of an evacuation or sudden move, it can be emotionally traumatic for a child who expected to return to their home abroad.

> *I felt very torn after a furlough was extended due to civil unrest – like I was being cheated out of returning to my friends/home but also like I was given a chance to give things a proper go in my passport country.*
>
> **Rebecca, 28 [1st: Australia; 2nd: Australia, Papua New Guinea, Solomon Islands; 8 moves. Family: mission. School: home (group), Christian international.]**

Children who are relocated with little or no warning need extra time and space to recognise and grieve all that they have lost. Walking through the grieving process is in some ways even more important as they had no opportunity to prepare and grieve in advance of the move.

Repatriation

Repatriation means returning to one's passport country after living in another country. For TCKs this experience is neither 'going home' nor 'just another move'. There can be a significant shift in identity. Some go from feeling local but thought of as foreign, to feeling foreign but thought of as local – an experience Norma McCaig and David Pollock describe as being a 'hidden immigrant'.

> *When we moved back to the States I had a really rough transition. It launched me into a battle against depression that went on for several years. I didn't understand who I was or why I was so unhappy in my new situation. It seemed my peers all had it figured out and I was the only one who didn't feel comfortable in my own skin.*
>
> **Megan, 30 [1ˢᵗ: USA; 2ⁿᵈ: Germany, USA; 6 moves. Family: military. School: local, international.]**

Repatriation can be difficult for all expatriates, not just TCKs. The longer a person lives outside their passport country, the more time it takes to feel comfortable again upon return. This may seem discouraging, but there is also a comfort – it is normal to feel out of place for a while after returning.

In her book, *The Global Nomad's Guide to University Transition*, Tina Quick comments, '*Repatriation is widely viewed as being just as or more difficult than expatriation. It is the same experience, but this time it is happening in your own country where you supposedly know everything. This is why it is such a jolt and can go unrecognized for quite some time. You are not expecting it.'*

For TCKs, there is often an added challenge – many have lived outside their passport country from a young age (if they ever lived there to begin with). 58% of TCKs surveyed spent more than half their childhood (up to age 18) living outside their passport countries; 30% spent fewer than three years of childhood in their passport countries. 67% moved overseas before age five. For a TCK, the passport country may essentially be a new place, more foreign than the host country.

It's hard to pinpoint exactly what made my transition back to the US difficult. Maybe it was because I had been away for so long (15 years). Maybe it was because I was suddenly lost in a sea of white people, instead of Asians. Maybe it was because I had chosen to go to college in a town where people thought that the next state over was a long distance. Regardless, I wish that I had been more prepared for living in the States. I knew who I was as a TCK within a foreign country. What I didn't know was who I was as a TCK in America. I suddenly found myself getting lost in malls, or wanting to cry from seeing how much food was readily available at grocery stores, or at baseball games, and not knowing the National Anthem.

Catherine, 24 [1st: USA; 2nd: Brunei, Indonesia, Malaysia, Russia, USA. 9 moves. Family: Business. School: local, international, home, Christian international, boarding.]

Repatriation as a new entry

It can be helpful to think of repatriation not as going *back* but as going *forward*. The person repatriating has changed, the people they knew in their passport country have changed, even the country or culture as a whole may have changed. TCKs may be surprised by changes in their passport country after only a few years away. The way children interact at age seven is very different to age 10, or 13.

It really is not possible to return to the way things were before – but that means the one repatriating can instead move ahead to something new, albeit it in a location that may be familiar.

> *We prepared for leaving by visiting all our favourite places, buying cultural souvenirs etc. There was a real sense of displacement. After all, if you can suddenly up and leave your life what stability does anything have? I don't know if there is a clear-cut way to make repatriation easy for anyone. Finding a 'new normal' is a long process.*
>
> **Rebecca, 28 [1st: Australia; 2nd: Australia, Papua New Guinea, Solomon Islands; 8 moves. Family: mission. School: home (group), Christian international.]**

There is a long adjustment period after repatriation, as a family remembers how to do things, catches up with how attitudes, pop culture, and technology have altered while they were gone, and learns to accept the more insular worldview held by monocultural people around them.

Emotional impact of repatriation

Every TCK I interviewed who had repatriated noted this as a particularly difficult experience. Talking about it prompted strong emotions and, in many cases, tears. 57% of TCKs surveyed said that repatriation was a painful experience. There were differences between certain subgroups, with 68% of MKs and only 40% of Business Kids saying repatriation was painful.

> *Repatriating was extremely hard. I became very sad, reserved, and insecure, and most likely struggled with undiagnosed depression, which I didn't realize until much later.*
>
> **Kendra, 24 [1st: USA; 2nd: Costa Rica, Ecuador, USA; 12 moves. Family: mission. School: Christian international.**

Repatriation can be a time of great loneliness, when TCKs may feel no one truly understands what they are going through. It can be difficult for a TCK to talk about aspects of the passport country and culture they are confused about or struggling with. There may be a fear of offending the people around them, who call this place home, and seem so comfortable in it. Monocultural peers (and even adults) may struggle to understand and accept the pain and grief the repatriated TCK is experiencing.

One of the hardest things for many repatriated expats is the sense that neither the depth of pain they are experiencing, nor the reason for it, is understood by anyone around them.

> *A lot of people didn't understand how much living overseas had changed my life. Also, because it was such a different lifestyle they didn't understand why I had a hard time readjusting to American life when that is what I have lived before. I feel like some were more sympathetic than others, but then there were those who just thought it was silly that I was so upset.*
> **Anna, 18 [1ˢᵗ: USA; 2ⁿᵈ: China, USA; 2 moves. Family: military. School: international.]**

Reverse culture shock and embarrassment

While many families are prepared for 'culture shock' upon entering a new country, very few expect 'reverse culture shock' upon repatriation. Even making regular visits to their passport country does not prepare expats for actually living there full time after repatriating. Everyone changes over time, whether they stay in the same place or move around. Regardless of their situation, the vast majority were completely unprepared for the inner turmoil they experienced – even those who knew to expect it.

Addressing TCKs preparing to repatriate, Tina Quick writes, *'You may remember going through culture shock when you first moved abroad. You may even have had some training before leaving so you came to expect the different stages of culture shock. You are not immune to experiencing this shock again upon repatriation, only now it is in reverse.'*

> *Being a kid who was constantly negotiating change and multiple cultures at once, I was pretty good at*

> *adapting. The difference this time was that it was permanent. I didn't have the solace of knowing I was 'going back' to what I loved. The vividness of my life so far was engrained in me – down to the smell of ripe mangoes and the sound of the rushing river. It's no wonder that when I came back to Australia nothing measured up. I didn't shy from letting people know that but in the same beat, I also felt I had no right or reason to complain. It wasn't until very recently that I let myself acknowledge that it was a big deal, that I had loved deeply so of course it hurt and that's okay.*
> **Lani, 25 [1st: Australia; 2nd: Australia, Ethiopia; 2 moves. Family: mission. School: home.]**

Things considered 'common knowledge' by passport country peers may be new to a repatriating TCK. Several TCKs I interviewed specifically mentioned the impact of pop culture references when it came to repatriation. Some found it difficult to engage in conversation when missing the references. Others talked of ways their parents had attempted to introduce them to their passport country's pop culture, and how much this had helped them when repatriating.

> *My university roommates would all talk about their grade school and middle school fixations on the Spice Girls, N'Sync, Britney Spears, Hanson, as well as TV shows and celebrities that I had little to no knowledge of. Once in a while when my husband now asks in disbelief, "You've never seen X?!" or "How have*

> *you never heard of Y?!" I'll just chuckle and remind*
> *him of what we both good-naturedly now call my*
> *'cultural vacuum'.*
>
> **Kendra, 24 [1st: USA; 2nd: Costa Rica, Ecuador, USA; 12 moves.**
> **Family: mission. School: Christian international.]**

While there may have been space for mistakes when learning the local ropes as a foreigner, in the passport country a TCK is seen as a local; when they display a lack local understanding and experience, TCKs may feel embarrassed, or even be ridiculed for gaps in their knowledge.

> *I've developed a 'good natured' response, which is to*
> *quickly acknowledge the 'hole' in my upbringing and*
> *say, "You've gotta remember, I missed the 90s and*
> *most of the 2000s here!" Sometimes when I'm self*
> *conscious, I'll talk about a similar fad that was going*
> *on in China at the same time so that I can still be a*
> *part of the conversation. Sometimes I will go home*
> *and educate myself about whatever the reference*
> *was so that I'll know better next time, and with smart*
> *phones, I can even look it up on the spot!*
>
> **Karissa, 23 [1st: USA; 2nd: China, USA; 9 moves. Family: mission.**
> **School: local, home (group), Christian international.]**

Personality change and anxiety

Several TCKs I interviewed spoke of experiencing temporary changes in personality after repatriating. This is something I have also heard from worried parents on several occasions.

Extroverts who enjoyed large groups suddenly became shy and insecure. Fairly detached people became emotional and even clingy. In most cases these TCKs found a new balance once they feel secure in their new location, but this helps illustrate what an upheaval repatriation is.

"Some of the personality changes are due to being lost in a new culture. Some are TCKs trying to fit into a new culture. Or it is their attempt to not be like their peers in that culture," Lois Bushong explains. "Some are dealing with depression or anger regarding the move. The best thing is to talk to the TCK and try to understand why they are doing what they are doing before making a judgment on the personality change."

> *I haven't been with another TCK since I was in China, and it's hard. I never felt out of place in China, but coming to America I suddenly started feeling awkward and nervous around a large group of people, which was where I usually thrived!*
> **Wendy, 16 [1st: USA; 2nd: China, USA; 3 moves. Family: unaffiliated, mission, adoptive. School: local, home (group).]**

For some TCKs, repatriation is a source of particular anxiety that their parents do not share. Differences between the host culture the child is accustomed to and the passport culture they are moving to can be upsetting, and in ways their parents do not feel.

> *When my brother came back to the States with us in 5th*

Grade he was absolutely terrified of America. It didn't matter that my parents told him that it was 'safer'; to him it was an open place without walls where any stranger could get at him. Anyone who's grown up in a country with as much crime as South Africa and India would have deep scars of mistrust for a more modern place like America where the houses aren't protected in the same way.

Rachel, 21 [1st: USA; 2nd: South Africa, Swaziland, Thailand, USA; 4 moves. Family: mission. School: Christian international.]

Other TCKs go 'home' to a culture that expresses respect and affection very differently to their host country, or even to the expat culture they live in. Some find themselves scolded for being rude to people, others feel their passport country is the 'rude' place.

South American culture is generally much touchier – personal space is not as much of a big deal. Everyone in Ecuador – in an office or at a party for example – will go around the room when they arrive and greet every single person with a besito (a kiss on the cheek – for women and women, women and men) or a handshake (men and men). American culture feels stiff and rude sometimes by comparison, and it took some getting used to.

Kendra, 24 [1st: USA; 2nd: Costa Rica, Ecuador, USA; 3 moves. Family: mission. School: Christian international.]

'Welcome home'

Regardless of how a TCK feels about their host/passport country, repatriation is difficult. Upon returning 'home' they discover just how different they are. There are so many things they have taken for granted about how life works – only to discover life works differently there.

> *Coming back to the States, we moved into a non-military community. I went to a regular public school instead of a Department of Defence school. Suddenly I was thrust into a kind of community I had never experienced before, and I felt truly lost. All the kids had grown up together. They had their own jokes I would never understand, a sense of style I couldn't figure out, and cared about things I had never really thought about. How was it I could relate with people so well who didn't even share the same mother tongue, yet when I was back in my 'home' country, I felt like a foreigner?*
>
> **Megan, 30 [1ˢᵗ: USA; 2ⁿᵈ: Germany, USA; 6 moves. Family: military. School: local, international.]**

The hardest part for many TCKs in this position is the pressure they feel to love their passport country. People say "welcome home" to a child who is visiting (or moving to) what is a new and strange place to them. 58% of TCKs born after 1985 (and 68% of MKs) surveyed said they disliked being greeted with the phrase "welcome home". Many TCKs I interviewed brought this up as a difficulty when repatriating. One said it showed immediately that these people, no matter how well meaning, did not understand what she was going through.

> *Moving back was so much harder than moving overseas because in coming back, I thought it would only be hard missing people, that I would feel at home here in the midst of that. But coming back was just so heart wrenching. My friends had changed, I didn't know anyone at my school, and I felt like I couldn't be myself. Before school started, everything felt normal because it felt like summer break and that I'd soon go back to Beijing, but once school started, the shock was enormous. No one knew about me. And I couldn't explain myself in the quick time period it takes to meet someone new.*
> **Elisabeth, 19 [1st: USA; 2nd: China, USA; 2 moves. Family: unaffiliated. School: Christian international.]**

Some may react with strong negative emotion, complaining about their passport country and wishing loudly to return 'home' to the host country. Others may wrestle with extreme homesickness but hide it, so as not to offend or upset their family and friends.

"This is often the case, as those around them may not understand what they are experiencing. Rather than shutting down emotionally or responding in anger, I would encourage them to reach out to those who do understand them," Lois Bushong advises. "This might be peers left behind in other countries or respected adults in their former schools. Encourage them to Skype or email or instant message these friends and share their feelings and experiences with reverse culture shock."

Repatriation with Family

TCKs who repatriate with their families (as opposed to those who repatriate alone to attend college) are in a different boat to their parents, emotionally.

Repatriation can be far more complex for the TCKs than for their parents, Lois Bushong explains: "The basic difference is that parents are returning to their home country or to their roots. While TCKs are often leaving their roots and transitioning to another culture where they do not have roots and yet are expected to be strongly connected to it just like their parents. Just understanding where the other person is coming from will help them on their road to a more harmonious transition."

It is important for parents to give their TCKs space to express how they feel – and permission to feel differently to their parents, and to one another. Every response, every emotion, is valid.

While I felt unhappy about leaving my school and friends, my parents seemed ecstatic about moving back to the States. They wanted me to have the typical

> *American high school experience and seemed fine with making me adapt once again. I was bothered that they didn't ask for my input about leaving Beijing. I wasn't allowed to act totally mopey; I was expected to see moving back to America as an 'adventure'. I was allowed to feel sad around friends, but not around my parents because they actually wanted to move back. I wish they would have been more sympathetic to why I didn't want to leave and that they would have been more supportive or given me a say in my choice about moving. Or at least asked how I felt.*
>
> **Sarah, 18 [1ˢᵗ: USA; 2ⁿᵈ: China, USA; 7 moves. Family: multicultural, returned immigrant expat, unaffiliated. School: international, Christian international.]**

It is also not unusual for children within the same family to feel very differently to one another – one may be ecstatic to return, while another is depressed about the whole idea. This can create tension between siblings – the one's excitement can seem like taunts to the child who is grieving.

Repatriation for university

When a TCK repatriates to attend university, several big changes happen at once. First, the TCK leaves the host country – which may feel like home and be desperately missed. Second, the TCK leaves their family – which may have been a source of security through a childhood of transitions. Third, the TCK begins studying at university – which may be a very different environment. These TCKs may be around many people who have also left home, but who do not realise their experiences are very different to the TCK's.

All of these changes are taking place at the same time that the TCK is going through the stress of repatriation. It is important for these TCKs, and those who support them, to understand the enormity of this change. Simply getting through is an achievement! It is also important to recognise that many people need help to get through. Counselling may be very helpful, and some universities even have on-campus services available.

'A huge amount of change goes along with becoming a new student, particularly in a new country or culture. Change is stressful. Some universities have mental health visits built directly into the cost of tuition and students are encouraged to take advantage of those services as soon as they feel the need to talk with someone. Many health insurance policies today cover mental health visits as well as counseling that might be needed above and beyond what the university health services offers,' says Tina Quick, who discusses many of the issues faced by TCK students returning to their passport countries for college in her book, *The Global Nomad's Guide to University Transition.*

Cultural translators

Third Culture experiences that are so key to the TCK's identity are not shared by passport country peers; without that shared ground repatriating TCKs may find it difficult to make friends and feel part of a group. Cultural translators – people who will come into their lives and help explain the passport culture to them – can be a great help.

A cultural translator is any person who helps bridge the gap between TCK and passport culture – introducing the TCK to aspects of the passport culture that may be unfamiliar, explaining things that are confusing, and preventing (or fixing) cultural missteps that might otherwise occur. College groups for repatriating TCKs can help with this – older TCKs who have spent more time in the passport culture can translate it for new arrivals. Non-TCK college roommates sometimes turn out to be great cultural translators, but this requires an almost instant chemistry that does not always happen.

> *I am incredibly grateful for my roommate my first year back in the States. She was totally goofy, but understanding. She took the time to teach me American nuances and the National Anthem. She patiently answered my dumb questions about if I'm allowed to walk around barefoot, or at what age people can go into casinos. None of my weirdness fazed her, and that helped me to not feel so self-conscious about how different I felt.*
>
> **Catherine, 24 [1st: USA; 2nd: Brunei, Indonesia, Malaysia, Russia, USA. 9 moves. Family: Business. School: local, international, home, Christian international, boarding.]**

Fence posting

The benefit of a cultural translator to a repatriating TCK leads to a phenomenon known among some TCKs as 'fence posting'. This describes a TCK who, having repatriated, enters a romantic relationship with a non-TCK who quickly becomes the centre of the TCK's emotional world – their stable fence post in the midst of confusion and transition. In a romantic relationship, the TCK has an 'excuse' to quickly go deep – to know and be known on a deeper level at a fast pace.

Several TCKs I spoke with intensely disliked the practice; some accused TCKs with 'fence post' partners of denying their TCK background. Few recognised the valuable role a fence post partner plays as a cultural translator, nor that it is possible to have this outside a romantic relationship.

There is a danger in fence post relationships if a TCK becomes socially or emotionally dependent on their partner, neglecting to create meaningful connections with others. A relationship like this can create further isolation rather than acting as a bridge to greater connection. When the relationship ends, the TCK may have even more difficulty connecting with the new culture.

> *I now realize I put so much emotion into the relationship that it was affecting the rest of my life. I remember feeling so foreign when I came back, not knowing all these various Internet terms. She helped me understand how to work the social media world. She wanted to hear my stories from China and I wanted to know more about her. Getting out of the relationship was hard, because I burned so many bridges that reconnecting was hard, like readjusting all over again.*
> **Pepper, 17 [1st: USA; 2nd: China, USA; 2 moves. Family: unaffiliated. School: Christian international.]**

This is not always the case. There is no reason a TCK cannot have a real and rewarding 'fence post' relationship. These partners do not have to be *just* cultural translators, *just* security in the midst of transition. I know a number of marriages that began as fence post relationships. The other things that attracted these TCKs to their partners were not invalid just because they also happened to act as cultural translators.

Benefits to repatriation

Repatriation is painful and emotionally charged for most TCKs, but it does not have to be a bad thing. In fact, taking the time needed to make one's legal country really feel like home has a lot of benefits for world travellers.

> *Near the end of high school, I realized I had no right to call Singapore home. I had never even lived there! And if I couldn't call Singapore home, where would home be? Thailand? All my memories of Thailand have long faded away. Germany? I must have been only four-and-a-half when I left. China? The place I lived for so many years, speak the language and have made so many life-long friends – but to call China home would be shameful, because I know that what I was exposed to when living there was the 'expatriate life', barely ever breaking out of the bubble. School, home, other housing compounds, high end shopping malls. I never really ventured beyond these places. So I decided I should get to know Singapore more, and finally earn the right to be a Singaporean.*
>
> **Stephanie, 20 [1st: Singapore; 2nd: China, Germany, Singapore, Thailand; 5 moves. Family: business. School: international.]**

Home Assignment

'Home Assignment' is a temporary repatriation common among missionaries. Most mission organisations require missionaries to return to their passport country for an extended period (usually at least 6 months) every few years. These trips are commonly known as home assignment, home leave, or 'furlough'. It is a chance to reconnect with family, friends and supporters, and to fundraise. It is often assumed to be a time of rest, away from the stress of overseas life. Unfortunately, many MKs I interviewed mentioned home assignment specifically as among the most difficult experiences of their international childhoods.

I don't like home assignments. We travel around to countless churches. Imagine that 'new kid' experience, but ten times worse. Even though I meet at least a hundred people a month I rarely feel more alone. I answer the same questions and say the same things over and over. But you have to be polite – you can't shout at the people who indirectly pay for your food. I do truly enjoy meeting new people and hearing their different stories and I've seen great things happen on our home assignments, but it doesn't take long before I need a rest from just being 'the missionaries' daughter' and need somewhere to just be myself again.

Jo, 14 [1ˢᵗ: Australia; 2ⁿᵈ: Australia, Cambodia; 3 moves. Family: mission. School: Christian international.]

Many families on home assignment simply exchange one set of stressors for another. Family traditions and routines are disrupted. They may travel frequently in order to see everyone. They may live with family or friends, or an unfamiliar place, rather than in their own home. They may feel out of place or misunderstood away from their international environment. The familiar 'foreign' things that were a part of everyday life are gone.

While there may be stresses to furlough for missionaries, in most cases the benefits outweigh the negatives. The same is not always true for their children. Many struggle with homesickness for their host country, the place they are emotionally connected to, the place their friends are, the place all their stories happened in.

> *I remember in grade four on home assignment, I was crying at lunch because I missed Ethiopia. I had a bunch of really great school friends who came to comfort me and said I must sad because soon I would have to go back to Ethiopia and leave them. I was touched but a little surprised by the fact that they really had no idea.*
>
> **Lani, 25 [1st: Australia; 2nd: Australia, Ethiopia; 2 moves. Family: mission. School: home.]**

Difficulty in building relationships

Many MKs on home assignment are enrolled in an unfamiliar school knowing they will leave again in a semester or two. It is always hard to be the new kid and break into a new peer group; it is doubly hard when you start knowing you will leave again before long. Some MKs feel it is not worth the effort, especially in the beginning. They may stay in touch with other TCK friends via the Internet and don't emotionally invest in new relationships in their passport country.

> *I didn't want to devote myself to new friendships because I knew it would just be another goodbye at the end of the six months. I knew that even if I was homesick for Cambodia, I couldn't easily mention it at school because there wasn't really anyone I knew who would fully get it.*
> **Eve, 15 [1st: UK; 2nd: Cambodia, UK; 5 moves. Family: mission. School: Christian international.]**

Another barrier to building relationships is that passport country peers may be reluctant to listen to a TCKs' stories from 'home' – a place they have no experience of. This reluctance is understandable, as they have little way of engaging with it as more than an abstract idea, but the lack of interest can be disheartening for a TCK who already feels disconnected.

> *I often feel like my parents don't understand how hard it is when we go back to the States for furlough. They know people there and have friends but I have to completely start over and am always the new girl, which is hard. Very few people my age cared about my*

experiences or my life in Cambodia. They didn't care to hear about where I lived though it was all I really had to talk about. I often complained about America and wished constantly that I was back in Cambodia. I wish people understood that I like Cambodia and don't have any great desire to get back to 'civilization'.

Faith, 17 [1ˢᵗ: USA; 2ⁿᵈ: Cambodia, USA; 2 moves. Family: mission. School: home.]

Many MKs said they felt they were 'biding their time' until returning to their host country. Several said it was a shock, however, to discover they had grown apart from host country friends, casting a shadow over a return they were looking forward to.

Four Stages of Starting Again

Relocation is a difficult experience for many TCKs. David Pollock and Ruth Van Reken created the acronym RAFT to teach TCKs some basic tools for how to transition well. Each step recognises the upcoming move will change things, and gives TCKs ideas of how to end this season of life well.

R – Reconciliation

A – Affirmation

F – Farewell

T – Think Destination

While it is a very helpful tool, teaching TCKs steps to help them process a transition, it is primarily about preparing for a move. While 'Think Destination' is about the shifting from one place to another, TCKs are often unsure of what to do after they arrive. The actual change has taken place, but the transition continues. Many TCKs I have talked to felt lost when they got to the other side of a move, particularly when moving to their passport country. They finished well, but had no idea how to begin again.

I talked to TCKs about their experiences of transition, looking for overlaps, and a pattern began to emerge – four stages TCKs commonly go through as they start again. In the Four Stages of Starting Again I describe common experiences among TCKs adjusting to a new situation.

1. **Isolation** – "no one understands me"; frustration at lack of shared experience or insular world-view held by peers.

2. **Investment** – deliberately attending events, consciously making friends (while still feeling disconnected).

3. **Enjoyment** – enjoying life in the new place; really interacting and filling emotional needs in the new place.

4. **Settling** – feeling "I could stay here"; being at rest in the new place and making a home there.

The Four Stages are particularly applicable to a TCK who is repatriating, but also apply to TCKs who have been left behind. They are a road map of landmarks to look out for, some experiences to expect (or recognise) and advice on how to proceed from there. The progression is not obvious to most

TCKs; they may resist doing the very things that will help them settle in and feel at home in a new place. Many begin adulthood believing it is not possible to find (or make) a new home – until the day they realise they feel at home in a new location.

Stage One – Isolation

A lot happens at once when a TCK relocates. They enter a new world, with its own culture, clothing, customs, cuisine, and vocabulary. While this newness can be exhilarating and adventurous it can also be stressful. 56% of TCKs surveyed felt isolated when they first moved to their passport country. Three quarters of these TCKs still felt isolated a year later.

While the newness and confusion of starting again is happening, the TCK is likely feeling a sense of homesickness for the place they left – a craving for its food, a desire to speak its language, etc. When the TCK wants to talk about these things, they often find the people around them have little or no knowledge about, or interest in discussing, that part of the world. 43% of TCKs surveyed said no one in their passport country wanted to hear stories about their life overseas. 49% of TCKs born after 1980 said they felt they could not be themselves in their passport country.

I started my junior year of public high school and it was a shock to my system. I distinctly remember feeling very lost. The lifestyles of people who had lived their entire lives without ever venturing out of the county in which they were born shocked me. I felt like I had nothing in common with them.

Kendra, 24 [1st: USA; 2nd: Costa Rica, Ecuador, USA; 12 moves. Family: mission. School: Christian international.

Different upbringings mean different perspectives, even very different views of the same events. This can frustrate and even anger TCKs, leading some to believe that "these people will never understand me."

Building friendships may feel extremely difficult, especially when the TCK sees no overlap in experience or interest as a foundation to build from. The TCK who has been left behind can also feel isolated. New friends, no matter how nice, cannot immediately replace the history shared with a friend who has left.

TCKs who feel isolated may refuse to meet new people or make new friends; this may seem counterintuitive on the surface, but the underlying belief is there is no point investing in people who will never understand.

Struggling with your passport country's ignorance of world affairs and your host culture is a very real phase of re-entry. Most TCKs I know definitely went through a period of anger at how detached their new friends, neighbours and countrymen seem from the culture the TCK had just moved from.

Karissa, 23 [1st: USA; 2nd: China, USA; 9 moves. Family: mission. School: local, home (group), Christian international.]

Some TCKs experiencing isolation want to give up on the whole thing – leave and find a new place. Some, especially students, adopt a get-it-over attitude, knuckling down to the work of graduating so they will be free to move on to another place.

> *My goal in finishing university and graduate school was to find the quickest path back overseas! And I know I'm not alone in that.*
> **Abbie, 40 [1st: USA; 2nd: Austria, China, Germany, Hungary, USA; 7 moves. Family: embassy, mission. School: local, international, Christian international.]**

Others may slide into a place of depression – seeing no point in trying if nothing will ever change. It is important for all of these TCKs to know their sense of isolation is normal, and will dissipate as they move through the next two stages.

Most TCKs are accustomed to meeting lots of new people. Either they moved frequently, or new people moved into their lives frequently. They are much better equipped to meet and get to know new people than their monocultural peers. This is why, while a sense of isolation may still occur when TCKs move into expatriate communities, it is more intense in a monocultural community.

> *When I had to move to three different schools in two years, I was amongst peers who moved just as much I did. In Canada, however, it seemed like everyone grew*

> up together and had the same friends from elementary
> school or even kindergarten. It made fitting in hard.
> **Shannon, 22 [1st: Canada, Hong Kong; 2nd: Canada, China,
> Hong Kong; 9 moves. Family: business. School: local, boarding,
> international, Christian international.]**

Extra complexities with repatriation

TCKs are often accustomed to going deep with life stories quite early in a relationship – this information is critical to their sense of self, something they all understand and are therefore interested in hearing about each other. This usually does not work for a newly repatriated TCK. When meeting new people, the TCK may feel an overwhelming urge to tell their life story, and especially to talk about the place they are grieving.

> I didn't connect with people at first. I would tell people
> about my life story and my grief and how much I
> missed Ecuador and my friends, and get that 'glazed
> over eyes' reaction from many people. It seemed I
> would never again experience the deep connections
> I had with friends in Ecuador.
> **Kendra, 24 [1st: USA; 2nd: Costa Rica, Ecuador, USA; 12 moves.
> Family: mission. School: Christian international.**

When the listeners' eyes 'glaze over' under the weight of information they cannot easily process, the TCK may think 'that didn't work; I guess I'll never fit in here', or even judge the listeners as being too small-minded or insular. Sometimes a sense of superiority over those with less travel experience may come up.

TCKs in this situation may feel no one cares about the country they have just left. What they often do not realise is others' interest may take longer to warm up. This is why they must be encouraged to invest in the new place, even when they feel isolated.

Ashamedly, it was my stupid bitterness that prevented me from making a lot more friends in my passport country. It was only later I realised: there are awesome people all around the world. If you look close enough, past the superficial differences, you'll find plenty of people you can relate to and connect with.

Justin, 23 [1st: Japan, Singapore; 2nd: Canada, Japan, Singapore, UK; 16 moves. Family: mission. School: local, Christian international, home, boarding.]

Stage Two – Investment

Investment is vital to developing a sense of home in a new location. It does not always come naturally, and almost always takes some work. The work of investment pays off, however, even when it is not immediately enjoyable.

Invest in people

The most important investment for a newly relocated TCK to make is investment in people. The people around them may have the potential to be their new best friends. TCKs tend to have very high expectations for very new friendships; they need to know the process and pace of making friends may be very different outside an expatriate community.

I thought I would integrate very easily because I had lived there earlier. But I had grown up and wasn't the same as when I was eight and moved away. I had a lot of trouble making friends because I felt like I couldn't relate to the typical American teenager. It took me a while to make true friends who understood where I came from. By making friends and taking part in activities, I felt more adjusted. People were wary about getting to know me, because I was totally different than they were used to. Now, because I made the effort to make friends, I feel I'm pretty popular and well known. Not just because I'm the 'China girl', but because I made an effort to have relationships and be a part of my school and friends' lives.

Sarah, 18 [1st: USA; 2nd: China, USA; 7 moves. Family: multicultural, returned immigrant expat, unaffiliated. School: international, Christian international.]

I encourage TCKs in transition to think about the close friends they have moved away from, and how many hours they have spent talking to one another throughout their friendship – usually hundreds. I then suggest they give new friends a minimum of 10 hours before writing them off. This gives the new friendship time to develop at a slower pace, and takes some of the pressure off the TCK to find their new best friend instantly.

During my first week of college I met so many new people and it was hard for me to tell them about myself.

> *I have never lived in a single area for more than four*
> *years of my life; everywhere I go I feel like a stranger,*
> *an alien. Where exactly was home for me? Instead of*
> *the short version (I'm Korean), I had to explain to them*
> *the entire thing: where I was born and where I lived. It*
> *took several months to feel at home. Once I found a core*
> *group of friends, I felt like I was home.*
>
> **Dan, 20 [1ˢᵗ: South Korea, USA; 2ⁿᵈ: China, USA; 9 moves. Family: mission. School: international, Christian international, home.]**

Sharing stories

Another helpful hint for TCKs learning to invest in new people is that they must 'earn the right' to talk about their international experiences, especially in their passport country. Once they demonstrate they are willing to listen to friends' stories and understand their backgrounds, new friends are much more willing to listen to TCKs' stories.

A good friend cares about what matters to others. If I am not willing to listen to a passport country friend's stories (even if they are of life lived in one house), how can I expect them to listen to my stories? Stories of life in a small town are just as valid as stories of jet-setting around the world; all stories are important to those who lived them.

> *I did feel very out of place in my initial group of*
> *friends – there were times where people's ignorance*
> *about world affairs was frustrating and made it hard*
> *to connect. After being angry at people for being*

unconcerned about the rest of the world, I realized that having an 'us vs them' mentality about people I think are globally unaware makes me guilty of being hateful too.
Karissa, 23 [1st: USA; 2nd: China, USA; 9 moves. Family: mission. School: local, home (group), Christian international.]

TCKs react to a lack of interest in their host cultures in several different ways. Some believe they will not be able to be close with passport country peers and seek out foreign or TCK friends in the new location. Others believe to have friends will require suppressing elements of themselves. They split off the international part of their experience and never talk about it, changing their identity in order to fit in. Whatever route they choose, this stage can be really difficult for TCKs. Many do not know what to talk about – all their stories and experiences from the recent past happened in places they feel they cannot talk about.

This is something Tina Quick addresses, writing: *'Just as home-country peers need to understand you in order to accept you, you need to make an effort to understand them. Be genuinely interested in other people's lives. Listen to other people's stories – everyone has one to tell. People find it easy to talk about themselves. It's what they know. So when you are caught in an awkward moment, try asking your peers some questions about how they were raised. Get them talking and they might just start to ask questions back to you.'*

Shared activities
A helpful way to invest in a new location is through shared

activities. Investing time and energy in joining activities passport country peers enjoy is a great way to build a foundation on which a friendship can be developed. A stumbling block for some TCKs can be that their new peers may engage in very different activities to those in the place the TCK has left. Perhaps they enjoy a sport or game the TCK is unfamiliar with, making the TCK feel awkward about a lack of knowledge or skill.

Some TCKs adopt a snobbish attitude, disdaining pastimes they are unfamiliar with, but this prevents a TCK from developing new friendships. A good rule of thumb is to try anything twice (even if they do not like it the first time). Without giving these activities a chance, they may miss enjoyable activities – and enjoyable people. These activities are often platforms for people to get together, so it is quite possible to go along and have a great time getting to know people at an event ostensibly about playing or watching something the TCK may not particularly enjoy.

> *It took several agonizing months of being lonely, sad and excruciatingly shy before I decided to get involved in extracurricular school activities. I joined the show choir and got a role in the spring play. I met people and began to have experiences that created common ground I could share with these people I'd just met. Those things were, it seems now, the ways I 'learned the language' – my system of translation.*
>
> **Kendra, 24 [1st: USA; 2nd: Costa Rica, Ecuador, USA; 12 moves. Family: mission. School: Christian international.]**

Difficult stage

Some TCKs have a stubborn attitude when it comes to investing in their new place. They just do not want to. They can give you long lists of why, but the bottom line is they are grieving. They have left a 'foreign' place they felt at home in, arrived at a 'home' in which they feel foreign, and no one around them understands what they are feeling – or why. What should be 'normal' and 'easy' – hanging out with peers – is fraught with potential social blunders.

TCKs often find the investment stage difficult, scary, and not fun. The more introverted, shy, or insecure a TCK is, the harder it is for them to take the plunge and get involved – and stick with it. Despite all these reasons to avoid investing, it is vitally important. Without investing, a TCK will not reach the point at which they really enjoy their new location. The more TCKs invest, the faster they start having fun.

> *TCKs should get involved in their "new life" quickly, regardless of whether they want to or not. It really is hard to let people get to know you. If you develop a habit in the new place of not letting people get to know you, it's going to be harder to change that later. We resist engaging because it's hard work! Also, involvement can have an emotional association with (eventual/inevitable) loss, or not being known, since that has probably happened in the past.*
> **Gabe, 22 [1st: USA; 2nd: China, USA; 5 moves. Family: unaffiliated, adoptive. School: home.]**

Stage Three – Enjoyment

While investment may feel like work, onerous and not fun, it leads to enjoyment. This is where interacting becomes less chore, more fun.

A key to enjoyment is engaging with people. There is a big difference between attending and engaging. One can attend and take part in an activity while remaining mentally and emotionally aloof from people. In the long run, continued investment that does not lead to engagement – when TCKs invest time in people and activities without ever engaging their true selves – leads to a greater sense of isolation.

'Some friendships students develop at the start of school will last a lifetime and others will be short-lived. Temporary friendships meet the need at the time, but then you find other people you can really connect with. Having 20 new friends immediately isn't what makes us happy. It's finding two or three people we can share with and trust,' writes Tina Quick.

Engagement – a two-way street

To truly engage – and move from investment to enjoyment – TCKs must feel they are known and accepted at least to some degree. They must feel there is both give and take – that they are not always bridging cultural gaps alone, but people in their lives have made some kind of effort to understand the TCK's perspective. Their investment in others must result in others' investment in them.

> *At times I still get really homesick, but having a community of people who can just be friends to me – not necessarily TCK friends, but just friends – has really helped. And when I do get a chance to share about China, I cherish it because it's an opportunity for me to re-live my experience. The key for me was to find a group of people who really were curious about who I was, where I was from, and were willing to not just listen, but to love on me too.*
> **Jonny, 20 [1st: USA; 2nd: China, USA; 3 moves. Family: returned immigrant expat, business. School: international.]**

A difficulty some TCKs run into is if passport country peers seem less open and welcoming to newcomers than the expatriate community the TCK left. When a TCK feels their investment in others is not paying off – that they are not developing a deeper friendship – they may give up, and return to a place of isolation rather than moving into a place of enjoyment.

> *When I moved overseas I was invited to a party the first week I was there. When I repatriated I felt frustrated with the lack of mutual effort to create new relationships. People in my passport country were okay being long-term acquaintances; I felt like I was hitting a wall and would eventually peter-out the relationship because it felt fruitless and insincere.*
> **Jes, 23 [1st: New Zealand; 2nd: Australia, Malaysia, New Zealand, South Korea; 7 moves. Family: multicultural, expat immigrant, unaffiliated. School: international.]**

Not 'home' yet

TCKs who have successfully engaged in a new place enjoy living there. They feel comfortable, although they may not feel totally comfortable referring to it as 'home'. They have connections – with people and groups – but these may be somewhat 'loose' connections. Being engaged in a place does not mean being rooted there; most TCKs at this stage are ready to leave again soon, whenever the next thing comes along.

TCKs who stop at this stage may feel a yearning for a stronger sense of home, a feeling they have not found in the place they belong. Some wonder if they will ever belong anywhere; others are sure they never will. These TCKs need to know there is one more stage – settling.

Stage Four – Settling

Many TCKs live with a sense their location is 'temporary', that they will move on again soon so there is no point in settling in. They are ready to leave for the next new thing at a moment's notice. This is why they may see no problem in uprooting after every year of college to go somewhere new – there were not many roots to be pulled up. Unless a family deliberately works to create a settled sense of 'home' throughout a TCK's childhood, it is unlikely the TCK will naturally understand how to settle anywhere, with anyone.

'In the end, many TCKs develop a migratory instinct that controls their lives. Along with their chronic rootlessness is a feeling of restlessness: "Here, where I am today, is temporary. But as

*soon as I finish my schooling, get a job, or purchase a home, I'll
settle down." Somehow the settling down never quite happens.
The present is never enough — something always seems lacking,'*
note Pollock and Van Reken.

While those who lived in a single country for a long time can
be better at this, it is a skill most TCKs must learn consciously
as adults. Settling is unfamiliar to TCKs and may even seem
illogical, but the ability to settle (by choice) is important in
the long run. Once TCKs learn how to settle, and do so, their
perspectives – and lives – can change.

Temporary homes

It is possible to live in a place for a long time without settling
there. I lived in China for six years before settling. Until
making the decision to *live* in China, I always considered it
a 'temporary' stay, a stop on the way to somewhere else. In
fact, I lived in China 'temporarily' longer than I lived there
settled. Being settled in a place has nothing to do with how
long one lives there, and everything to do with one's attitude
toward living there. Settling has a sense of permanence, and
peace. Perhaps a better way to express the concept of settling
is being 'at rest' in a place.

A person who is *not* settled may:

· Have no reason/plan to leave but still not expect to stay.

· Frequently think about or look for the next thing/place.

· Put more effort into long-distance relationships than
  into friendships with people in their local area.

· Be very pro-active about visiting nearby tourist spots –

there is no sense of 'I can just do it another time' as they do not know how long they will be in the area.

- Avoid deeper commitment to activities they attend regularly and enjoy.

- Decide against certain purchases because they are 'too permanent'.

- Deliberately purchase cheap items rather than quality so they can be left behind.

- Have few decorative items, especially larger things like framed pictures.

- Move house frequently (within the same general area).

Fear of settling

Many TCKs have a fear of settling, a sense of dread they find difficult to articulate. This is understandable in the light of childhood experiences. Childhood was spent in places they knew were not 'really' home. No matter where they were physically, part of their heart was elsewhere. They may have felt they could not truly be at rest anywhere – because nothing lasts, and everything changes.

When I was five I said to my grandmother, "I love that I have so many homes. I saw anywhere I could unpack my suitcase as home. Even in hotels I would create 'home' by emptying my belongings and neatly arranging them. I still have the tendency to make myself at home wherever I am, but it's no longer an excitement of 'I have homes everywhere.' My childlike

> *excitement has switched to a grown-up fear of "wait...*
> *where is my home?" What was once fun and exciting*
> *has now become exhausting and emotionally wearing.*
> *This has created a deep rooted feeling that eventually*
> *everything has to go back in and get zipped up and*
> *move onto the next place.*
>
> **Corrie, 20 [1st: USA; 2nd: China, USA; 11 moves. Family: mission.**
> **School: home, international.]**

A family on a two-year assignment is aware of a lack of permanence in their situation (though investing and engaging remain critical). The upheaval of friends coming and going can interrupt a sense of permanence even for families who do not move around. This means many TCKs live in a constant state of 'temporary' during childhood; as adults, they do not know any other way to live.

Some TCKs continue moving as adults, never living anywhere long enough to truly settle there. It is not rare for a TCK to equate a desire to travel with a need to move to a new place; rather than go on holiday, they move to a new city (or country). They may even see settling down as a negative thing – 'settling' for something less interesting, less meaningful than globe-trotting. University can be confronting – the idea of living in one place for three or four years may feel like being chained in place. Thus it is not surprising a large number of TCKs will undertake a semester abroad during their time at university, and others will transfer to a new place one or more times during their degree. Ann Cottrell writes that 19% of TCKs studied at three or more different institutions during their undergraduate degrees.

> *I still have trouble with the concept of 'settling'. Home has always been people for me—my family, my closest friends, and now, certainly, my husband: people I know will always be permanent. Maybe someday we'll 'settle' in a geographical location.*
>
> **Kendra, 24 [1st: USA; 2nd: Costa Rica, Ecuador, USA; 12 moves. Family: mission. School: Christian international.]**

Learning to settle

There are a lot of pieces to truly settling in a place, but for many TCKs the biggest step is being able to accept a single seemingly simple fact: "I live here". Just like that – with nothing added. Not "this is where I'm living now" or "... but home is (somewhere else)". For most monocultural individuals, this comes naturally. Of course I live in the place where I live. For most TCKs it is not that easy.

> *I fear saying "I live here" would mean I'm tied down and not allowed to move anywhere. I know that's not true. But that's how I feel when I think of making that statement.*
>
> **Liz, 23 [1st: USA; 2nd: China, Nepal, USA; 10 moves. Family: unaffiliated. School: home (group).]**

Many TCKs have trouble owning a single location – rather than several homes in several different places (perhaps on different continents). To settle in one place may feel like a betrayal of another place – especially when settling in one's passport country. It may feel like a betrayal of loved ones living in different places – especially when the idea of home is linked to people rather than places. Or it might just feel strange. When you grow up attached to multiple 'homes' choosing just one can feel odd.

Ruth Van Reken encourages TCKs in this, writing, *"Listen to what my ATCK father told me: 'Where ever you go, unpack your bags and plants your trees. Live fully in that place as long or as short as you are there. If you spend your life waiting until the next move, you will never live.' But beyond that, I want you to know you can never lose what you have been given and what has been planted in you in each place. Sometimes I have seen TCKs afraid they will lose their pasts and all they loved if they embrace the next place and people. Don't fear. You can't lose the past. It is your strong foundation upon which you will build your future. Don't be afraid to move on. Growing up as a TCK is one part of your life story and am important part, but it is not the only part."*

The important thing is to invest in the location – in one's house, or city – and develop a sense of permanence. Once a TCK makes the decision to settle, to own a single place as '*my* place', several things can be done to help cement the decision and contribute to being truly settled:

- Commit to groups (become a member, join a committee, go on a volunteer roster).

- Acquire some 'permanent' items, whether practical or decorative – the item does not matter, only that it be something the person considers goes in a 'permanent home' (for me, it was a Christmas tree and a chest of drawers).

- Do things that will create stories and memories based in the new home location (have fun with people).

- Get to know the place better: explore, read history, look at maps – whatever interests you.

- Develop a sense of ownership – adopt a local custom or take part in a local celebration/festival (equally important in a TCK's passport country).

- Learn the language, even if that just means picking up the local slang/dialect of a language you already speak.

> *To me, home is not just wherever your family and friends are, but when you go out and explore the place you live in. Should it be small cafes or a street that you enjoy, as long as you find places you feel comfortable having some alone time, and places where you can hang around with your friends. It is appreciating the memories and time spent with yourself and the people you meet in that certain place that leaves an impression within you which makes it feel more like home.*
>
> **Vanka, 19** [1st: Indonesia; 2nd: Australia, Canada, Fiji, Germany, Indonesia; 7 moves. Family: embassy. School: local, international.]

Creating 'home' anywhere

Settling in a place does not anchor one there forever. There will always be the possibility of moving. Settling is about accepting the possibility of staying. Settling is about having a life centred in the place I physically live. Should I then move elsewhere, I can create a new home by settling in a new place. Home ceases to be a place that has never existed and becomes, instead, a place I create as I interact with others.

The ability to create home is literally life changing for TCKs – people who are stumped by the question 'where are you from?'. Many spend their lives believing they will never fit in, they will never be understood, and they will never have a home. This is not true. Settling in a place changes a TCK's life because it answers all these heart cries.

In some ways this is like Dorothy from *The Wizard of Oz*. Having been on a long and arduous journey in search of home, Dorothy is told she has had the power all along. This is true also for TCKs as they go out into the world as independent adults. Home is not, as many believe, a physical place (or person) they must find – the treasure at the end of a long quest. Home is, instead, something they choose to create – anywhere, anytime.

CHAPTER FIVE

THE INNER LIVES OF TCKS

Common Threads

This chapter discusses ways the childhood experiences shared by many TCKs can affect their beliefs and actions. It explores the hidden hearts of TCKs – things they think and feel which may not be obvious on the outside.

The preceding chapters established the variety of the Third Culture in which TCKs grow up. While each TCK is unique, and many different experiences fall under the TCK umbrella, the term would not exist if there were not also some common themes in the lives of TCKs.

Many of the common threads that connect TCKs stem from ways in which they cope with frequent change, and the journey to create personal identity in the midst of transition. These traits are *logical reactions* to the pressures of circumstances in which TCKs find themselves. While they may sound like personality characteristics, they are instead reactions to, and coping strategies for, international living and constant transition.

Childhood experiences cause TCKs to internalise certain beliefs about the world. Actions prompted by these deep-held beliefs may not be clearly connected to underlying feelings. Adults can easily misinterpret a TCK's behaviour, not understanding the emotional trigger prompting it. This then contributes to a TCK's feeling of being misunderstood.

Individual Experiences

This chapter is not a cheat sheet to explain how every TCK ticks; rather it is a window into how experiences *may* have influenced an individual, and therefore how they *may* feel, and how to better understand and serve them. The specific feelings and strategies described will not be found in every TCK, and when they are evident may not be deliberate.

Ideas for how to help TCKs grow into healthy and happy adults are not a one-size-fits-all approach, but hints that may help when judiciously applied to unique individuals. Some ideas will be most helpful to parents, others to any adult who spends time with TCKs. Some can be helpful for TCKs themselves, especially those already living independently, or to those who know and love them.

The goal is to give you insights that lead to questions and greater understanding – to give you ideas of what *might* be affecting TCKs you know, and questions you might ask to understand them better. Many TCKs find it difficult to articulate the things described in this section. Learning about the things hidden in the hearts of many TCKs can help you approach these topics with specific TCKs – opening lines of communication, giving them permission to agree or disagree, and to start sharing their own experiences.

If while reading this section you think *ah, so that's what's wrong with them*, you have missed the point entirely.

If, however, you think *wow, I never realised how that experience might affect a young person*, you are right on target.

Nomadic Life

One of the biggest common factors in the lives of TCKs around the world is connection to multiple places. Continual change is a normal part of their lives – different places, different people. Whether they live most of their childhood in one country, or move frequently, most TCKs visit a lot of places and say goodbye to a lot of people.

A common term for TCKs and other cross-cultural individuals coined by Barbara Schaetti is 'global nomads' – a term that embraces lives of travel and a sense of rootlessness. While not all TCKs feel rootless, they do tend to move about the world a lot, often including regular visits to other countries.

The 'global nomad' lifestyle of many TCKs can be confusing to monocultural individuals. Interactions with well-meaning people who do not understand add to the feeling many TCKs have of being a sojourner, a wanderer, rather than being 'at home' in any one place. 70% of TCKs born after 1985 feel misunderstood by friends in their passport countries, and only 11% feel host country friends understand them.

Home

'Home' is a complicated concept for children who grow up internationally. 'Passport country' is straightforward. Either I do or do not have a passport from a particular country, regardless of whether it feels like 'home' to me. 'Home' is more elusive.

'Home connotes an emotional place – somewhere you truly belong. There simply is no real answer to that question for many TCKs. They may have moved so many times, lived in so many different residences, and attended so many different schools that they never had time to become attached to any,' say Pollock and Van Reken.

Most TCKs know what country they are *supposed* to call home – and know the 'correct' answer expected in each context – but the country they are trained to call home may in fact feel strange to them. Many feel caught between two or more countries, none of which are completely home – certainly not in the way monocultural people mean.

Singapore has always been very foreign to me, but when people asked where I was from, I replied: 'Singapore.' It was a reflex. In high school, when people asked where I was from, I still said Singapore, but I knew it simply meant the country printed on my passport.

Stephanie, 20 [1st: Singapore; 2nd: China, Germany, Singapore, Thailand; 5 moves. Family: business. School: international.]

TCKs grow up in a place they know is not 'home' – a place they will ultimately leave. They are caught between conflicting emotions. A TCK naturally feels attached to the place in which he lives, but is legally attached to a place he may only have visited briefly, if ever. This conflict can create identity struggles.

As a TCK now back in his passport country, I feel like this place is the foreign country and these people are the foreign people. If asked where my home is I want to say Cambodia but I know it really isn't. It's where I feel I'm meant to be, it's what's familiar to me, but I'll never be accepted in that country as one of them. And I cannot call America my home because I cannot accept myself as one of them. They aren't like me. I long to go back to what is familiar but even as I long I realize that when I go back it won't be the same place I left. TCKs are the only ones who really understand this. We are like our own nation, but we are scattered and do not have one place to say we all live.

Caleb, 19 [1st: USA; 2nd: Cambodia, USA; 6 moves. Family: mission. School: home.]

For many TCKs 'home' is not a single location. There may be many places around the world they consider 'home'. Being asked to choose between the places that matter to them is very hard. Well-meaning friends and family, trying to understand their experience, ask about their 'favourite' place to live, or the place they like the most. In many ways this is like asking a parent, "Which is your favourite child?" Each one has different strengths and weaknesses, but each one is loved greatly.

Because my father is German and my mother is American, I get the question, "But where do you feel most at home". This is a difficult question to answer.

I grew up for 14 years in Bangladesh, I speak English with a strong American accent and German is only my third best language. I went to high school in a boarding school in Germany. Before I just chose to answer with whichever country I felt the person would be happier with. Now I say something like, "I choose depending on the day and the situation". I honestly believe this is fair because I've had a full array of situations in Germany, USA and Bangladesh. Some days, I'm all for Germany and I think there's no other place in the world I'd want to live. Other days, when I get weird stares in the German grocery store for speaking with a slight American accent, all I want is to go to the States where my accent would be normal. Most of the time, I want to answer with Bangladesh. However, I get very weird looks as I don't look Bengali with my blonde hair and green eyes. Most people cannot fathom that a girl like me would feel so at home in a country like that. Many have not met someone who is fluent in a language other than English before and don't even believe that I can speak other languages. It really is a tough question.

Hannah, 20 [1st: Germany, USA; 2nd: Bangladesh, China, Germany, USA; 10 moves. Family: NGO. School: local, boarding.]

'Where are you from?'

Simple questions like 'where are you from?' are very complex for TCKs, and often the head and the heart give totally different answers. In fact, the question leaves many

TCKs stammering for a response that fits the context. It is difficult to give an answer that adequately describes their experiences and feelings. A one-word answer will not be the full story, but only one word is expected.

> *I always used to joke about the answer to 'where are you from' being a story rather than a one word answer. People expect a one-word answer, so they often tune you out after the first couple words. This often makes me feel they don't care and just asked the question to be polite.*
>
> **Rachel, 21 [1st: USA; 2nd: South Africa, Swaziland, Thailand, USA; 4 moves. Family: mission. School: Christian international.]**

Many TCKs have told me one of the only times they are relaxed when answering the dreaded 'where are you from?' is when it is asked by another TCK – someone who has shared the experience of 'home' being several different places at once. Once I overheard a TCK ask, "You're from Canada, right?" The second TCK replied, "Well, I have a Canadian passport, but I've never been there. Does that count as being 'from Canada'?"

> *I answer the 'where are you from' question by saying, "I am living in..." Most of the time that's what they want to know, and if they hear the difference, they might be one of those people who listen without their eyes glazing over when I try to explain where I'm from.*

Emily, 21 [1ˢᵗ: USA; 2ⁿᵈ: DR Congo, Kenya, Rwanda, USA; 20 moves.
Family: mission. School: local, international, boarding.]

A broader concept of 'home'

Often a TCK's feeling of home is connected to people rather
than to places – home is where their family/community
is. While this can be distressing for a TCK trying to answer
questions or fit in, some find comfort in knowing that
'home' is not limited – it can be found in many places, with
many people.

"Home for me now is many places or situations where I feel
'at home'," Ruth Van Reken says. "I may not easily answer
where I'm from if someone means place of origin [...] but
I feel deeply contented and 'at home' all over the world in
these strangest of ways. I consider it to be one of my gifts
and find so much joy in each differing experience of being
'at home'."

*Where are you from? Where do you live? Who are
you? Are the most difficult questions that I have been
asked. Not only are they confusing to me but they are
confusing to the inquirer as well. The interactions,
although hilarious, just leave most people frustrated.
"What language was that?" "Mandarin." "Oh my!
How did you learn that?" "I lived in China." "You live
in China?!" "No, I live in Qatar." "Where is that?"
"In the Middle East." "Oh you mean East Houston?"
I don't know where I belong. My passport says
America, my ethnicity says American and Middle*

Eastern, my mother says wherever she is, and my heart says everywhere.

Callie, 17 [1st: USA; 2nd: China, Qatar, USA; 6 moves. Family: business. School: international.]

Patriotism

Patriotism can be a touchy subject among TCKs. Some TCKs are so ardently biased toward either their passport country or their host country it can be off-putting (or even offensive) to others. Others are quite ambivalent on the issue. However a TCK feels, nationalism can be a subject which highlights their different experience of the world.

Any kind of statements about patriotism or nationalistic comments from adults can be somewhat disheartening and make me feel bad about not loving a country. It can also create a significant mental gap between me and them.

Jacob, 19 [1st: New Zealand; 2nd: China, New Zealand, USA; 6 moves. Family: unaffiliated. School: local, home, Christian international.]

"I think it can be a turn off when others are super patriotic as if this is the only country of value in the world," says Ruth Van Reken. "I think a sense of patriotism also depends on where you are. In Africa at the US embassy, if I hear the national anthem, it was a great song from 'home', but I also absolutely love the Liberian national anthem when I am here (in the US) and hear it played at a Liberian gathering. I can feel connected to lots of places and countries too!"

Global patriotism

Adults in a TCK's life can help greatly by recognising the pluralistic nature of patriotism in the Third Culture. Rather than telling a child what they should feel, and about which place to feel it, adults can help a child to celebrate *all* the places they feel a connection to.

> One thing my parents did that was really helpful was to help my sister and I appreciate foreign cultures. I always felt a sense of respect for German culture – appreciating their unique cultural bents, while also seeing their weaknesses. My parents were instrumental in shaping this view of foreign cultures. As much as I was taught to appreciate other cultures, I am still thankful to be an American. I wouldn't say I'm "proud to be an American", but rather humbled. I think the best lesson in patriotism that my TCK experience taught me was a sense of balance – embracing the good of other cultures while being able to look with a less critical eye at their weaknesses.
>
> **Megan, 30** [1st: USA; 2nd: Germany, USA; 6 moves.
> Family: military. School: local, international.]

When a TCK believes patriotism does not have to be exclusive, they are free to feel (and express) love for all the places to which they feel a connection. This freedom saves them from trying to show something on the outside, which does not match the way the feel on the inside – a heavy burden for anyone to carry.

> *I only claim to be 'somewhat' proud to be an American. It's important for kids (and adults) to recognize that they don't have to feel patriotic, that it's enough to be thankful for the heritage their parents have given them through their passport country.*
>
> **Abbie, 40 [1st: USA; 2nd: Austria, China, Germany, Hungary, USA; 7 moves. Family: embassy, mission. School: local, international, Christian international.]**

Some TCKs find a way to balance all their allegiances. They may openly use and share the languages, foods, or cultural traits of many places. They may support multiple countries in international sports competitions – their passport country, their host country (or countries), and even the passport countries of TCK friends.

> *I love my home country, and am still patriotic. It is possible to love them both, or all three, I believe.*
>
> **Esther, 28 [1st: USA; 2nd: Dominican Republic, Guatemala, USA; 3 moves. Family: mission. School: home.]**

A different connection to their passport country

It is important adults, and parents in particular, understand TCKs will bond very differently to their host and passport countries than their parents. TCKs do not experience their passport countries in the same way as children living there. Even life in an expatriate community is very different to a monocultural life in one's passport country. An expatriate child in an international school may have classmates from many countries and cultures, travel extensively, and have (or lack) access to services such as household help. At the same time, they may miss common childhood experiences from their passport country – celebrating certain festivals, watching or playing a popular sport, and rites of passage such as part-time work or learning to drive. Sometimes these differences are not apparent until a family repatriates – which can make for a bumpy re-entry.

While many TCKs do maintain strong ties to their passport country, and benefit greatly from the ways their parents work to promote that cultural identity, it is unrealistic to expect them to have the same emotional connection to it that their parents have. Parents who expect this strong emotional connection may frustrate their children or be frustrated by them – or both.

My family would take me to Syria every summer, but I never truly immersed myself in the Syrian culture. I never made real friends, I couldn't speak the language. It was not a fun place to go for the summer. It was so

> *unfamiliar to me. It was underdeveloped and lacked the average landmarks I had been accustomed to. Malls, grocery stores, two story houses. So to shelter myself from that I stuck close to my English-speaking siblings, spending only time with the family I stayed with. I feel a continuous frustration with my parents for their feeling of entitlement to their children's sense of home. They just didn't get that there would be a permanent gap between their perspective of Syria and mine. And that that separation would never be closed.*
>
> **Dialla, 18 [1st: USA, (Syria); 2nd: Qatar, UAE, USA; 3 moves. Family: immigrant expat, business. School: international.]**

I have talked to many parents who were upset their children did not express love and patriotic sentiment for their passport country, or the parent's hometown. Some felt their children were ungrateful, not recognising how great a place they come from; some felt guilty for failing to instil this in their children; some were simply sad they could not share this attachment with their children.

Alternatively, a TCK may say the 'right' things about his passport country, but not have the depth of feeling his parents do. Some TCKs learn to say and do the right things to make their parents happy (for example, expressing love for or pride in their passport country) without actually feeling it.

Some TCKs feel their passport country is their parents' home but not their own. They may feel obligated to call it home, but the emotion is not always there. They may feel disconnected, or feel they do not belong there. When these feelings go unnoticed by parents, or are discouraged by parents who want their child to fit in 'at home', the child may feel isolated and alone – unable to share their heart with the people closest to them.

> *I feel my passport country is my parents' home, not mine. I refer to it as the 'motherland', not my homeland. My parents tried to make me eat traditional food and expected me to know the language, but it's really hard. In the end it irritates me. Re-entry was a huge culture shock. Although Zambia is my 'home' I feel it's just a place where family lives.*
> **Longa, 18 [1st: Zambia. 2nd: China, USA, Zambia; 4 moves. Family: unaffiliated. School: local, Christian international.]**

Language and Identity

70% of TCKs born after 1985 said they had multi-lingual influences in childhood. Some learn multiple languages from birth – perhaps including one their parents do not speak. Others pick up the basics of a new language with every move. Even those using a single language are usually exposed to more than one dialect, such as the different forms of English, French and Spanish spoken around the world.

Language is not simply utilitarian – a means to communicate – but is closely related to a sense of identity. Dialect and accent, part of international life, are also markers of identity –

of where a person belongs. The influence of multiple cultures and languages can affect the way TCKs see themselves, the way they interact with the world. Their identity is wrapped up in the languages they speak, and when a language changes, identity can change with it.

> *I feel like a different person when speaking Finnish than when speaking English. Maybe because my Finnish is not sophisticated enough to allow me to express myself to the same level as I can in English. I feel frustrated when I'm away with friends, say for a week, and don't get any chances to speak Finnish. Even though I am limited by my Finnish, I feel constricted when I don't get to be my 'Finnish self'.*
>
> **Elisa, 19 [1ˢᵗ: Finland; 2ⁿᵈ: China, Denmark, Finland, France, Switzerland, USA; 6 moves. Family: business. School: international.]**

"For TCKs starting out as [...] monolinguals, living as an expat or in another culture can give them the opportunity to be bilingual, which will bring advantages to them. For all children living as TCKs, having access to the different cultures that are part of them is important, so many will be exposed to, and pick up, varying amounts of different languages along the way," says Eowyn Crisfield, language expert and educational consultant.

The languages TCKs speak – or do not speak – are usually very important to them. The TCKs I interviewed often raised the subject of feeling pride or shame when discussing their language abilities or lack thereof. Speaking the host country's language fluently was a source of pride – setting the TCK apart from tourists. Lacking fluency in the language of one's passport country, however, could be a source of shame, and meant a sense of distance from passport country peers.

One TCK said his parents teased him for his lack of fluency in his passport country's language, and his lack of familiarity with its geography and customs. He knew it was meant as a joke, but he felt the sting of their disappointment.

Language and education

20% of TCKs surveyed were not educated in their parents' native language; 8% of TCK born after 1985 were educated in a language their parents do not speak (compared to less than 1% of older TCKs). Others are educated in a different dialect of their native language (such as an Australian or Singaporean student attending an American school).

When a TCK is educated in a language their parents do not speak natively, they may end up with a different 'heart language' to their family. Others do not develop fluency in the language of their passport country – leaving them unable to communicate comfortably in the one place they legally belong. Even if it is a different dialect rather than a different language altogether, some TCKs end up sounding foreign no matter where they are.

Exposure to parents' languages

23% of TCKs born after 1985 speak the language of their passport country with an accent, compared to less than 10%

of TCKs born before 1985. 4% of younger TCKs were not fluent in the language of their passport country, compared to less than 1% of older TCKs.

"Many TCKs add languages into their repertoire along the way, especially if English is not their first language," Eowyn Crisfield explains. "No matter how many other languages they acquire, it's critical to not abandon the development of the parents' languages. These are key to allowing TCKs to function as a part of their heritage culture as adults. Allowing a family language to lapse is denying a child the potential to be a part of all their cultures."

Some TCKs are dismayed to discover passport country peers consider their command of the language quite poor. Careless comments by native speakers can make a TCK feel embarrassed, or cut off from the country/culture they consider their own.

One time when I was visiting at the Finnish boarding school I was introduced to a new student by an older student, "This is Thongfaa, she doesn't speak Finnish very well." I was very hurt by this as Finnish was my mother tongue and at that point perhaps my best language. At university I faced this same frustration: my English was compared to an international student's English.

Thongfaa, 24 [1st: Finland, USA; 2nd: Finland, Laos, Thailand, USA; 5 moves. Family: multicultural, NGO. School: home (group), international.]

Parents may also suffer shock or embarrassment when they realise their children lack assumed language abilities.

> *Some languages have different words to address people of levels – e.g. parent to child, child to parent, child to older people, child to child (peer), and general address to people in public. When we were visiting Indonesia (our home country), my children spoke to our neighbours in a way that sounds really impolite – they addressed them in the way one would address someone of lower status, such as a child or employee. As parents we don't realize these gaps in our kids' language until we see them interact in our home countries. While they seem fluent, there are things I picked up as a child that don't come naturally to them.*
> **Yuli, parent of TCKs [1st: Indonesia; 2nd: Australia, China, Indonesia, Japan. Family: business. School: international.]**

Lacking fluency can have an academic impact, as it puts a child at a disadvantage – especially when parents are unable to understand the language of homework or assignments. TCKs educated in a different dialect of the same language also encounter challenges. Despite a common language, they are marked by their accent.

> *I even had teachers make fun of my accent. I was 15 and the Spanish teacher in Colombia laughed at me when I answered her question in my Argentine*

Spanish. It wasn't even a different language, but a different accent/attitude. I swore to myself I was going to hide my identity from now on. So I copied my classmates' mannerisms and their tone, their accent, until nobody could tell I wasn't Colombian any more. But I would speak Argentine Spanish at home.

Melody, 31 [1ˢᵗ: Argentina, Germany; 2ⁿᵈ: Argentina, China, Colombia, Germany, Mexico, Uruguay, USA. Family: multicultural, mission.]

Creating their own dialects

Several TCKs I interviewed talked about having a special way of speaking with siblings – a mixture of the various languages they have been exposed to. This seems to be more common among younger TCKs, with 40% of young TCKs saying they shared a special language with their siblings, compared to just 16% of older TCKs.

A shared language often mixes the vocabulary from various languages the siblings have been exposed to. This may include their parents' native language(s), languages they are educated in, languages their school friends speak, and languages of host countries. Even if the mix includes just two languages, there is a sense of comfort and 'home' that comes from speaking a personalised multi-lingual vernacular.

This sort of mixed-language also happens among international school students, especially those who live long term in a single host-country. Regardless of ethnic background, these students all have two languages in common – the language of the host country, and the language they are educated in.

> *I don't know all the vernacular of the kids my age in America. I often find myself asking what things mean and most kids laugh at my ignorance. It is the same with texting; I prefer proper punctuation, spelling and grammar to most of my peers' slang and text spelling. Something about being exposed to so many languages has made me value how sophisticated the languages are.*
> **Callie, 17 [1ˢᵗ: USA; 2ⁿᵈ: China, Qatar, USA; 6 moves.**
> **Family: business. School: international.]**

Accent switching

International influences usually show in a TCK's accent. Some develop an accent that melds elements of different dialects they have been exposed to. TCKs who grow up long term among peers with a different accent may adapt the different speech patterns – and lose their 'home' accent. Passport country peers may tease them, or have trouble understanding their 'foreign' accent.

Others 'accent switch' – changing accent depending on the situation, such as speaking in an accent that matches the person they are speaking to. Some switch accent frequently during a single conversation if the group they are speaking with includes people from different places.

> *Apparently I speak however the person I'm speaking to speaks. Singlish, American, Australian, occasionally a Chinese accent when speaking Chinese, not to mention a Kiwi twang if I speak to friends from New Zealand. It's not a conscious thing, but my peers find the accent switch funny. I can talk to two people at the same time and unknowingly switch accents within a single sentence. The reaction is usually either amusement or a judgmental attitude. I have been called a 'fake' because of the 'default' American accent I developed growing up in an international school, despite not being an American and never having lived in the USA.*
>
> **Jaey, 23 [1ˢᵗ: Singapore; 2ⁿᵈ: Australia, China, New Zealand, Singapore; 11 moves. Family: business. School: Christian international, international.]**

Many TCKs I interviewed spoke about being teased for subconscious accent switching. Several related incidents in which a person thought their 'accent switching' was a form of mockery. One TCK, working a retail job in her passport country, accent switched to match a customer of a different ethnicity; the customer became upset at her 'racist' behaviour, leaving her confused and frightened.

"In my experience, mixed accents are a mixed blessing," says Chris O'Shaughnessy, ATCK, speaker and advocate of TCKs, and author of *Arrivals, Departures and the Adventures*

In-Between. "As a young child who was initially raised in the UK, my accent (and accompanying British vocabulary) was a huge hindrance when my family moved to the US. I was made fun of in school, and the second I opened my mouth my accent would trigger those around me to stop listening to the meaning behind my words and simply hear the 'oddity' of their pronunciation."

Some parents, hoping to spare their children these difficulties, work to correct a child's pronunciation of their passport country's language. Several TCKs I interviewed found these efforts distressing; some felt ashamed for disappointing their parents, and most felt misunderstood. While it is helpful to speak like a native, once a family moves abroad a TCK's accent is affected by factors outside their control. Instead of fighting a losing battle to 'fix' an accent, parents can make home a safe space, allowing their children to speak freely without worrying about their audience. This can be of great comfort to children who struggle with reactions to accent.

Defending and 'betraying' dialects

Some TCKs get very defensive about language – especially accents and vocabulary between dialects. They may consider one dialect to be superior, and look down on those who speak differently.

I went from an American international school where everyone spoke in a flawless 'American accent' to

> *a country where everybody spoke English with a Singaporean accent. Worse still was Singlish, the local English mixed with Chinese and Malay dialects, which was grammatically incorrect. I struggled to take anyone seriously. Unfortunately, I looked down on everyone and adopted an irrational superiority based entirely on the fact that I spoke good English and no one else did; thus, I must be better, smarter, and wiser than them. I now know better and find English accents to be different 'languages'. Coming to the UK for university, I've adopted a British accent. I then switch back to an American accent when I return to Japan and interact with my American English speaking friends.*
> **Justin, 23 [1st: Japan, Singapore; 2nd: Canada, Japan, Singapore, UK; 16 moves. Family: mission. School: local, Christian international, home, boarding.]**

Even more common, TCKs may feel an emotional bond to a particular accent or dialect. A changed accent can feel like a betrayal, or like losing a piece of oneself. In my own case, maintaining my Australian accent and vocabulary was very important to me on an emotional level when I lived in the US – it was the one way I could obviously show myself to be different, that I had a reason for not understanding everything about the new situation I was living in.

> *I went back to Laos for an internship for four months. But I lived in a different part of the country so I picked up the regional accent. I realized this by the comments Lao people were making – I would say I grew up in*

> the south and they would ask why I didn't have a
> southern accent. I felt like I had betrayed my roots.
> **Thongfaa, 24** [1st: Finland, USA; 2nd: Finland, Laos, Thailand,
> USA; 5 moves. Family: multicultural, NGO. School: home (group),
> international.]

Cultural Chameleons

Most TCKs become cultural chameleons – changing
their accent mannerisms and attitude depending on the
circumstances.

> I had a hard time transitioning into a public school in
> Indonesia. I would always find myself feeling much
> more comfortable hanging out with my family or
> fellow TCK friends than with my junior high friends.
> However, as time passes, you learn this skill of being
> able to adapt yourself and have different behaviours
> within different settings. Being able to travel and jump
> to different continents for more than half my life has
> taught me how to adapt to different kind of situations
> and how to fit in different social environments.
> **Vanka, 19** [1st: Indonesia; 2nd: Australia, Canada, Fiji, Germany,
> Indonesia; 7 moves. Family: embassy. School: local, international.]

A life moving between cultures teaches TCKs to change who
they are on the outside in response to the situations in which

they find themselves. The different cultures they inhabit use different verbal and body languages, dress and move differently, and show respect in different ways.

> *The necessity of switching to fit in with where you are is something I and my siblings have grown up knowing. This is an automatic response to a new environment. No one wants to be pointed at and whispered about, and to minimize the personal damage, we change to belong. Subconsciously, I even change my style of dress. For instance, wearing sneakers for anything but exercise is something I would not do in Estonia. Too American, too casual. It's an automatic, "Hey, she's not from here".*
>
> **Chelsea, 21 [1st: USA; 2nd: Estonia, Hungary, USA; 11 moves. Family: mission. School: local, Christian international, home (group).]**

TCKs develop a chameleon nature because it helps make life smoother. For many this happens on a subconscious level; they are not deliberately acting, or trying to deceive. They are doing what makes sense in their situation – and it feels normal. It makes life easier. This may sound self-serving, but it can be a show of cultural sensitivity.

> *Many explanations of the chameleon tendency I've read seem to paint it in a negative light – as if TCKs were trying to be deceptive or are acting only out of self preservation. I think it is often a gesture of respect*

> and affection to behave in a way that seems natural
> to the other.
>
> **Lani, 25** [1ˢᵗ: Australia; 2ⁿᵈ: Australia, Ethiopia; 2 moves.
> Family: mission. School: home.]

Personal values and identity

TCKs get on a plane and go to a totally different culture (often several times a year) where they are required to act differently.

This act can feel constant and wearying. A TCK's passport country may not be a place of respite – the act may actually be less familiar there. This means many TCKs feel they are *always* acting. The only respite is when they are with other TCKs, hence the importance of them spending time together. It can be very difficult for them to learn who they are and be themselves in any other context. Anywhere else they are, by necessity, watching and acting.

While adaptation is a skill that can be useful in certain contexts, many TCKs I interviewed spoke of experiencing confusion as young adults. After years of adapting to fit in everywhere, they were not sure which traits and ideas were truly their own.

> *Because I always had to control what I said and what*
> *I talked about so I'd be accepted by kids my age, I still*
> *struggle to understand who I am. I have no clue what*
> *my true personality is and what is a habit I learned*
> *to fit in. It's as if I've had to paint spots and stripes*

> *of specific colours onto my skin so that I could be*
> *accepted, while erasing past paint strokes so people*
> *would like me more. Now that I get to stand in front*
> *of the mirror, I'm not entirely sure which stripes and*
> *spots were originally on my skin and which ones I*
> *painted myself. I look like an abstract piece splattered*
> *with vibrant, clashing colours, and I'm not sure how to*
> *untangle myself from years of camouflage, because I*
> *don't have a clue where I end and the fake begins.*
>
> **Aurelie, 19 [1st: France; 2nd: Belgium, China, France, UK; 5 moves. Family: business. School: international, local.]**

The ability to change outwardly can affect the expression of opinions or development of personal values. Several TCKs I interviewed said they noticed in themselves a tendency to speak differently about an issue depending on their audience. One spoke of the struggle to identify his personal values, an identity struggle he also watched other TCK friends go through, connecting this to their habit of adapting to each social environment.

> *Adaptability is a hallmark of a TCK. I think because*
> *TCKs sense their inability to impact the many changes*
> *in their lives, they are generally more able and willing*
> *to do what it takes to fit in. This means you might find*
> *as TCKs move they may change what is important,*
> *and what they believe, in order to fit in.*
>
> **Johanna, 25 [1st: USA; 2nd: Mexico, South Korea, UK, USA; 6 moves. Family: embassy. School: international.]**

'Some ATCKs may outwardly continue to be successful chameleons, but inwardly the questions "Who am I?" "Where am I from?" and "Why can't I seem to move on in life?" still rage. They can't figure out why they've always felt different from their peers,' observe Pollock and Van Reken.

Empathy

There are advantages for cultural chameleons beyond the initial skill of fitting in. The time spent working out how to adapt to different situations teaches these TCKs how to see a situation from another's point of view. Many TCKs I interviewed do either paid or volunteer work that includes advocacy for diverse, neglected, or downtrodden people groups.

> *I love the world-view I acquired. I feel like being a TCK has really grown in me a compassionate heart for social justice worldwide.*
> **Karissa, 23 [1st: USA; 2nd: China, USA; 9 moves. Family: mission. School: local, home (group), Christian international.]**

Another way this can manifest is sensitivity to the feelings of others. They may be sensitive to the atmosphere of a group, or pick up on emotional stress others have not expressed. For some TCKs, this extends to feeling a great sense of grief for a loss in their community even if not close to the person involved.

> *The way regular people feel about something that happened to a good friend is the same way a TCK would feel about someone who was an acquaintance.*

> *Everything is felt deeper. The bond you make with people when you are living overseas is unexplainable, even as a community.*
>
> **Christyn, 30 [1st: USA; 2nd: Egypt, Israel, Jordan, UK, USA; 12 moves. Family: mission. School: international, home.]**

Feelings of isolation

There is also a negative side effect to the chameleon skills many TCKs possess. In most situations the chameleon is adapting to others – being like them, being what they expect. This can lead to feeling no one really knows them, and a sense of emotional isolation. Losing close friends regularly due to relocation compounds this.

Some TCKs end up self-isolating, in what can become a vicious cycle. They feel different, that they do not belong, so they act to fit in; the acting makes them feel distant from people, so they feel more isolated.

> *Loneliness is extremely common, I still struggle with loneliness! I don't have very many close friends, because when we do start getting close I feel like I'm acting, and I don't want to hurt them.*
>
> **Wendy, 16 [1st: USA; 2nd: China, USA; 3 moves. Family: unaffiliated, mission, adoptive. School: local, home (group).]**

It is important for TCKs to learn they do not *have* to be isolated, that it is possible to share their innermost thoughts and feelings – and be truly understood.

"I have encountered a number of TCKs who have these same feelings at some point in their lives," says Lois Bushong. "But when they are introduced to other TCKs who share these feelings of being disconnected, they come to the realization that they are not alone and even though they may not be connected to just one country, they can proudly hold high the banner of being a 'global soul'."

Connecting with chameleons

Another consequence of learning adaptation is a tendency to cover emotions well. Many TCKs are skilled at showing positivity while feeling negative emotions. Seeing beneath the surface to what is really happening in their hearts may not be easy, but is worth the effort – both for the TCK and for the person getting to know them.

Many TCKs have 'tests' they use to decide if a person can be trusted with their deeper thoughts and feelings. Some have a sort of secret code – words and phrases they throw out, wondering if someone will notice their subtle request for help. It is that same deep question rearing its head –'can anyone understand me?' If these hidden messages are missed, the TCK might not try again for a long time. Many TCKs who do this are unaware of it – they are not trying to be difficult to know. It is simply a self-defence mechanism developed over time.

"Nobody likes being hurt. People naturally grow adaptations to avoid being hurt, or at least to limit the degree of hurt that might occur," Doug Ota says. "In this degree, the TCK 'test' is a specific manifestation of how all humans try to protect themselves socially."

"Because the TCK has accurately assessed the landscape, and because the TCK has realized that the vast majority of people cannot identify with and validate a TCK way of life, the TCK often shows one card at a time. If the other 'player' doesn't recognize the suit that's been played, the TCKs knows – and perhaps rightly – that subsequent cards from the 'deck' of his or her experiences would also get ignored or misread."

The overwhelmed kid who will not tell anyone they feel like they are drowning might say, "I'm pretty busy with all the work that needs to get done, but I'm good." In offering a less-than-perfect response a TCK opens the door for a question to be asked, an opportunity to dig deeper. Asking that question, seeking to know more about what is happening in that TCK's life, shows you really do care, really are interested.

Pressure to Excel

Many TCKs come from high achieving families. Their parents are chosen by a sending organisation (whether a company, a government, or a mission organisation) most of which look for exceptional people. In addition, some countries require expatriates to have a university degree (or other qualification) to be eligible for a work visa.

This is not, as one might suspect, seen only in 'elite' circles – among highly paid expatriates or in expensive international schools. Even TCKs who live immersed in the local culture and/or outside expatriate circles tend to have high achieving parents – 80% of MKs have at least one parent with an advanced degree. MKs are just as likely to feel pressure to excel and to succeed academically. 94% of adult MKs surveyed by MK–CART/CORE went on to become university-level students; 73% received a degree, and a third of these graduated with honours.

Academic excellence

Many TCKs grow up in elite circles without seeing them as elite. They may think this level of intelligence and achievement is normal – the minimum acceptable standard – because in their world, it seems to be.

For example, at each of two international school graduations I attended one year more than 70% of graduates had a GPA higher than 3.5. Another school, the British School of Beijing, states on their website that 55% of their students received IGCSE and A Level results of A or A+; 90% of all grades were IGCSE C (US B) or higher. In the world of international schools, straight As are not an exception, but the norm.

I've always excelled academically — it was a point of pride for me that I had always been 'good at school'. I was never particularly pressured by my parents to get outstanding grades. I knew, of course, that if I ever brought home an assignment or midterm grade report with a D or F that my parents would ask me why,

> *probably express some disappointment, and work with me to find solutions for how to bring the grade up. But the thought of bringing home even a C to my parents was unthinkable — I would have been much too disappointed in myself to let that happen. I graduated 11th in my class of 200 students but remember feeling very cheated. My first two years of high school had not weighted honours classes, so when my transcripts and credits were imported to my new high school my GPA was lower than it would have been.*
>
> **Kendra, 24 [1st: USA; 2nd: Costa Rica, Ecuador, USA; 12 moves. Family: mission. School: Christian international.]**

Most of the TCKs I interviewed spoke about feeling pressure to excel academically. One spoke of moving from a public school in his passport country to an international school abroad. Although the school was chosen because it taught the same curriculum, the pace of study and study habits of his new classmates was radically different. He went from feeling happy with his study habits and results to feeling lazy and slow.

In Beijing I listened to many young TCKs speak (even cry) about letting themselves, their families and their teachers down, because they received Bs or perhaps a C. I also heard the parents of these same children express pride in how hard a child was working – then astonishment as they began to realise the pressure a child had put on him/herself.

Considering university

Most TCKs go through high school expecting to attend
university – indeed, many do not even think to consider
other options. Guidance counsellors at international
schools often work on the assumption every student will
attend university.

It is not a bad assumption, as statistics gathered by
Denise Bonebright (*HRD Challenges and opportunities*) and
Ann Cottrell (*Military Brats and other Global Nomads*) show.
95% of TCKs receive at least some tertiary education, and
nearly a third attain an advanced degree. In comparison,
60% of high school graduates in the US enrolled in university
in 2001, and 20-30% of adults in Western countries have
university degrees.

> *When my daughter was in Grade 8 her international
> school ran talks about preparing for university. I was
> concerned there was no mention of other tertiary
> options. Some kids do not wish to go to university, and
> it is not the best fit for every individual. I talked to the
> guidance counsellor responsible to ask her opinion,
> and what other options the school could/would
> present. After I explained my concerns she gave me a
> blank stare and said "Don't you want your child to go
> to university?" That wasn't the point. Children need to
> know there are other options available.*
>
> **Eleanor, parent of TCKs** [1st: Australia; 2nd: Australia, China,
> UK; 5 moves. Family: business. School: international.]

Some students feel pressured to attend the most prestigious university possible. I have spent many hours listening to TCKs nearing the end of high school discuss their options going forward; quite often I heard a pull between what they felt suited them, and what they thought was the more prestigious option.

> *I watched my sister drawn to big name schools as she graduated. All her friends went to Yale, Pepperdine and NYU, but she got a wonderful scholarship to a wonderful school which nobody had ever heard of in Qatar. She felt as if she was letting herself down by going to this lesser known school even though she fell in love with it. I am experiencing this now as I formulate my list of colleges to apply to. I have found myself with an elitist mindset when picking schools.*
> **Callie, 17 [1st: USA; 2nd: China, Qatar, USA; 6 moves. Family: business. School: international.]**

Fear of failure

TCKs from various backgrounds spoke about a fear of failure. Often it seemed to be more of an internal pressure these TCKs placed upon themselves, not just an external pressure exerted by peers or authority figures.

> *I always felt I was expected to do well and be above average even though I was never explicitly told this.*

> *Failure wasn't really an acceptable option – or at least I never felt like it was. I had travelled a lot and I always felt I should know more than the average person.*
> **Maddie, 18 [1st: USA; 2nd: Germany, Japan, USA; 9 moves. Family: military. School: home (group).]**

Several TCKs I interviewed spoke of feeling the weight of their parents' occupations – whether they worked in an embassy, a mission organisation, a school, or the corporate world. Several expressed the sense that everything they did would reflect on their parents, their parents' employers, and even their entire country. For others there is a more general sense that failure is inexcusable given the advantages they receive from international life.

> *I remember my parents always being 'on', or as my mom says, "dressed for press". For kids with parents in jobs that are very political, like embassies, and living with and going to school with people whose parents know yours, there is a strong feeling that your actions, successes and failures will be reflected on your parents.*
> **Arielle, 24 [1st: USA; 2nd: China, India, Kazakhstan, Kenya, Thailand, Uganda, USA; 9 moves. Family: embassy, NGO. School: local, international.]**

A fear of failure is certainly not limited to TCKs, but it was a topic that came up in most of my interviews. Many TCKs spoke about the fear of failure as a significant part of their experience growing up. Learning how a fear of failure can present may help in understanding a TCK's point of view.

Four ways students approach success and failure

Psychology professor Martin Covington of the University of California, Berkeley, identified four different approaches students have toward success and failure:

· Success-oriented

· Failure-avoidant

· Failure-accepting

· Overstrivers

Success-oriented students find challenges encouraging, as they anticipate the positive feelings of success. In contrast, Failure-avoidant students are discouraged by challenges as they anticipate the negative feelings of failure. These students may see new activities are new opportunities for failure; this can add an extra stress to an already stressful relocation.

Failure-accepting students give up trying to succeed, probably having already experienced several failures, and are very difficult to motivate. 'Overstrivers' or 'closet achievers', however, are very motivated – by fear. They push themselves far beyond what is reasonable, and exhibit a range of self-protective strategies.

Overstrivers
While TCKs can fall in any of these categories, it is the Overstrivers who figured most prominently in my interviews. Many of Covington's descriptions of Overstrivers mirror stories TCKs told me of their experiences as students. One

such example is 'defensive pessimism', in which students create such low expectations that success is a relief and failure just what they had expected anyway.

Overstrivers can experience significant emotional stress, especially when considering the possibility of failure, no matter how successful they may seem. In his article, "Self-Worth Theory: Retrospection and Prospects" in *Handbook of Motivation at School*, Covington writes, *'Many otherwise successful students cannot endure even a single, minor setback, grade-wise, without feeling totally devastated. One might think that a superior record of noteworthy accomplishments would easily offset the single exception. No, not if those prior successes were motivated by fear in an attempt to prove one's worthiness [...] a single, uncharacteristic failure serves to remind Overstrivers of their inadequacies, and of what they have feared all along, despite their accumulated successes: they are not perfect. [...] A high GPA is simply evidence of an endless struggle to avoid feelings of shame and self-doubt, a struggle that is never completely resolved. Little wonder that successful performances among Overstrivers can bring only temporary relief.'*

Mistakes can be good

While the prospect of failure terrifies many TCKs, mistakes are part of the process of learning and growing. There can be freedom in failure, when nothing terrible happens, and people continue to offer love and support.

'There is no need to be afraid of being wrong. Mistakes are the "stepping stones" to achieving success,' note Pittman and Smit in *Expat Teens Talk*.

> *I definitely have a great fear of failure. I got my first C this semester, and hardly getting Bs I was shocked! Had I bitten off more than I could chew? Would my family and friends be disappointed and upset with me? Instead I got a sympathetic, "I'm sorry, but at least you passed!" and it was never mentioned again. Every time I fail (which is rarely, but with grace and love I'm slowly learning it's okay), I feel more loved and supported than when I succeed. My fears were of my own invention.*
>
> **Wendy, 16 [1st: USA; 2nd: China, USA; 3 moves. Family: unaffiliated, mission, adoptive. School: local, home (group).]**

Many TCKs I interviewed felt they had no space to fail, internalising a pressure to live up to the standards of their parents' occupations. Foreign service and MKs were most likely to make these comments; several had been told outright, often in a serious sit-down talk, that their actions had repercussions for others – reflecting negatively or positively on their parents, their country, or even their God. Adults can help TCKs by talking about success and failure – that mistakes are not the end.

> *It was wonderful to know there was someone who wasn't expecting me to always be perfect. A lot of TCKs need a place where they can fail safely, a place where they know failure won't cause someone to look down upon them, their family, or their company/organization.*
>
> **Grace, 25 [1st: Singapore, USA; 2nd: China, Hong Kong, USA; 4 moves. Family: multicultural, mission. School: home.]**

Anxiety

Many TCKs struggle with moderate to high levels of anxiety. Anxiety is experienced by many young people, but the specific challenges of international life (such as change, loss, and identity issues) can compound these anxieties.

'When I work with a TCK in my counseling office, they sometimes present all of the symptoms of anxiety. Some talk about full-blown, panic attacks. Some have been on medication for anxiety for months. Yet the source of all of this anxiety can be a mystery to a therapist who lacks experience in counseling TCKs or expats. The life of the globally mobile looks picture-book perfect. Most will report a loving, stable family, travel to some of the most exotic places in the world, the best of education, and wonderful job opportunities. Yet underneath this idyllic world, some experience a silent struggle with anxiety,' observes Lois Bushong in *Belonging Everywhere & Nowhere*.

Hidden Anxiety

On many occasions I have talked to teenagers so adept at hiding the cycles of anxiety they are caught in, their own parents have no idea of the stress they feel. Many told me of times in which they reached out to a parent (or other significant figure) to share a fear, only to feel the adult in question dismissed or downplayed the issue.

Almost every TCK I know knows how to hide their anxiety from their parents. Very few TCKs are completely open with their emotions with their

> *parents. I know my parents are oftentimes afraid to*
> *know what I'm feeling, because I act like a time-bomb*
> *around them, bottling it up then exploding.*
> **Pepper, 17 [1st: USA; 2nd: China, USA; 2 moves. Family: unaffiliated.**
> **School: Christian international.]**

When a TCK expresses fear or anxiety, it should be taken seriously. To dismiss or give a flippant answer to their anxiety can hurt deeply. Even saying "it will be okay" without first taking time to understand their feelings can be counterproductive. It may be they are sharing the surface of a deeply hidden anxiety, which will take time and patience to sort out.

Something normal to an adult may be frightening to the TCK because of their very different experience of life. One example I heard was a young child frightened by blue toilet water – something normal to her parents was unexpected and scary to her. An experience I heard many times was that of older children who grew up with walled compounds feeling insecure in towns and cities without fences and walls around everything. These fears and anxieties are valid – even if there is no true danger, they represent something new and uncertain for the TCK.

> *What makes me anxious is very different than what*
> *makes my peers anxious. For example, long car trips,*
> *long flights, packing a suitcase or shipment, meeting*
> *new people, etc. does not faze me anymore. It's the*
> *decisions related to whether or not I will stay in the*

> *same state or country for college or how long I will be*
> *in one place. The nomadic mindset is not one that can*
> *be easily dissolved.*
> **Callie, 17 [1st: USA; 2nd: China, Qatar, USA; 6 moves.**
> **Family: business. School: international.]**

Making decisions about the future

Many TCKs feel incredibly stressed when required to make
decisions about the future. Some get so stressed over school
results and applying to universities they become physically
sick. Others finish university successfully only to encounter
unexpected stress concerning their next steps. Having
always put their energies into study and doing well, many
have never taken the time to work out what direction they
want their life to take.

> *Leaving university can be a really hard process. I*
> *realized this between moving from college to graduate*
> *school and being asked by my grandfather to reflect*
> *on the decisions that had transformed my life, and*
> *besides answering, "I'm 22, I haven't started my life,"*
> *I had no answer. I realized later it was because up until*
> *this point all my decisions had been made (or strongly*
> *encouraged) by my parents. Beyond the choice of*
> *college and my major (done with extensive consultation*
> *with them) I had not made any substantive decisions*
> *about the direction of my own life. I think there are*
> *probably a lot of TCKs who feel similar anxiety, faced*

> *suddenly with being able to shape their own lives*
> *without bringing their parents into it.*
> **Arielle, 24 [1ˢᵗ: USA; 2ⁿᵈ: China, India, Kazakhstan, Kenya,**
> **Thailand, Uganda, USA; 9 moves. Family: embassy, NGO.**
> **School: local, international.]**

For some TCKs, decision making is made difficult because of unexpressed emotion. These TCKs have all the information they require to make a good decision, but powerful feelings make it difficult to see clearly. Their feelings about the decision – about the change, loss, or fear of getting it wrong – cloud their judgment.

When the inability to make a decision is clouded by emotion, more information will not help. These TCKs need to articulate what they *feel* about the situation, and especially any anxieties. At times what TCKs need most is not advice, but someone to listen, until the root of the problem – the anxiety – raises its head. Once the anxiety is defused, an answer often becomes clear.

> *I happened to be at a youth camp as I was trying to*
> *decide between two universities on opposite sides of*
> *my home country. Most people I asked were more*
> *interested in giving their opinions about the schools,*
> *or sharing their university experiences, but one of my*
> *youth leaders let me sit on her bed, lay my head in her*
> *lap and cry while I talked through the pros and cons*
> *of each school and worked through this huge, life-*
> *altering decision. I am incredibly grateful to her for*

> *just listening to me. All she said, at the end, was*
> *"I think you know where you need to be," and I did.*
> **Johanna, 25 [1st: USA; 2nd: Mexico, South Korea, UK, USA;**
> **6 moves. Family: embassy. School: international.]**

Expressing the Inner Life

Many TCKs experience a lot of emotional turmoil during their early years. Separation, transition, and goodbyes often form a continual backdrop to their childhoods. Many become overwhelmed by emotions they do not have the resources to fully process as children. When these emotions are not adequately addressed, TCKs may bury their emotions, suppressing grief, and use 'chameleon' skills to appear fine on the outside despite inner turmoil.

Experiencing and expressing emotions is healthy, and an integral part of growth and maturity. Children who habitually suppress emotions miss out on opportunities to grow emotionally. This can result in emotional expression that is 'out of sync' with a child's age. Suppressed emotion may be expressed with an outburst that is seen as rebellious or childish. As TCKs grow older, these 'immature' emotional outbursts are less tolerated by parents and other adults, who see them as a discipline problem. TCKs in this situation suppress their emotions even more, drawing on chameleon skills to act more like adults.

> *My three-year-old son refuses to say goodbye on many occasions when he is feeling really sad. If we didn't know better it could be misconstrued as rudeness. However, we have realised that he doesn't want them to leave, and can't bring himself to say goodbye. We warn people in advance so they also understand that this is actually an expression of great sadness because of great love.*
>
> **Anne, 37 [1st: Australia; 2nd: Australia, Burundi, Canada, Liberia, Malawi, South Africa, South Sudan, Sweden, UK, USA; 30 moves. Family: mission. School: local.]**

Safety in academic success

Many TCKs find that academic success brings praise from authority figures (parents and teachers). These authority figures are likely to treat students with increased trust and respect as they succeed academically and act like adults. School can become a comfort zone – a place where TCKs know the rules, a known way to excel and be accepted. Even those who do not pursue academic success usually feel they *should*, and generally prioritise intellectual growth over emotional expression.

The combination of these two factors – suppressed emotional growth and accelerated intellectual growth – leads to a gap between the inner life and the outer life of many TCKs. This gap widens over time if they continue to grow faster intellectually than they do emotionally.

Catching up

While these TCKs look 'fine' on the outside, and may do so for many years, it is important for them to stop and process their experiences at some point. There comes a time when each TCK must process the grief suppressed in childhood and un-learn techniques for suppressing emotion.

Many TCKs I interviewed spoke of going through a period of emotional upheaval after leaving home, usually to attend university, often in a different country. Many labelled this period as a 'rebellious phase'. While these TCKs were also dealing with transition, or repatriation, they indentified this 'rebellious phase' as something different. For some it was a time of 'finding' themselves, what they really cared about and wanted from life, which seemed rebellious to others (even to the TCKs themselves in some cases).

Most said they had felt a sense of freedom upon leaving home and high school; they had space to act 'immaturely' without it reflecting badly on people they cared about. Some TCKs felt very guilty for this phase – for giving into 'feelings' or being 'weak'.

Other TCKs told of significant episodes of depression or anxiety. Long suppressed emotions rose to the surface, sometimes so strongly the TCK felt confused, overwhelmed or lost. Several of these TCKs talked about hitting a 'wall' or running out of steam – being unable to maintain the coping mechanisms that had enabled them to suppress years of unresolved grief, but knowing no other way to live.

While these experiences may look 'messy' or seem a backward move, for most of these TCKs it was a time of 'catching up' on emotional growth that had been slowed by unresolved grief. Once they took the time to address their grief and learn new strategies, these TCKs felt more confident about moving forward. For many it is a painful process, perhaps requiring intensive counselling or a change of plans, but one that is worth the effort.

It is never too late – or too early – for a TCK to do this sort of processing. The rest of this section will discuss several tools to help TCKs of all ages strengthen the ability to experience and express emotions.

Emotional vocabulary

It is possible to be intellectually articulate while lacking the ability to articulate one's emotions. Many young TCKs are capable of contributing intelligently to adult conversations well beyond their years, yet lack the ability to describe and express their emotions in a measured and comfortable way. Their thoughts are articulated with ease; feelings require more exploration and effort.

As children develop emotionally, they learn to name their feelings. This does not happen automatically. *'The ability to label emotions is a developmental skill that is not present at birth – it must be learned,'* writes Julia Simens. The more words children know to describe their feelings, the better they are able to communicate their emotions. Simen's book, *Emotional Resilience and the Expat Child: Practical Storytelling Techniques That Will Strengthen the Global Family,* is a wonderful resource for parents; she explains this concept in detail, including tools that help parents teach young children words to describe their feelings.

Suppressing grief and other emotions leaves a child with fewer opportunities to practice and develop this emotional vocabulary. TCKs who have suppressed grief, or buried emotion, for a long time may find it difficult to re-learn how to experience and express their feelings. Several TCKs I interviewed spoke of struggling to label strong emotions they expressed. They knew words for labelling emotion, but had not learned to connect the definition of a word with the experience of feeling it.

One TCK told me she unintentionally gravitated toward peers in helping professions, particularly those with psychology or counselling backgrounds; they could see when she was experiencing an emotion she could not express, and coached her through naming the feelings so she could process them.

Self expression through the Arts

Art is a form of communication and expression that does not require one to have all the right words in the right order. This sort of self-expression can be very helpful for TCKs. It gives them a way to explore unresolved grief, and any emotions they do not have words to express.

"In my opinion, the arts are the best way for people to express stories or emotions that they would not otherwise feel 'safe' to explore and share," says Elizabeth (Lisa) Liang, ATCK, writer, actress and creator of the one-woman TCK show, *Alien Citizen: An Earth Odyssey*. "The artistic form is both the conduit and the buffer for the TCK's story, message, feelings and needs."

I have seen TCKs express themselves through a variety of art forms including music, photography, videography, dance, drama, writing (including poetry), sewing, and visual arts (painting, drawing and more). Some excelled, others were mediocre, but all of them created for enjoyment and with freedom of expression. In so doing, they learned to bring some of their innermost feelings into the open through their art form.

Having an artistic avenue to express myself in was extremely beneficial to me. For about a year I decided I was going to attain academic excellence and pretty much 'Spock' myself out of society. I had one or two close friends, but the majority of my time was spent studying. This resulted in a fantastic GPA, but a stunted emotional maturity. I didn't allow myself to grow socially and emotionally, which was a barrier when I moved again a year later and had to make new friends. This problem was nowhere near as bad as it could have been though, because six months earlier I turned the focus of my life away from my studies and expressed myself much more through art and music. Even though I never showcased what I did, it helped me get out emotion that seemed difficult to deal with. This was a massive aid in allowing me to grow socially and emotionally and preparing me for another move.

Jacob, 19 [1st: New Zealand; 2nd: China, New Zealand, USA;
6 moves. Family: unaffiliated. School: local, home,
Christian international.]

Many TCKs feel a core part of who they are is hidden inside,
separate from the face they show the outside world. Art can
form a bridge between the outer (intellectual/adaptive) and
the inner (emotional/suppressed) lives of TCKs, showing a
hidden heart to the outside world. In creating art, TCKs do
not need to be able to rationally explain what they feel but
are free to simply be.

This emotional freedom can be confronting, even scary,
to TCKs who have survived emotional overload by bottling
everything up. When they first start expressing through art
these TCKs may be surprised at the 'darkness' that emerges.
Some wish to hide this, afraid it will be misunderstood.
Others feel a need to flaunt it – wanting someone to see
what is happening beneath a calm exterior. This 'darkness'
is often an expression of unresolved grief that has finally
been given an outlet.

*Recently, I dug up past rants or rambles I had written
during my army days – boy, are they dark. But if I
hadn't bothered penning my desolate thoughts and
emotions back then, they would have undoubtedly
remained and plagued me internally – who knows
what might have consequently happened?*

Justin, 23 [1st: Japan, Singapore; 2nd: Canada, Japan, Singapore, UK;
16 moves. Family: mission. School: local, Christian international,
home, boarding.]

"David Pollock and Ruth Van Reken taught us that TCKs have experienced more loss in their formative years than many adults experience in a lifetime. Moreover, many are not afforded an outlet for their loss, or even worse, they are made to feel guilty any time their natural anger or sadness arose," Doug Ota explains. "It may even be unfair to label that which comes out later artistically as 'darkness'. It may just be loss, finally being given an opportunity to surface and be seen."

Sharing one's inner life is an important part of emotional growth, and art is a way for TCKs to progress in this area. Over time, continued artistic expression can help TCKs connect with suppressed grief and share their inner lives with others.

"Whether TCKs express their feelings and ideas in abstract visual art forms, or in plays with fictional characters based on real people, or in dances that they choreograph [...] they are expressing their truth – which can be therapeutic and cathartic for them – via art, which can also be therapeutic and cathartic for the people who witness it," Lisa Liang says. "And that can lead to new friendships, alliances, mentorships – connections that will help to support and guide the TCK as he or she navigates life."

The power of storytelling

One reason art can be such a powerful tool for TCKs is because it is about telling stories, whether through words, images, sounds, or motion. Stories engage our hearts, painting parallels between one situation and another by pointing out the emotional resonance they share.

"I believe we were built to respond to stories," Chris O'Shaughnessy shares. "Part of having a healthy sense of self and grasp on our identity is being able to appreciate we have a story and our story is linked to that of others; and ultimately we are part of a bigger story."

The process of storytelling helps a TCK move from feeling isolated and misunderstood to connection. Sharing stories builds intimacy and attachment.

"The more people truly know our story, the safer we are likely to feel with them. The safer we feel with people, the more we are inclined to gradually feel attached to them. And this works in reverse too: the more others know our stories, the more likely it is we know theirs, meaning they feel safe and attached to us, too. In other words, attachment develops hand in hand with our knowledge of people's life stories," says Doug Ota.

Uncovering stories

When an adult wants to learn a TCK's story, their first approach is generally to ask questions. For many TCKs, however, a string of questions can feel confronting. They go into chameleon mode, trying to calculate the expected/desired response. Even when a TCK feels a person really wants to hear their story, and is willing to share it, he may not have the words to explain his inner life.

"TCKs often face the challenge of not having the language or framework to explain parts of their own story. Aspects like culture, home and a sense of permanence aren't as clear-cut for TCKs as they are for those of other cultures," Chris O'Shaugnessy explains.

As soon as a sensitive issue comes up, a TCK may deflect questions with dismissive language ("that doesn't bother me" or "it's not a big deal"), or share the bare bones of a situation while glossing over the emotion of it. They may even just stop replying. I have witnessed TCKs stare mutely at an adult asking questions the TCK does not want, or does not know how, to answer.

"These are classic signs of a dismissive attachment style," Doug Ota says. "This can be a natural adaptation to an attachment landscape that one can't seem to trust. Remember, we evolved living in clans of a limited number of trusted people. We did not evolve to cope with repetitive loss."

One way to help uncover a TCK's story is to engage them in a creative art form. Another way is to enter the storytelling world with them, and do it together.

Often when talking with a TCK struggling to express their feelings about something, I take time to tell a story from my own life – preferably one that parallels the emotion of their own experience. This takes the spotlight (and the pressure) off the TCK, allowing them to observe a demonstration of storytelling. I talk about how I felt in a situation, offering emotional vocabulary options the TCK may be able to use subsequently. I tend to choose stories in which I 'failed' in some way, as a reminder that mistakes are okay. Often, a TCK will then reciprocate, telling a story of their own that reflects emotions I expressed in the storytelling.

Family Bonds

When a child moves a lot, or their friends move away, family becomes very important. For many TCKs, family members are the only constants – the only ones who are there to stay.

> *I still feel that I'm extra close to my family and that they know me the best (except for my husband now, but even after we'd been dating for years, I still thought my family knew me better!). It was always hard for me to explain how close I was to my family, despite that we are not overly affectionate or even confide much in each other.*
>
> **Karissa, 23 [1st: USA; 2nd: China, USA; 9 moves. Family: mission. School: local, home (group), Christian international.]**

This is especially true for families living in remote places, or constantly on the move. When a child spends their early childhood years in this sort of situation, the family bond becomes very important. Even if a family is not particularly close there is rarely anyone else in a TCK's life who can take on that role – someone who has been in the same places and situations.

> *When I'm homesick, I don't miss a place or a country; I miss my family. We were moved so much they had become my home; I couldn't rely on a place, so I relied*

> *on people. It's terrifying, because now that I'm away*
> *from them I have to rely on myself.*
>
> **Aurelie, 19 [1ˢᵗ: France; 2ⁿᵈ: Belgium, China, France, UK; 5 moves.**
> **Family: business. School: international, local.]**

Fear of upsetting family members

With many TCKs feeling a sense of security connected to family relationships, it is not surprising some are afraid to 'rock the boat'. Some TCKs deliberately choose not to tell parents how they *really* feel about a move, a location, or an activity – for fear it will upset them. They do not want their parents to feel guilty for initiating a move which prompted the child's frustration or sadness. In these cases the TCK may feel a sense of distance they regret, but prefer to shoulder that burden rather than potentially upset a parent.

> *The only time I am forward about emotions is to my*
> *mum, but that happens sparingly because I don't want*
> *her to feel residual guilt about being so far away or*
> *regret that my parents relocated us several times.*
>
> **Jes, 23 [1ˢᵗ: New Zealand; 2ⁿᵈ: Australia, Malaysia, New Zealand,**
> **South Korea; 7 moves. Family: multicultural, expat immigrant,**
> **unaffiliated. School: international.]**

TCKs with dysfunctional family relationships are often unwilling to share their problems with others, worrying it may reflect badly on a family member. They may not give themselves permission to feel hurt, instead internalising their feelings or self-blaming.

Home life and family relationships profoundly impact a child no matter where they live. The impact of a broken or unhappy family runs deep in the lives of TCKs, for whom so much else is in flux. Even in a generally happy family, small conflicts can have a deep emotional impact.

Family rituals

Children in general respond well to regular family rhythms – daily routines, annual events, family holidays. TCKs in particular seem to hang on to the familiarity of these rituals in order to feel safe and secure. There is so much change in TCKs' lives, and none of it under their control; knowing their family rhythms will not change helps. Family traditions can be very special to them.

'Children tend to love family rituals, even if they don't admit it. Rituals provide a sense of security and can be soothing. Rituals are emotionally enriching. It is never too late to start a ritual. Some children may resist being involved in such rituals. But if rituals are presented in a non-controlling manner and you manage your expectations, all family members will 'get on board' much more readily than you thought,' advises Julia Simens in *Emotional Resilience and the Expat Child.*

One family I know would decorate cookies together every Christmas, and each child would invite a friend to join the family for the cookie party. Even after moving to a different country and with kids in university this remains a beloved family tradition.

Another family I know always has a Saturday morning breakfast treat – a special something that can be made just about anywhere in the world. This weekly routine helps their young children feel at home no matter where in the world they are.

Sibling friendships

Many TCKs have told me a sibling is their closest friend – the only one who has been through all the things they have been through, and seen all the things they have seen. 40% of TCKs born after 1985 said their sibling is their closest friend. Siblings usually share the same legal cultures and the same geographic cultures. The Third Culture itself is all about shared experiences – and siblings have the greatest overlap of experiences.

I would definitely call my sister one of my closest friends, if not my closest. She's the one who knows me best and has shared my background and experiences with me, and we've always had each other to rely on, even though we're radically different people and we had a strained relationship when we were young.
Kendra, 24 [1st: USA; 2nd: Costa Rica, Ecuador, USA; 12 moves. Family: mission. School: Christian international.]

TCK siblings might not always get along but there is a strong bond borne out of a lifetime of shared experiences no one else truly understands. TCK siblings are not just family – they are friends who have been through everything together. For many TCKs, siblings are the closest approximation of long-term, childhood friends. Even if they do not consider themselves close friends they can be quite protective of one another and value the stories they share.

Many TCKs take the bond they have with their sibling(s) for granted until after repatriating. They assume the closeness between them is fairly ordinary until spending time with monocultural friends – at which point it suddenly becomes clear not all siblings are so close.

> *When coming back from my passport country I quickly realized not everyone could speak a second language. What took longer to recognise was not all siblings were as close as mine. I talked about my siblings a lot, and it confused people, as they really only hung out with their siblings when they had to, not by choice.*
>
> **Wendy, 16 [1st: USA; 2nd: China, USA; 3 moves. Family: unaffiliated, mission, adoptive. School: local, home (group).]**

Sibling separation

TCK siblings are often close because of their shared experiences. When siblings go separate ways, this shared experience diverges – they begin to have different experiences in different places with different people. The constant presence of someone who really understands is removed.

While it can happen earlier (especially if one attends boarding school) the most common sibling separation experience among TCKs is when an older sibling leaves for university.

The grief of having a sibling leave is often compounded by how unexpected the depth of grief is. It is not the same as losing a friend. Family is forever – which means a TCK may think "this will hurt less" only to discover it actually hurts more. They cannot 'move on' from a lost/changed relationship with a sibling the way they can with a lost friend. Then, each time they reconnect, the pain of leaving begins all over again. Visits to, or from, a sibling who lives far away can be a bittersweet mixture – the joy of being together followed by another wave of grief when they leave.

> *Recently I've been dealing with having siblings on the other side of the world. It is a type of grieving completely different from grieving friends. Family, however, are always going to be a part of me. Every time I see them I get closer to them and it hurts 10 times more when we have to leave. I was never really prepared for it to be so much harder.*
> **Laura, 18 [1st: USA; 2nd: China, USA; 3 moves. Family: education. School: home.]**

The grief of seeing a child leave is very different to the grief of seeing a sibling leave, and means parents may have trouble understanding why younger siblings are so upset.

A parent raises a child with the knowledge they will leave one day. In fact, for many parents a key goal is to prepare their child to become independent, to go out into the world with confidence. For this reason, while it can be sad or stressful to see a child go, and there can be a lot of anxiety about their being alone (especially in another country) there is also an element of pride and peace – this is how things are supposed to be.

A sibling does not have the same perspective. The sibling leaving may have been a playmate, a roommate, a classmate, a confidant, an advice-giver, a source of hugs and other comfort, and many other things besides. The sibling left behind is therefore losing a lot of irreplaceable things, not least of all the shared Third Culture experiences.

As with many things in a TCK's life, this loss is something that cannot be prevented or 'fixed'. It is a very real loss, one that needs to be grieved. A TCK grieving after being separated from a sibling may need extra attention and compassion. As with any other loss, they cannot just 'get over it' but need space to grieve, and to have their feelings validated.

It can also help to give siblings the opportunity to individually farewell one another, just as they would a friend. This might include a one-on-one outing for the siblings, or having each one write a letter to the other, sharing what they appreciate and will miss, but also what they look forward to in the future. This process helps each one recognise that while the relationship is changing, it is not ending forever.

CHAPTER SIX

THE FUTURE FOR TCKS

Choosing a Future

The oldest 21st century TCKs are now in their late twenties. They are graduating from university, pursuing careers, marrying, having children. As I interviewed these TCKs about their adult lives, certain trends became apparent. These included several core questions, which shape what they choose to pursue in life.

These core questions concern places, people, and occupation. Often the TCKs I interviewed felt a conflict between certain options, and used these questions to determine their priorities – sometimes only realising this upon reflection.

Move around or settle down?

This core question concerns place, and how a TCK will decide where to go, and where to live.

Many 21st century TCKs are excited about, and even seek out, opportunities to experience new things. This can manifest in frequent travel, lots of post-graduate study, or pursuing careers that require regular travel or relocation.

After graduating college I joined a two-year rotation program and moved to a new state every six months. I did this to get more experience in different job functions but also to delay the idea of settling down somewhere. When the two years were up,

> *I stalled again and took on a three-year assignment to Germany. I'm not ready to get comfortable and stay rooted to a single location. There's too much to experience for me to stay still.*
>
> **Lee, 24 [1st: USA; 2nd: China, Germany, USA; 6 moves. Family: returned immigrant expat, business. School: local, boarding.]**

Other TCKs are looking for a place of peace and rest following a childhood full of transition. These TCKs may still value travel and cultural experiences quite highly while seeking, building and maintaining a strong sense of 'home' rooted in a single location.

> *I feel I'm often looking for a place that will tick the boxes – perhaps now why I'm so willing to move – but all the same, I want stability. I do get itchy feet, but there is a definite desire to stay put. It's nice to know there is always the option to move on if we need to or want to.*
>
> **Rebecca, 28 [1st: Australia; 2nd: Australia, Papua New Guinea, Solomon Islands; 8 moves. Family: mission. School: home (group), Christian international.]**

Place or person?

This core question concerns the desire to find a 'home'. Many 21st century TCKs going out into the world believe they must *find* home. Some are looking for a place; others are looking for a person.

Those looking for a place may move frequently, hoping they will eventually find somewhere that feels like home, a place they belong. Some have a sense they will settle down one day, or when the time is right. These TCKs may have internalised a belief that they will know home when they find it. Learning how to settle can help them create home, rather than seeking it 'out there'.

Those looking for a person may quickly get serious in relationships, or idealise marriage as the introduction of a permanent person – their new home. Others may struggle to strike out on their own, preferring to be close to parents or siblings.

> *My experiences definitely put me very close to my family. Through all the moves and changes, we were each other's constants. I think that's one reason it was so hard to move away and live completely by myself for the first time, which I didn't even do in university. My experiences left me with the feeling that I function better in a family context and having those close, safe relationships that I see as a source of stability.*
>
> **Kendra, 24 [1st: USA; 2nd: Costa Rica, Ecuador, USA; 12 moves. Family: mission. School: Christian international.]**

Many young married TCKs I interviewed described their spouses as 'home'. One TCK told of returning to the city his wife was in after months living apart while he studied abroad. As the plane landed he felt that he had come home – not because of the place, but because of the person he was coming home to.

> I definitely feel like my wife is 'home' for me, and I will be okay as long as we're together.
> **Logan, 24 [1ˢᵗ: USA; 2ⁿᵈ: China, Hong Kong, USA; 6 moves. Family: mission. School: home (group).]**

Location or vocation?

This core question also concerns place, and the conflict between choice of location and choice of occupation.

Most people can readily understand the decision to choose a location based on vocation – to live where one has fulfilling work. A TCK who has a clear sense of what they want to do in life will make choices about location, and whether to move frequently or not at all, based on where they can best do the thing they want to do. They will usually invest most deeply in relationships with people who support their vocational choice.

A struggle for some TCKs comes when the occupation they pursued clashes with other priorities – such as places, or people.

> *I am starting to feel more strongly that I'd like to settle in one city. I'm feeling less compulsion to travel, and especially now that my family is back in the States, I'm starting to think about what it would be like living close to them. However, I feel pretty strongly about wanting to do work which would necessitate moving somewhere not entirely of my choosing. That has been kind of stressful.*
> **Logan, 24 [1ˢᵗ: USA; 2ⁿᵈ: China, Hong Kong, USA; 6 moves. Family: mission. School: home (group).]**

Prioritising location

There are several reasons a TCK may prioritise location. They may feel strongly about a particular country or city, want to be near family, or just to settle in one place. These TCKs may still value travel and multicultural influences, but establish themselves in a single home location.

A TCK who prioritises a specific location will choose a vocation (and relationship) that allows them to be there. These TCKs may avoid developing romantic connections with people who are not committed to the specific location(s) the TCK has chosen. They may pass up work or study opportunities that, while appealing, would take them away from their chosen location.

The chosen location may, however, be a series of locations. After a period of time in one chosen location, they may look for opportunities in another specific location.

> *Nearly every job I have taken has been due to me*
> *wanting to be in a certain location. I wanted to be*
> *in Mexico − so I took a job there. I wanted to be in*
> *Alaska − so I took a job there. Now, the job I will take*
> *will be centred on a relationship − where my husband*
> *needs to be. I have always chosen location over people*
> *− and have risked relationships willingly to do so.*
> *That includes family relationships, friendships, and*
> *romantic relationships. My husband remembers one*
> *of the first things I said to him when talking about if*
> *we had a future or not was, "you had best be willing to*
> *move around, because I'm not staying in one place."*
> *Luckily, he quite agreed!*
>
> **Lisa, 24 [1st: UK; 2nd: China, France, Malaysia, Mexico, Peru, UK,**
> **USA; 7 moves. Family: unaffiliated. School: international.]**

Several TCKs I interviewed who prioritised family relationships had a repeating pattern − they would move somewhere for a vocational reason (to study or work) but not last long before moving close to a family member. This created a sense of uncertainty regarding their occupation and future, but being near family was more important to them than pursuing a particular vocation.

Another way TCKs prioritise location is by choosing transience. Some TCKs are not comfortable staying still − they get itchy feet and feel the need to move on. For others this is simply all they have known − after a childhood of frequent moving they do not understand, or want to learn, a different way to live.

I was not accepted fully in Japan, and I can say that while I plan to live and work in the US and now speak English fluently, I never really feel like I belong anywhere here, either. Many people ask me where I'd want to settle down, and I never have an answer. Europe? Asia? US? To me, adventure awaits in any of those places and I would not be afraid to go because I already know that by not belonging anywhere, I can go anywhere. It's a lonely life, yet a fulfilling one.

Gabrielle, 23 [1st: USA; 2nd: Canada, Japan, USA; 4 moves. Family: multicultural, unaffiliated. School: local.]

Military Service

A particular vocation that warrants individual consideration is that of military service. A number of countries practice conscription, in which citizens are required to serve a certain amount of time in the military. I interviewed both male and female TCKs who serve (or have served) in the military forces of nine countries. Some served voluntarily, others due to conscription requirements.

When training in a national military force, a strong sense of patriotism is espoused and expected. Since TCKs have a different sense of cultural identity and patriotism than their monocultural peers, military service can be a particularly challenging experience. A TCK may feel allegiance to more than one country, or lack a strong emotional connection to the passport country. This can be an especially difficult hurdle when military service is compulsory.

Mandatory military service

In countries where military service is mandatory it is common to enter a special military program following completion of secondary school. In these countries military service is a rite of passage shared by peers. A TCK who has been living abroad leaves their high school peers in order to begin military service, rather than joining alongside them. These TCKs often feel a sense of disconnection – both from other recruits, and from TCK friends.

One TCK spoke of being seen as an outsider by fellow recruits throughout his service, as he had never lived in his passport country before. Another told me his years of required military service created a great gulf in his relationships with high school peers – they had no comprehension of the significant experience he had been through, and began university or careers years ahead of him. At the same time, his fellow recruits had no comprehension of his international upbringing, and saw him as a foreigner.

Repatriation is a difficult time for most TCKs, and for a TCK repatriating straight into a military setting the difficulties may be compounded. External conformity may increase the feeling of being different on the inside.

> *I returned to Singapore after graduating from high school in order to serve my two years of compulsory national military service. Those were the toughest two years of my life, not because of the physical training but because of perpetual confusion: 'I thought Singapore was my home – why do I feel like such an outsider?' On the first day of orientation the sergeant major started yelling, "You are going to die for your country!" I almost burst out crying; it took all my willpower to stay in my seat. Internally, I was screaming: 'I am not here by choice! You forced me here!'*
>
> **Justin, 23 [1st: Japan, Singapore; 2nd: Canada, Japan, Singapore, UK; 16 moves. Family: mission. School: local, Christian international, home, boarding.]**

Choosing the military

For some the military is chosen for practical reasons – consistent employment, tuition assistance, or other benefits. For others it is a way to deliberately identify with the country named on their passport. Some TCKs believed that military service would make them truly belong in their passport country, or 'earn' them a sense of belonging and citizenship.

Having control over the decision to serve does not necessarily prevent inner conflict, but makes a very different experience to undertaking mandatory service. TCKs who choose the military can weigh options and decide whether it is worth pushing through to gain what they want.

> *During training all recruits are 'broken' as people, and then 'rebuilt'. As a TCK the primary issue you face is questioning whether or not struggling through is worth it, and this ties in with patriotism. I enlisted to be at the very frontline and to fight for my country, however it begs the question, is it really my country? I've never lived in the UK before; my personal 'favourite' country is China, as I spent the majority of childhood there and it holds the most positive memories for me. It was a question of whether this was what I really wanted to do for a living. It's about finding balance between what's comfortable and what you really want.*
>
> **James, 21** [1st: UK; 2nd: China, UK; 3 moves. Family: military. School: international.]

Conformity

In a military setting, new recruits are generally required to conform – to look and act the same. While some TCKs find this very challenging, others particularly enjoy this aspect of military service. The recruit is a clearly recognised member of the group, and knows exactly what to do in order to fit in. Structure gives these TCKs a sense of stability and security.

> *It was easy for me to let go and see the way things are done here and then just do it. I also love the structure – it's so easy to succeed. Just do what you are told.*
>
> **John, 23** [1st: USA; 2nd: China, USA; 3 moves. Family: mission. School: home.]

Some TCKs see the military as another new culture to learn and fit in to – and the adaptation skills they developed over the years help them thrive. What might rub other recruits the wrong way these TCKs simply see as 'the way things are done here.'

> Going into boot camp I knew my drill sergeants were doing their jobs, instructing me to do what I signed up for. My mother and I realized during our travels that things are not going to go how you want. I learned the ability not to hold a grudge, to adapt, and realize that everyone has a boss and everyone has a job to do. It helped me not take things too personally, or get too homesick.
>
> **Isaac, 21 [1st: USA; 2nd: China, USA. 4 moves. Family: unaffiliated, adoptive, non-traditional. School: local, home, boarding, Christian international.]**

Commitment and Children

Most TCKs grow up with immediate family being the only constant in their lives. Friends and locations changed, but those few people were still there. For some TCKs this leads to a subconscious belief the only way to feel truly at home is to have a family.

While for some this leads to a strong desire to marry, for others it leads to a fear of being in a long-term relationship.

The reason for these kinds of desires (or aversions) may be unknown to TCKs themselves – they see it as a personal preference with no understanding of the root of it.

Several TCKs I interviewed told me they associate the idea of marriage (or even a long term commitment) with being confined. TCKs who value travel and prefer transience may see a committed relationship as an impediment to a world-travelling life.

Several TCKs I interviewed related this to watching one parent follow the other's career around the world. The lesson internalised was that to commit to a relationship is to give up the freedom to travel.

Committing to property

Another area where some TCKs struggle with commitment is with owning property. There is a sense that owning a home will tie them down to a single location.

> Buying a house will be one of the biggest life decisions I will ever make next to getting married, bigger than choosing a career I think. It will be a choice to tie myself permanently to a place, something I have never had before in my life.
>
> **Emily, 21 [1st: USA; 2nd: DR Congo, Kenya, Rwanda, USA; 20 moves. Family: mission. School: local, international, boarding.]**

In most cases this is an emotional opinion rather than one based in any sense of research; telling these TCKs they can always rent it out and move away does not make a difference.

Even the paperwork, the taxes and so on will tie them to a particular place. They won't be 'free' of that location, no matter where they go. On the other hand, some TCKs think of a house as a place to return to – rather than a place to stay in.

> *I would love to own a home. Because then when money is short from travelling, there is always somewhere to go and crash for a while. To have a base. Travelling can be hard when you don't have a base.*
> **Lisa, 24 [1st: UK; 2nd: China, France, Malaysia, Mexico, Peru, UK, USA; 7 moves. Family: education. School: international.]**

Long distance relationships

Related to commitment is long-distance relationships, which were very prevalent among the TCKs I interviewed. Many had been involved in long distance relationships, whether near the beginning of the relationship or even after marrying their partner. While there are many reasons for this, it does seem short-term separation is something many TCKs see as normal and are able to incorporate into their own lives even at an early stage of a relationship.

> *I'm very comfortable with long-distance relationships, largely due to how much I've travelled and lived far away from people I love. I was in a long-distance*

relationship when I left Ecuador for almost a year after moving back to the States. Later, my husband and I were in a long distance relationship for almost a year. My husband is a touring actor currently, and is gone for weeks at a time. I don't like it when he's gone, but it's certainly manageable and we communicate so easily that we make it work well.

Kendra, 24 [1st: USA; 2nd: Costa Rica, Ecuador, USA; 12 moves. Family: mission. School: Christian international.]

This openness to long distance relationships may be in part because many TCKs have watched adults manage relationships long distance. Frequent (and sometimes extended) work trips are a normal part of life in the international business and foreign service worlds especially. Children who grow up watching parents, or friends' parents, go through regular or protracted periods of separation have a framework for what this can look like in their own lives.

Most TCKs are adept at multiple forms of long distance communication, and know how small the world can be – factors that serve them well when working to maintain relationships despite a physical separation. For some there is a sense of comfort in knowing this particular separation will not be permanent – that they will be with the person again – making it very different emotionally (even redemptive) in the light of so many lost friendships over the years. I saw this happen with my own parents. They've been separated by their jobs multiple times over the years and recently I've seen how the separation makes the times together sweeter. But I also know it's challenging in the context of their relationship. I assume that at some point whomever I end up with and I will be separated for job/travel reasons.

Johanna, 25 [1st: USA; 2nd: Mexico, South Korea, UK, USA; 6 moves. Family: embassy. School: international.]

To marry a TCK or not?

Many single TCKs I interviewed talked of hoping to end up with a partner who shares their international experience of the world. The young married TCKs I interviewed mostly married non-TCKs, however – and find encouragement in it.

I married a non-TCK with an open mind and willing heart. I sometimes wonder if marrying a TCK would be different but I think once you have been married for a bit and you really get to know each other it really doesn't matter if they had the same upbringing as long as there is good communication between you. He has learned a lot about my life and he balances me with the knowledge he has.

Thongfaa, 24 [1st: Finland, USA; 2nd: Finland, Laos, Thailand, USA; 5 moves. Family: multicultural, NGO. School: home (group), international.]

'*Most of the time, they [a couple composed of a TCK and a non-TCK] grow together in their understanding of one another and the non-TCK slowly learns to recognize the impact on the spouse and their marriage of the other one's having grown up in the third culture. There needs to be an understanding that this is, in fact, a marriage between two (or more) cultures,*' writes Lois Bushong.

Many TCKs told me that being in a relationship with a non-TCK was comforting; through their partner's love and understanding these TCKs came to realise that being a TCK does *not* mean they will always be misunderstood.

Raising children

Many TCKs have *very* strong opinions about where they will raise any future children. Some are very definitive about the fact they will of course raise their children as TCKs, living overseas for at least part of their childhood. They cannot imagine any TCK would deprive their children of such valuable experiences.

There are so many ways in which this life has affected us but I don't think I could name anybody that wouldn't say they'd do it all again or that they want the same for their kids!

Pia, 21 [1st: UK; 2nd: China, UK; 2 moves. Family: business. School: international.]

Others are very clear they do not intend their children to be TCKs – they plan to make sure their children have a clear sense of home in a single home country.

> *I wouldn't really wish my kids to be TCKs except that I do badly want them to have an interesting and rich childhood – and am still looking for ways to make that happen in the new context that is now my life. I am slightly mortified that they might grow up in the one house/place/way but don't want them to have that same uprooting that I experienced. I do believe that this is possible but have yet to find a good solution.*
>
> **Rebecca, 28 [1st: Australia; 2nd: Australia, Papua New Guinea, Solomon Islands; 8 moves. Family: mission. School: home (group), Christian international.]**

I think this illustrates a core dilemma of the TCK life. While they may love their experiences abroad, and deeply appreciate all they have learned and gained from growing up internationally, they may also feel a sense of loss at not having had a clear home.

> *I love the way I grew up, but feel a void (I'd be willing to call it a wound, even) of not having a place to call home.*
>
> **Logan, 24 [1st: USA; 2nd: China, Hong Kong, USA; 6 moves. Family: mission. School: home (group).]**

TCKs recognise it is not possible to have both – when it comes to raising their own children, they have to make a choice.

Those who choose international life do think about the sense of home their children will miss out on – but believe they will understand this and be able to help their children in a way their own parents were perhaps less equipped to do.

Those who choose a settled life do think about the experience of the world their children will not have – but believe they can have the best of both worlds by ensuring their children are educated about the world, have cultural experiences, and travel as finances and schedules permit.

In reality, I would not be surprised if many TCKs who currently have a strong opinion one way or the other end up doing something very different in 10 or 20 years' time. They may have kids in their home country, planning to move away after a few years, and find they actually enjoy being settled and rooted as a family. Or an opportunity may arise which feels worth the sacrifice of leaving the place their kids call 'home'.

> *I have strong feelings on raising my kids in terms of the level of education I want them to have. I had always wanted to raise them abroad – but since meeting my husband, and seeing the sense of family unity his family have, nearly all living in the same state, it is just so wonderful and so much fun – I really like it. Having family around and growing close to them is marvellous! It is something I totally missed out on. So now, I am up in the air about it. I really am not sure anymore. I believe that I would be happy either way – but if we were to have our kids grow up in one place, I would*

want to travel with them lots and make sure they are
exposed to the grand and beautiful world around them.
Lisa, 24 [1st: UK; 2nd: China, France, Malaysia, Mexico, Peru, UK,
USA; 7 moves. Family: unaffiliated. School: international.]

Growing into happy and healthy adults

The thoughts and opinions of the young TCKs I interviewed
may not reflect where they end up in 10 or 20 years. I spoke
with TCKs who, in their twenties, are already making
commitments and parenting choices they had not predicted.

How TCKs choose to live their lives is not important;
what matters is that they have the tools to develop into
emotionally mature adults – so their choices are not driven
by unacknowledged fears rooted in childhood experiences.

An international upbringing is not a curse on TCKs growing
up, entering into relationships and forming their own
families – it is just part of a unique blend of experiences that
makes up each individual's background.

Hope for TCKs

While some TCKs are overwhelmingly positive about their
experiences and lives, others are quietly wondering if they
can ever be normal, or truly understood. I believe the stories
shared in this book show there is great hope for every TCK
who feels they are missing something.

TCKs who feel they are the only one struggling with the issues of an international childhood can see many others feel the same way.

TCKs who feel misunderstood can discover emotion as a human language – something everyone can understand, regardless of specific experiences.

TCKs unsure of what they want out of life, with a need to 'find' themselves, can try expressing emotions through art and stories.

TCKs searching for home, or mourning the lack of home, can learn how to create home wherever they live.

TCKs are not strange or weird or impossible to understand. They may have grown up differently, and had a wide range of interesting experiences, but that does not prevent them from having deep and meaningful interactions with others.

Being a TCK is not a bad thing. It is not something to erase, get over, or 'cure'. Being a TCK is an opportunity, and a wonderful blessing – even though it comes with its own pitfalls and problems.

TCKs around the globe have a wealth of stories, experiences, and perspectives to share. If you know some TCKs, you are fortunate. TCKs are wonderful, warm-hearted people with a lot to offer the world – whether as family members, friends, employees, partners, or parents.

GLOBAL CONTRIBUTIONS

In the interviews and survey I conducted while writing this book, I was careful to connect with TCKs from a wide variety of backgrounds. This meant TCKs from different countries, languages, religions, and family backgrounds. One illustration of the breadth of input in this book is the list of countries and territories the contributors identify with. I interviewed TCKs from every continent – even one who spent time living in Antarctica as an adult.

Below is a list of the 165 territories represented (including 153 of the 193 member states of the United Nations), categorised by continent. There are 86 legal cultures and 158 geographic cultures (in which non-citizens lived). (Some legal countries are not on the geographic list, as I did not interview anyone who lived there as a foreigner).

Africa

Legal: Burkina Faso, Burundi, Cameroon, Central African Republic, Chad, Côte d'Ivoire, DR Congo, Egypt, Madagascar, Malawi, Niger, Nigeria, Rwanda, Senegal, South Africa, Tanzania, Togo, Zambia.

Geographic *(non-citizen):* Algeria, Angola, Benin, Botswana, Burkina Faso, Burundi, Cameroon, Chad, Congo, Côte d'Ivoire, Djibouti, DR Congo, Egypt, Equatorial Guinea, Eritrea, Ethiopia, Gabon, Ghana, Guinea, Guinea-Bissau, Kenya, Lesotho, Liberia, Libya, Madagascar, Malawi, Mali, Mauritius, Morocco, Mozambique, Namibia, Niger, Nigeria, Rwanda, Senegal, Sierra Leone, South Africa, South Sudan, Sudan, Swaziland, Tanzania, Togo, Tunisia, Uganda, Zambia, Zimbabwe.

Americas

Legal: Argentina, Bolivia, Brazil, Canada, Chile, Colombia, Costa Rica, Cuba, Dominican Republic, Ecuador, Guatemala, Guyana, Honduras, Mexico, Panama, Peru, Puerto Rico (USA), Suriname, United States of America (USA), Uruguay, Venezuela.

Geographic *(non-citizen)*: Argentina, Bahamas, Belize, Bermuda (UK), Bolivia, Brazil, Canada, Cayman Islands (UK), Chile, Colombia, Costa Rica, Dominican Republic, Ecuador, Guatemala, Guyana, Haiti, Honduras, Mexico, Netherlands Antilles (Netherlands), Nicaragua, Panama, Paraguay, Peru, Puerto Rico (USA), Suriname, Uruguay, USA, Venezuela.

Asia

Legal: Cambodia, China, Hong Kong (China), India, Indonesia, Israel, Japan, Kazakhstan, Lebanon, Macau (China), Malaysia, Mongolia, Pakistan, Philippines, Singapore, South Korea, Sri Lanka, Syria, Taiwan, Thailand, United Arab Emirates (UAE), Vietnam.

Geographic *(non-citizen)*: Afghanistan, Bangladesh, Brunei, Cambodia, China, Hong Kong (China), India, Indonesia, Iran, Israel, Japan, Jordan, Kazakhstan, Kuwait, Kyrgyzstan, Laos, Lebanon, Macau (China), Malaysia, Mongolia, Myanmar, Nepal, Oman, Pakistan, Philippines, Qatar, Saudi Arabia, Singapore, South Korea, Sri Lanka, Syria, Taiwan, Thailand, Turkey, UAE, Uzbekistan, Vietnam, Yemen.

Europe

Legal: Albania, Austria, Belgium, Denmark, Finland, France, Germany, Hungary, Ireland, Italy, Netherlands, Norway, Poland, Portugal, Slovakia, Slovenia, Spain, Sweden, Switzerland, United Kingdom (UK).

Geographic *(non-citizen)***:** Albania, Armenia, Austria, Belgium, Bosnia and Herzegovina, Bulgaria, Croatia, Cyprus, Czech Republic, Denmark, Estonia, Finland, France, Georgia, Germany, Hungary, Iceland, Ireland, Italy, Kosovo, Macedonia, Netherlands, Norway, Poland, Portugal, Romania, Russia, Serbia, Slovenia, Spain, Sweden, Switzerland, Turkey, United Kingdom (UK), Ukraine.

Oceania

Legal: Australia, Fiji, New Zealand, Papua New Guinea, Vanuatu.

Geographic *(non-citizen)***:** American Samoa (USA), Australia, Fiji, Guam (USA), New Zealand, Norfolk Island (Australia), Northern Mariana Islands (USA), Papua New Guinea, Solomon Islands, Tonga, Vanuatu.

GLOSSARY

There are a lot of technical terms and acronyms used when talking about cross-cultural experiences. Understanding what they all mean, and how they differ, is important to understanding the world of TCKs (and this book).

Adult Third Culture Kid (ATCK)
An adult who grew up as a TCK – spent a significant portion of their life (before the age of 18) outside their passport country. An ATCK may *or may not* live as an expatriate as an adult. Regardless of their location as adults, they are affected by their experiences as children.

Cross-Cultural Adoption
When a family adopts a child born in a different country/culture or of a different ethnicity.

Cross-Cultural Kid
A person who meaningfully interacts with two or more cultures during childhood.

Culture Shock
A period of adjustment upon arriving in a foreign country. Characterised by difficulty accepting or adjusting to the differences of a new place, feeling out of place, difficulty fitting in and making new relationships, general stress, and emotional overload. For some expats this process takes 12–18 months.

Expatriate (expat)
A person living abroad as a foreigner. That is, a person living

in (not just visiting) a country he/she is not a citizen of. Different to a tourist, who only visits the host country, but does not settle down there.

Expat Immigrant
An immigrant who, having settled and gained citizenship in their adopted country, moves again to another country to live as an expatriate there. For example: a Brazilian who moves to South Africa and becomes a South African citizen, and later moves to India to live as an expat. Upon first moving to South Africa this person would be an immigrant; once living abroad as a South African citizen they become an expat immigrant.

Foreigner
Any person outside their passport country. Also a more common word used for expatriates, sometimes in a derogatory way. The word 'foreign' has a strong implication of difference, and 'otherness'. Some TCKs do not feel like foreigners in their host culture; some TCKs feel like foreigners in their passport culture.

Geographic Culture (2nd culture)
Any culture a person has lived in, whether as a local or as an expatriate.

Home Assignment (Home Leave, Furlough)
An extended period of time (3-12 months) a mission family spends in their passport country, often mandated by their mission organisation. This time is used to report on the work they have been doing and reconnect with supporters.

Host Country (Host Culture)
This is the country (and culture) an expatriate lives in as a foreigner.

Immigrant
A person who leaves their passport country and settles in a new country where they become a naturalised citizen – changing their citizenship.

International School
A school using the curriculum of a country other than the one it is located in, e.g. an American School in Kenya, or a French School in Indonesia. Some international schools are open only to expatriate children (local students cannot attend).

Legal Culture (1st culture)
Any country a person has legal standing in (the country that issued their passport, or in which they have official permanent residence).

Missionary Kid (MK)
A child whose parents go overseas with a religious group.

Monocultural
This term describes a person influenced by a single culture – they are born in their parents' homeland and live their whole lives there. (Anyone who does not have a cross-cultural experience).

Multicultural
This term describes a person who has multiple cultural influences *within their family*. This usually means their

spouse comes from a different country/culture (or a child of such a relationship), but can also include immigrant families and families who adopt cross-culturally.

Passport Country
The country a person has legal standing in – the nation that issued their passport. This is often called a person's 'home' country, but some people living cross-culturally have *never* lived in their passport country; a few have never even visited their passport country.

Repatriation (also known as re-entry)
Expatriation is leaving one's passport country; repatriation is returning. Repatriating is the process of moving and adjusting to one's passport country after an extended time away. Often includes a period of reverse culture shock.

Returned Expat Immigrant
An immigrant who, having settled and gained citizenship in their adopted country, returns to the country in which they were born, to live as an expatriate. For example: an Egyptian who moves to Germany and becomes a German citizen (giving up their Egyptian citizenship), and later moves to Egypt, now as an expatriate in the country they were formerly a citizen of.

Reverse Culture Shock (also known as re-entry)
The period of adjustment following repatriation. This takes many expats by surprise, especially as for some it can last 12–18 months.

Third Culture Adult (TCA)
A person who lives as an expatriate for a long time, with

the first international move occurring after age 18. May also include adults who spent only a short time abroad as children (and do not identify as TCKs), and later spent a long period as an expatriate in adulthood.

Third Culture Kid (TCK)
A child who has spent a significant portion of their life (before the age of 18) outside their passport country. Generally speaking a child who spends three or more years abroad between ages 7–17 will identify as a TCK. Some who have spent less time abroad may also feel like TCKs. A person's feeling about the experience is more important than the numbers.

BIBLIOGRAPHY

Besanceney, Valérie (2014). *B at Home : Emma moves again.* Great Britain: Summertime Publishing.

Bonebright, Denise (2010). "Adult Third Culture Kids: HRD challenges and opportunities" in *Human Resource Development International*, Volume 13, Issue 3. Routledge.

Bruner, Kay (2014). *As Soon As I Fell: A Memoir.* CreateSpace Independent Publishing Platform.

Bushong, Lois (2013). *Belonging Everywhere & Nowhere: Insights into Counseling the Globally Mobile.* Indianapolis: Mango Tree Intercultural Services.

Cottrell, Ann (2002). "Educational and Occupational Choices of American Adult Third Culture Kids" in *Military Brats and Other Global Nomads.* Praeger.

Covington, Martin V. (2009). "Self-Worth Theory: Retrospection and Prospects" in *Handbook of Motivation at School.* New York: Routledge.

Grubbs, Dr. Jim (2014). *Growing Up in the Military: 25th Anniversary Reissue.* San Francisco: QSKY Publishing.

Hervey, Emily (2014). *Setting Sail! The Family Workbook.* Worldwide Writings.

Janssen, Linda A. (2013). *The Emotionally Resilient Expat: Engage, Adapt and Thrive Across Cultures.* Great Britain: Summertime Publishing.

Kübler-Ross, Elisabeth (2011). *On Death and Dying: What the Dying Have to Teach Doctors, Nurses, Clergy, & Their Own Families*. New York: Scribner.

ed: László-Herbert, Eva; Parfitt, Jo (2014). *The Worlds Within: An anthology of TCK art and writing: young, global and between cultures*. Great Britain: Summertime Publishing.

Marzano, Robert J. (2006). *Classroom Assessment and Grading That Work*. Alexandria: Association for Supervision & Curriculum Development.

Melkonian, Lois (2015). *Hybrid: The transformation of a cross-cultural people pleaser*. Lois Melkonian.

Murray, Taylor (2013). *Hidden in My Heart: A TCK's Journey Through Cultural Transition*. BottomLine Media.

O'Shaughnessy, Christopher (2014). *Arrivals, Departures and the Adventures In-Between*. Great Britain: Summertime Publishing.

Ota, Doug (2014). *Safe Passage: How mobility affects people & what international schools should do about it*. Great Britain: Summertime Publishing.

Pittman, Lisa; Smit, Diana (2011). *Expat Teens Talk: Peers, Parents and Professionals offer support, advice and solutions in response to Expat Life challenges as shared by Expat Teens*. Great Britain: Summertime Publishing.

Pollock, David C.; Van Reken, Ruth E. (2009). *Third Culture Kids: Growing Up Among Worlds*. Boston: Nicholas Brealey Publishing.

Quick, Tina L. (2011). *The Global Nomad's Guide to University Transition*. Great Britain: Summertime Publishing.

Rockson, Tayo (2015). *The Ultimate Guide To TCK Living: Understanding The World Around You.*

Sand-Hart, Heidi (2010). *Home Keeps Moving*. Hagerstown: McDougal Publishing.

Silver, Margarita Gokun (2012). *The Culture Shock Tool Kit: Three Strategies for Managing Culture Shock*. GCC Expat Publications.

Simens, Julia (2012). *Emotional Resilience and the Expat Child: Practical Storytelling Techniques That Will Strengthen the Global Family*. Great Britain: Summertime Publishing.

ed: Smith, Carolyn D. (1996). *Strangers at Home: Essays on the Effects of Living Overseas and Coming "Home" to a Strange Land*. Bayside NY: Aletheia Publications.

Useem, Ruth Hill (1993), "Third Culture Kids" in *Newslinks*, Newspaper of the International School Services, Volume 12, Issue 3.

Van Reken, Ruth Ellen, (2012). *Letters Never Sent: A Global Nomad's Journey from Hurt to Healing*. Great Britain: Summertime Publishing.

Zilber, Dr Ettie (2009). *The Children of Educators in International Schools*. Woodbridge: John Catt Educational Ltd.

Online Articles Referenced

The 3 'Third Culture Kid' Cultures (Libby Stephens)
http://www.libbystephens.com/blog/third-culture-kids/
31-the-3-qthird-culture-kidq-cultures

Outlawed Grief, a Curse Disguised (Jonathan Trotter)
http://www.alifeoverseas.com/outlawed-grief-a-curse-
disguised/

Don't ask where I'm from, ask where I'm a local (Taiye Selasi)
https://www.ted.com/talks/taiye_selasi_don_t_ask_
where_i_m_from_ask_where_i_m_a_local

How To Know If You Are Pre- or Post-Griever (and why
it matters)
http://velvetashes.com/how-to-know-if-you-are-pre-or-
post-griever-and-why-it-matters/

Successful Students (The British School of Beijing, Shunyi)
http://www.nordangliaeducation.com/our-schools/beijing/
shunyi/our-students/successful-students

RESOURCES

Sea Change Mentoring (Ellen Mahoney)
http://seachangementoring.com/

Transition Dynamics (Barbara Schaetti)
http://www.transition-dynamics.com/

RNG International (Becky Grappo)
http://rnginternational.com/

Navigating Life's Transitions (Becky Matchullis)
http://www.navigatelifecoach.com/

On Raising Bilingual Children (Eowyn Crisfield)
http://onraisingbilingualchildren.com/

Alien Citizen (Elizabeth Liang)
http://cargocollective.com/aliencitizen

Families In Global Transition (FIGT)
http://www.figt.org/

Communicating Across Boundaries (Marilyn Gardner)
http://communicatingacrossboundariesblog.com

Missionary Care: Resources for Missions and Mental Health
http://www.missionarycare.com

Brats Without Borders
http://www.bratswithoutborders.org/

Denizen Magazine
http://denizenmag.com

TCKID: A Home For Third Culture Kids
http://tckid.com/

ABOUT THE AUTHOR

Tanya Crossman grew up in Sydney and Canberra, Australia, and lived in Greenwich, Connecticut, USA for two years of high school. She had TCK friends as a child, before her own experience of life overseas, and long before hearing the phrase 'Third Culture Kid'.

She received a degree in Asian Studies from the Australian National University, and a diploma in Mandarin from Beijing Language and Culture University. She worked several bilingual jobs in China, including interning at a publishing company and Office/HR Manager for a small textile trading company.

After years of volunteering her time to mentor TCKs, Tanya left her job to work with TCKs full time. She coordinated over 35 camps and conferences for teenage TCKs in China and Cambodia, and was invited to speak to groups in China, Thailand, Cambodia, and Singapore.

After 11 years in Asia, Tanya is currently studying in Sydney. She is still passionate about advocating for TCKs, even in her passport country. She plans to return overseas in time to continue working with, and on behalf of, TCKs.

You can contact Tanya at:
tck.tanya@gmail.com
misunderstood-book.com/
Facebook.com/misunderstoodTCK
Twitter.com/TanyaTCK

CPSIA information can be obtained
at www.ICGtesting.com
Printed in the USA
LVOW10s0328081117
555442LV00007B/206/P

9 781909 193857